D0845014

DISCARD

REF

T
339
.G74
1991

Griffin, Gordon D.,
1930-

How to be a
successful
inventor.

$37.95

DATE			

BUSINESS/SCIENCE/TECHNOLOGY
DIVISION

© THE BAKER & TAYLOR CO.

How to Be a
Successful Inventor

Turn Your Ideas Into Profit

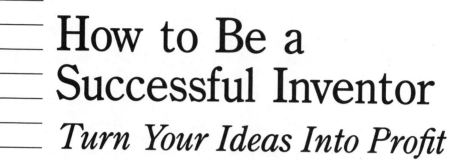

How to Be a Successful Inventor

Turn Your Ideas Into Profit

Gordon D. Griffin

John Wiley & Sons, Inc.

New York • Chichester • Brisbane • Toronto • Singapore

In recognition of the importance of preserving what has been
written, it is a policy of John Wiley & Sons, Inc. to have books of
enduring value published in the United States printed on acid-free
paper, and we exert our best efforts to that end.

Copyright © 1991 by John Wiley & Sons, Inc.

All Rights reserved. Published simultaneously in Canada.

Reproduction or translation of any part of this work beyond that
permitted by Section 107 or 108 of the 1976 United States
Copyright Act without the permission of the copyright owner is
unlawful. Requests for permission of further information should be
addressed to the Permissions Department, John Wiley & Sons, Inc.

This publication is designed to provide accurate and authoritative
information in regard to the subject matter covered. It is sold with
the understanding that the publisher is not engaged in rendering
legal, accounting, or other professional service. If legal advice or
other expert assistance is required, the services of a competent
professional person should be sought. *From a Declaration of
Principles jointly adopted by a Committee of the American Bar
Association and a Committee of Publishers.*

Library of Congress Cataloging-in-Publication Data

Griffin, Gordon. 1930–
    How to be a successful inventor : turn your ideas into profit
/ by Gordon Griffin.
      p. cm.
    Includes bibliographical references.
    ISBN 0-471-53444-7 (cloth : acid-free paper).
    ISBN 0-471-53446-3 (paper : acid-free paper)
    1. Inventions. 2. Patents I. Title.
T339.074 1991
608--dc20   90-25076

Printed in the United States of America

91 92 10 9 8 7 6 5 4 3 2 1

To my wife Dionis, who is without guile and gives
me much joy and also to my children who often do!

Illustrations by Peter Lee

Contents

Preface ix

Acknowledgments...xi

Chapter 1   The Simplest of Inventions 1
Need 2
Ideas 8
Prototype 9
Inventing While Working for
Someone Else..19
The Problem with Over-Secretive Inventors........................22
Solicitations to Give You Help...24
Inspiration for Inventors 28
Concluding Remarks 30

Chapter 2   Left/Right Dominance and Inventors 33
Balancing the Brain...35
Education Needs 35
Left-Brain Inventing..37
Taking Left-Brained Action...38

Chapter 3   Licensing Large Companies 42
Licensing Middle Sized Companies 43
Left-Brain/Right-Brain Bargaining 46
The Individual Entrepreneur...46
The Importance of Attitude to Infringement 48

Chapter 4   Your Involvement in Marketing...53
Mail-Order Sales 68

Chapter 5   The Cost Approach to Selling...72
Pricing Our Boomerang 78
Personal Protection through a Corporation 82

Chapter 6   Don't Rely on Trust Alone 87
Finding Qualified Licensees...91
Demonstrate A Working Model to Your Potential Licensee 93

Chapter 7   No Patent "Know-How"...109
A Basic License Agreement...114

Chapter 8   Patent Attorneys...139
Searching for Other Related Patents...................................143
Applying for a Patent Yourself...146

Examiner's Response to
Your Patent Application 151

Chapter 9 Publication of Your Patent 166
Disadvantages of Patent Application...171
Invalidation of Patents...172
Invalidating An Existing Granted Patent.....................................173
Two Major Breakthrough Inventions...173
The Importance of Action
Against Infringers 177

Chapter 10 Third-World Technology 185
You and Your Patent Attorney..188
Game and Toy Inventions..188
Help for Prototypes 189
Independent Verification of Tests 189
Non-Disclosure Agreements 190
Agreements for Helpers 193
Keeping a Diary or Log...194
Disclosure Document in the
United States..196
Sources for Locating Trade Associations.....................................197
Evaluation of Your Patent 198
Patent Searching by Yourself...200
Direct Government Help...203
Getting Help in Business 205
Proper Evaluation by Interested Corporations and Others..............208
Would-Be Help from Developers and Brokers.............................208
Finding Licensees 211
Evaluating the Competition...212
Starting a Corporation 215
Getting Outside Investment 216
Whole or Partial Manufacture of Your Invention by Others 216
Mail Order Possibilities and Direct Marketing 217
The Sales Representative 217

Bibliography 219

Appendix Acknowledgment 223

Appendix A 225

Profile 235

Preface

When I was a young lad everything around me was modern. I remember that the latest "wireless" was a great delight to me. Special innovative programs would announce it was the first time such programs had been broadcast. Television was stated to be the ultimate wonder of the world! Surely we had reached the pinnacle of man's achievement, and you know, we had, but as time went on, new wonders appeared, creating new pinnacles. Each time a new wonder appeared I thought how great it was to be living at a time when all these things were happening.

Since those times over fifty years ago, I have come to realize that man's progress has been almost continuous from the stone age. I think it is the escalation of this progress that surprises us all. Where does it come from? Primarily, I believe, from that part of us which conceives an idea in our mind, then proceeds to take that germ, nurture it and bring it to fruition—perhaps not in its perfect state, but enough to prove its new place in society; in other words, the inventive side of us.

One might suppose the inventors who are originators of today's affluent society would enjoy the height of personal financial success. Unfortunately history and my personal experience indicate somewhat the opposite! I believe almost every individual has the potential to invent something worthwhile. There is a handyman or a problem solver in all of us. Whether our ideas can be patented or can make money for us is another matter, and one that this book is directed to.

A penny saved is a penny earned. On that basis, this book can make many individual inventors a great deal of money. Many inventors unknowingly waste money needlessly. On the other hand, this book also deals with how to be financially successful with a really good viable invention. The inventor needs to know how to reap his just rewards in partnership with that other essential type of person, the "get up and go" type entrepreneur who can make things happen! Facts and figures are the entrepreneur's stock in trade, together with knowledge of how to get things to the right market, maneuver people and situations, as well as make money.

Having had a lifelong experience in inventing and in business, I have had the unique experience to view both sides of the usually confrontational attitudes of each, that is, inventors and entrepreneurs. This book stresses the need for co-operation between them for greater, more equitable profits for both.

To this end, therefore, I have included suggestions to help the (often weaker) inventor type, obtain some of the skills of the (more dominant) entrepreneur type, to enable him to have a fairer share of his primary efforts, all described here, with practical workable suggestions, and with, it is hoped, sufficient detail to be really helpful to the many inventors and would-be inventors in this world.

—Gordon D. Griffin

Acknowledgments

I, like others who write, must give due thanks and appreciation for the many people who have helped make this book possible in its present form. It is said that we are part of all those we have associated with. Mr. Roger Petit, Patent Attorney of Paris, France and Mr. Gordon Overton, Patent Attorney (deceased) of Melbourne, Australia have both had considerable beneficial influence on me as a person and as an inventor. Special mention must go to Lori, Bonnie, Pam, Holly and Susan for typing, re-typing and yet re-typing again, gratefully made necessary by the guiding technical help and constructive criticism of Steve Walker, professor of English at Brigham Young University, Provo, Utah, USA; Mr. Roy Sanford, Inventor, of Springville, USA; Mr. Mr. Greg Munt, Patent Attorney of Melbourne, Australia; Mr. David Devons, highly gifted European Patent Attorney of London, England; Mr. Reid Russell, Patent Attorney of Salt Lake City, Utah, USA and my dear, long-time friend, Mr. Roy Gilham, Patent Attorney (retired) of London England, who, over the years, has helped me to begin to understand the real world of inventing from the legal and litigation side. Finally, I must give my greatest appreciation to my wife, Dionis, for her understanding, encouragement, and literary guidance, that may enable you to make some sense out of what I have written.

Gordon D. Griffin

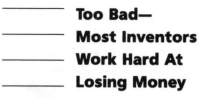

**Too Bad—
Most Inventors
Work Hard At
Losing Money**

1 Inventing Something: An Overview

Now, more than ever, inventing is a global exercise. With emerging Third World countries and the tremendous need for improved products by the former Eastern Bloc countries, one cannot deal with inventing in isolation. So although certain emphasis is given to the United States in inventing procedures, almost all the information in this book is very relevant to the inventor (or would-be inventor) on a worldwide basis. I do not claim to give legal advice or to be an authority on the patenting laws of all countries. Probably no one legal authority could encompass all that is within this book anyway. But as a practicing inventor, I can help you get a good overview of the real world of inventing. I have been there.

If you like the idea of inventing something useful, this chapter will give you some helpful tips.

Inventing is basically the realization of a need—making or developing something that is perceived as needed. If you perceive yourself as a good trouble-shooter—that is, a person who, besides being a good handyman, can be presented with a problem and, using intuitive solving powers, can solve or fix the problem—then you will probably make a good inventor. Note that I did not say a successful one; read on to have a hope.

The Simplest of Inventions

Often a person with a handicap will invent something for his or her own convenience. A man with poor foot control who normally uses a walking stick, for example, might still feel afraid of slipping on grass or packed snow in winter, so he might put studs on his shoes and at the base of his walking stick to give him a greater sense of security. That is a type of functional invention. The fact that in this case the "invention" probably is not patentable or commercially marketable should not detract from this inventive step. There was a need. Thought processes were used to satisfy that need. The idea was developed and a functional unit was made.

You may have your own pet idea for which you think there is a need. To test your belief, you must go through various steps. A faint heart or a hesitant spirit can jeopardize your success. Failing to take each step in the proper order can also cause later hardship.

Need

Let us say you perceive a need for something. You need to look at this first step closely, and you can usually discuss it with others, without specific details, at no risk to a subsequent patent. For example, say I had an idea for a new type of flying vehicle that traveled over water. I can say to someone, "I have an idea for a flying vehicle to cross over water. Do you think such a vehicle that could carry two (or more) people at up to 60 miles per hour would sell if the price was within, say, $5,000?" Such disclosure lets the other person know nothing about how I would achieve such an end result. If the reply is, "Yes, I do (or no, I don't)—tell me all about it," I would say it's at the idea stage. With a potential licensee I would tell the person more only if he or she signed a nondisclosure statement (see Chapter 10). If reactions to my vehicle were positive, I would now have a long way to go to bring my idea to a practical reality. If reactions were negative, now would be the time to go on to my next idea! I cannot have ideas in isolation from reality. Your approach to your idea should be to ask yourself the following:

1. Would I (or anyone, for that matter) buy this product if it were available?
2. How much would I (or anyone) be willing to pay?
3. Will it have a restricted market or is it needed by a great many people?
4. Does it have defense or security aspects?
5. Is something like it already out there?

Necessity Is
Always The
Mother of
Invention

     Then ask several friends in general terms. Say, "I have an idea for a new kind of product" (again, don't go into specifics). "Would you buy one if you could? What would you be willing to pay for one?" If the idea is in a specialized field, you might need to approach those in that field. If the answer to "Would you buy?" keeps coming back "no" and there are no extenuating circumstances, then you had better try for another idea or else face possible great heartache later. I will now examine these five areas more closely.

Would You Buy One Yourself?

This requires a lot of soul-searching. You know how it is when you go to a garage sale. Are you the type who buys things on impulse, then brings them home only to allow them to accumulate along with all the other things you've previously bought, or were given as presents but never used—more clutter awaiting the time of your own garage sale? Or are you circumspect in your purchases? Mind you, some people might think it all right to invent something that is bought on impulse even if it is never used. Large chain stores are full of impulse–purchase merchandise that quickly finds its way to garage sales. Your own family and friends should help you decide this question.

     It seems to me, however, that people today are becoming more circumspect in their buying habits, giving more intelligent thinking to what they buy.

     If your invention is either nonconsumer, for a specialized market such as light or heavy industry, a new design, a new type of weapon, or perhaps something more esoteric, then you may already be able to give an unequivocal answer of "yes," knowing that there is a market for what you envision. Of course, at the right (lower) price, the market would be self-evident for the new product.

How Much Could It Be Sold For?

Getting a good idea as to what your new invention would sell for (rather than what it could be made for) is very important. (See "Pricing," Chapter 5.) Pricing will give you a much more reliable idea as to its viability. The cost of making the product is variable and tends to escalate higher! It also depends on the volume made. Starting with what it will sell for can instantly give you a good idea as to whether to continue as is, or be forced to go back to the drawing board.

     For example, I can visualize a new road-making machine. But its size and servicing requirements, as well as its cost, would make it prohibitive to use. Such a machine would be ahead of its time. Therefore, I do nothing with this idea. At the other end of the scale, how about a kitchen machine that quickly punches out a hole in a container and sucks out the contents into a saucepan or dish? Sounds fine and would work well too, but would you use it? And if so, would you be willing to pay ten or more times the cost of a can opener, electric or not?

People of today want not only utilitarian products easily stored. They want them used often. And, most importantly, they want them at the right price. Industry looks at the whole cost of new machinery, maintenance included, and the rate of profit to be returned to them. New paper-printing machines that cost over $1 million each are greatly sought after by certain types of printing firms just because of their high rate of profit return. So do not be deterred by the cost of your new invention. Industry wants productivity and profits at any price. But a lower price is always better.

The free enterprise Western Hemisphere society and industry are always striving toward greater productivity and lower costs. It's all part of the Western culture. Can your new invention meet this challenge? If not, stop right now and carefully reevaluate it to see where it can be made to do so. Even if you eventually get it off the ground, your efforts to refine and reduce costs must always continue. So, in short, if the answers to "How much could it be sold for?" indicate a price lower than that for which it can be made and marketed, then you had better go back and see if you can simplify your idea before proceeding. The price must fall within the range of acceptability to the customer. You would be very fortunate if the product you envision were so valued and indispensable to the buyer that its price was of secondary importance. The response to the price question is also very important to your whole marketing approach (see Chapter 4).

What Is the Market Potential?

Complicated Inventions May Be Too Costly To Be Successful

Inventors often (indeed, usually) get carried away with their new ideas—myself included. It takes some level of self-discipline to stand back far enough to get a clear view of your product's sales potential. Of course, almost all inventions have some sales potential, if only to the inventor. But if you intend to try to patent your idea, then it is normal to expect an eventual profit after all expenses.

For example, suppose you have this wonderful idea for helping your neighbor who has only one leg and one arm. Your idea is a new type of walking stick not expected to cost very much to manufacture, say $7. But overheads bring it up to a sales price of $21.95, out of which you expect a 10% royalty, or $2.19. (Ten percent is very high, but you do not expect to sell a great quantity, and you want to try to recover costs as well as make a profit.)

"Fine," you say. But wait. Have you stopped to consider how many one-legged, one-armed people there are and what percentage of them might buy a special walking stick? Your personal time and expenses and the patenting costs might well reach $10,000 during the first two years from when you file your patent. Then there is interest on your money, maintenance fees, and wear and tear on yourself.

You might be lucky to find 1,000 people willing to buy your specialized walking stick. Your royalties would equal $2,195, giving you a minimum loss of nearly $8,000 and a gain of a few more grey hairs and perhaps an ulcer or two. You think the foregoing is too farfetched? If so, take time to browse through issued patents for inventions that clearly are, or have been, nonviable in the marketplace.

There is prestige in obtaining a patent, I suppose, but it comes at a costly price if there is no return or, as is more likely, a considerable loss. This book is

Question
Inventions
With Limited
Sales Or
Monetary
Return

designed as much to help you not spend your money unwisely (lose it), as many inventors do, as to help you make a net profit. The former will help you reach the latter more quickly! It is an old, yet accurate truism that money saved can be money earned.

Military, Defense, or Security Interest

Whether your invention has defense or security applications is not easy to answer. Only you can say. Government security needs change from year to year. The virtual collapse of traditional Communism in Eastern Europe and the resulting shift in international relations has made the future uncertain for this area of invention. But the lesson of world history tells us that conflict somewhere in the world is ever present, perhaps just around the corner! There will always be wars and rumors of wars that will keep the world's armaments industry in continued prosperity, though the type of defensive and offensive weaponry will change dramatically, as it has over the past 4,000 years, allowing the inventive process to continue. Unfortunately, inventions need not be respectful of humanity; it is somewhat sad to think that the inventive process can as readily take away as give life.

Nevertheless, it is safe to say that all patents are screened in some manner for government defense or security applications by the government, which issues the patent, and dealt with by the particular government accordingly. You would certainly find yourself less free to promote your invention if it had great defense or security applications. Perhaps you would receive an arbitrary financial settle-

AH! I JUST HAVE AN IDEA FOR A NEW MULTI PURPOSE WALKING STICK.

ment that may be fair according to the government in question but not to your liking entirely. Your negotiating parameters would certainly be limited.

Getting Someone To Take Your Invention Under Their Wing Is Great

If you think there is some possibility of government or security interest, your best approach would be to first confidentially approach a government supplier of a similar product, or more than one if there are more, in order to get an existing supplier interested in taking your invention under its wing, so that you will then have more support during the prosecution of your patent. Beware of *vested interests* (government or industry) that might wish to suppress your ideas or buy them out in order to safeguard their existing line or product. This is where the importance of a proper license agreement comes in (see Chapter 6).

Similar or Related Products

If something similar to what you have invented is already in the marketplace, but you know yours is better, life could be better and easier for you in almost every area. But the very first thing you will need to do is make a thorough search for any patent that may have been granted on that other product to see if its claims already anticipate what you have "invented." If they do—or if the prior product makes your new invention an obvious improvement—you can without more expense dispose with any further action and proceed to your next invention.

However, *you* should not make the determination as to whether your invention (or any aspect of it) is patentable or not. This can best be done by an expert patent attorney or patent agent who may be able to point out possible patenting claims (strong or weak, broad or narrow) that may be granted upon your applying for a patent. You may then find it easier to locate and license manufacturers or tap into their existing markets. Manufacturers are always looking for less expensive improvements. If this looks good to you, first go into the pricing procedure as outlined in Chapter 5 so that you can be assured that your improved product will not price itself out of existence (even if it's better than the competition).

Please remember that each country in the world has its own peculiar ways of dealing with patent applications. You will certainly need to be aware of these

Inventive
Inspirations
May Come
At The Most
Odd Times

peculiarities in your countries of interest and to get qualified help from a registered patent attorney or agent in each country you deal with. While most major countries, including the United States, are signatories to a General Patent Convention Treaty, many countries vary the specifics and have kept on changing their own stands on the specifics over many years. This is likely to continue as each government strives toward but never reaches its own brand of perfection.

For example, all convention countries now grant patents for 20 years, but this is not strictly correct. The United States is presently alone in granting patents for 17 years from time of grant, generally two to four years after filing—whereas all other convention countries grant patents for 20 years from time of filing. The end result of 20 years of cover is therefore about the same.

Remember that you cannot start legal proceedings against infringers until your patent is actually granted. It is my opinion that the invention that has applications in only one country is very much a rarity. That fact forces one to view any invention as potentially global in nature, irrespective as to whether the inventor or applicant can afford the costs of multicountry patent applications.

These global possibilities are why I will stress ways in which inventors need not always prematurely exclude themselves from overseas filings. Worldwide there are calculated possibilities to extend valuable patent income while minimizing exposure to sometimes heavy, unnecessary expenses. The following is the real world for inventors as I see it, found out by me over many years through the school of hard knocks and Murphy's law!

Ideas

Soon after you perceive a need, you should begin to develop an idea as to how this need could be satisfied—first in your mind, then by scribbling on bits of paper, even on the odd table napkin at a restaurant! Your mind is dwelling on this item and perceives difficulties and problems. Something almost magical is happening. Without your knowing it, your mind is working for you and will throw out solutions and insights at the most unexpected times.

For this reason it becomes essential always to have a pen or pencil handy— a small notepad also, especially at night. Inventive thoughts come at the most unexpected moments and are often fleeting. If you are not prepared to jot down the essentials of the thoughts as they come, you may lose them, perhaps forever. These thoughts may take one day or one year or more. But as you dwell on the problem, they will come, and you need to be prepared at all times.

I once invented a new type of bed that I was trying to refine by lessening its retail cost and the complexity of manufacturing. I knew what I wanted. I even knew what functional part I wanted. It was something that had to have lateral stability, yet at the same time vertical movement. My mind brought out many ideas over an 18-month period, all to be tried, all failures.

Then, just as I was going to sleep late one night, a wisp of an idea came to me, so wispy that pencil and paper could not capture its simplicity. Out of bed I stepped, gently visualizing the solution. I moved downstairs, gathering a pair of scissors and some plastic fabric, then used the scissors to cut the fabric as I saw it in my mind's eye. It was a thrilling moment when I found that this simple unit before me really was the basis for the successful solution to 18 months of periodic concentrated thought on a difficult problem. I slept well that night.

I suppose for many people one of the most relaxing times to get ideas is while taking a bath or shower. I frightened my wife once by letting out a great wail of despair while in the bath. She thought that something terrible had happened. It had, but not to me. I had suddenly received new insight on an invention I had been working on for a whole year and found that I could achieve the same end result more simply and at considerably less cost. All my previous year of hard thought and work was now obsolete! It was a shock to the system.

So be prepared to get solutions to your problems at any time. Don't be afraid to think of the whole idea often so that your mind can deal with those thoughts subconsciously.

> **Almost Nothing Is Made Perfect The First Time**

Prototype

The prototype step may be simple, complicated, quick, or lengthy. You may first make a drawing and then construct a model, or construct a model and then make a drawing of it. Each approach is appropriate, depending on the complexity of the invention. In general I have found that the simpler the invention and the fewer moving parts it has, the greater the need for an exact final drawing.

Conversely (though you may have some scribblings on odd pieces of paper for reference), the more complex the invention and the greater number of parts it has, moving or otherwise, the less able you are to put it down as a precise

Keep Good
Control Of
Prototype
Costs From
The Outset

drawing. So often it would be a waste of time or even counterproductive to try to do so. The more complex an invention, larger or smaller, the more you need to be free to use your creative imagination to overcome the inevitable changes in details as you proceed. So a prototype is usually best for a complex invention. The exception to this case is if you were skilled in detailed drawing and the company you were approaching had higher management who could understand, three-dimensionally, what the drawing represented. The savings a detailed drawing can bring to a more complex invention could be considerable, as there *might* be no need to physically make a (working) model. Complex inventions usually do not work initially—resulting in much trial and error. Therefore any "bugs" that can be worked out in a drawing stage prior to costly prototypes could be highly beneficial.

If you think this situation appeals to you and your prospective licensee, but you do not personally have the necessary drawing skills, you might like to do what I did many years ago with my first composting machine, which I originally developed in Tasmania, Australia. That spark of an idea first came to me while I was visiting a composting facility in Holland. There were several machines present, doing quite well quite slowly (one was broken down in the middle of a pile of compost with its steel conveyor belt broken).

For some reason, I squinted my eyes to look at another machine that was enveloped in that hot steam of the compost. I seemed to see the compost going into the machine at one end and out the other, but the middle part was a cloud of white, hot moisture vapor. In a flash I imagined two rotary moving parts in the steam cloud, one picking the compost up and the other throwing the picked-up compost onto a new pile being formed. It was like a blinding revelation. I just knew it would work if the proper speeds were worked out. A new, revolutionary concept— only two moving parts instead of what were now hundreds of cogs, chain links, and several conveyor belts. As a mushroom grower I was almost overwhelmed by the possibilities: higher speeds, less power used, fewer breakdowns, less maintenance, more cost-effective production. The benefits seemed endless for the mushroom (composting) industry—and indeed they proved to be so.

However, here I was in the middle of a composting yard with this flash of inspiration. How was I to capture the essentials? I had no notebook or paper with me. Desperately I looked around. There on the ground was an empty Players cigarette packet. Eagerly I snatched it up and started scribbling furiously before I overlooked or forgot any essential detail. Never was an empty cigarette packet more treasured or protected than during the next few days. My nights were somewhat sleepless through my excitement, as I planned the details of how the machine would work and look! I had had no formal drawing training of any kind, but I was good at sketching ideas. I also had no mechanical machinery training, though I could fix problems and breakdowns.

While in England, in my excitement I rashly approached an acquaintance who was a professional mechanical engineer, though not associated with the mushroom industry in any way. I generally outlined my new approach for a machine to pick up organic hot compost entirely with tines (spikes) and comb it off the first set of tines, throwing it at high speed into the air for aeration and watering, to finally come to rest in the new pile thoroughly mixed, watered, and aerated. Imagine my

feelings at his crushing remark, "It won't work. The tines will get clogged up and
the whole thing will grind to a halt in a heap of compost." He said it was better
to keep to established mechanical principles.

Too Soon—
Too Long
Regretted!

Essentially he was saying to me that I, as a nontrained engineer, should not
think that I could come up with something new. If it were possible to do what I
said, engineers in the trade would already have done it! Such left-brained arrogance!
Though his remarks did sober me, rather than stopping me, they made me all the
more determined to prove him wrong—a typical right-brained inventor's response,
I might say!

Upon my return to Tasmania I was to be consumed with the need to proceed,
but where to start? I needed an engineering workshop to make one, but securing
that required at the least some rudimentary drawing to scale. So I approached a
draftsman friend and he agreed to help me. I insisted on paying him. You must
never, NEVER get help with your invention from anyone—even relative or best
friend—without paying for their work or help and getting a receipt for it. This is
because you have to establish that he or she is working for you and is being paid
for services rendered. It is also necessary for you to first establish that all drawings
become your property and will be assigned to you permanently. This can become
very valuable both in any future litigation and for copyright.

My friend drew and redrew my ideas for the machine in all elevations needed,
together with the two main component parts, the rotary spinners. I took my
completed drawings to the proposed manufacturer of the first working prototype.
The manager said that, though the drawings were not of a professional standard,

he felt his shop could make my machine to my satisfaction. "How much will it cost?" I asked. "I don't know," he said. "Not too much."

Fortunately I had had sufficient experience to know that one can never get something made (especially a first model) without an escalation in price. I told him I wanted his closest estimated price, then I wanted a price that my final cost would not exceed! I told him that I could not to give him the job unless I was able to pay him. If his maximum cost was beyond my resources, I could not proceed. For some reason the medium-sized engineering workshop wanted to take on the project. Whether because the manager liked me or because of possible future mass production, I never did find out. But what I did find out later was that their estimated maximum cost to me turned out to be about two-thirds of their actual cost. If I had not insisted on a maximum price I had to pay them, I would have been left in an embarrassing situation. The foregoing actually happened. I hope some of this you recognize and the balance you are able to put to good use.

When Should You File for a Patent?

Some of my inventor friends might wish to interrupt me here to advise you strongly to seek patent protection before you make a model. But I would counter that when you go to make that first prototype, you may encounter great difficulties, as I did, because the product is expensive, temporarily nonfunctional, or not what you envisioned. Pre-expense for patent protection could be, and usually is, totally wasted because your product may change while you build it, and the end result may need a substantially different patent application wording. You have little enough covered time as it is—only one year from the time of filing—to warrant spending it on lengthy prototype development before you have anything to offer the prospective buyer or licensee!

However, you could consult a patent attorney with a view to obtaining a country- or worldwide search in the relevant product area of your invention to see if your idea is patentable (see Chapter 7). This has the added advantage of establishing you as the first inventor of the new product. This is also the time to use nondisclosure statements literally!

The concept obtained in my first "flash" in Holland has since developed into the most-used composting machine in the mushroom industry, and it is used extensively throughout the world. The fact that I did not gain the financial rewards I should have does not detract from a certain feeling of pride in my being the first to develop a breakthrough in technology in a particular industry.

In those days I did not have the knowledge and expertise, now detailed in this book, to maximize my rewards and minimize my heartache. I found out the hard way that the better the invention, the greater the likelihood of infringement if you are not vigilant and do not have proper safeguards.

Should you make your own prototype or get someone else to do it for you? This will depend on your own skills and the size of your invention. If you have specific skills that can be applied to your invention, then fine, you can do it yourself. If, however, you know what you want but do not have the equipment or skills to make it, then you need to get the assistance of someone who has. But make sure you pay them.

For example, I once invented a series of plumbing fittings—six basic fittings that could be used by a plumber to effect repairs or connections to 6,480 different requirements. First I had to make the fittings in bronze and aluminum because they were easy to machine. I had no lathe or lathe skills, so I went to a machine workshop and asked them to make these fittings for me, giving them detailed drawings of each unit. They were happy to sign a nondisclosure statement. With the aid of my visual sampler I was able to approach plumbing hardware manufacturers and physically show them the fittings and what they could do.

At the same time I had what I called a "hand-tight" fitting, to connect polyurethane high- and low-density pipe by hand (that is, without the use of any tools)—great for field use by farmers and so on. In this case, I felt obliged to have made an experimental steel die for the ejection molding of samples for actual use. I approached a toolmaker specializing in making dies and got what I wanted at an acceptable price (about $5,000). It was not a fully functional, long-lasting stainless steel commercial die, but it was functional enough to make several thousand units so as to prove that my invention did what it was designed to do, and to satisfy an interested company with field tests.

With another of my inventions, a motion transmission mechanism to replace tracks on such machines as earth-moving equipment, bulldozers, and tanks, I had a friend with a wood lathe turn out a unit of the main working component for me so that I could see precisely the three-dimensional nature of the key component part. It was eventually put on the back burner because it needed a large heavy-machinery manufacturer to do the research and development on it, and I could

Inventions Are Often Resisted When They Change The Status Quo!

Help In Need,
Is Help To
Heed

not find one to take it on. It could not have just been added to any existing product a company was manufacturing; it would have been a multimillion-dollar project for them, requiring a total redesign of their equipment line. In any case, I realized then that if a manufacturer took on the development of my new invention, it would impact their profits short term. A business is very often reluctant to go out on a limb when it is already making a profit. Also, a company often tends to be comfortable in its own niche.

This happened to me with my wind power generator. I had developed a new type of blade to catch and convert wind power at lower speeds, which could be automatically self-aligning to the wind direction. Its efficiency was not high, but its cost/power ratio was! In other words, the system was low-tech and low-cost in comparison to the power output—good for pumping water from vertical wells!

The company I approached was Southern Cross of Queensland, Australia, a well-established old company making mostly farm windmills with reciprocal pumps (up-and-down stroke) that were prone to break down at higher wind speeds and gave very poor performance (if any) at low wind speeds. The basic design dated back to the late 1800s.

My thinking was that my design could give them a new lease on life for future generations, but their chief engineer saw immediately that it would mean a total retooling of their plant *and* retraining the existing staff, who had gotten used to the old ways (many employees had been with the company 20 to 40 years). They were selling their product well and had extensive outlets all over Southeast

Asia. Why should they make a competitive product that could have made their existing line and equipment obsolete? I could understand his reasoning.

Use A "Sprat To Catch A Mackerel"

I had a parallel response from the manager of a large bed mattress manufacturer when I approached him to be licensed for the manufacture of my Relax-a-Flex Comfort System. My design was too advanced, too revolutionary and would have disturbed the status quo. In any case, older management (probably for good reasons) is generally the least likely to make radical changes to their operations.

I was forced to return home and build a full-scale prototype of the wind power generator, with the considerable help of a sheet-metal fabricating workshop. In proving the basic concept I found operational flaws that pointed the way to further refinement and efficiency. It too has been put on the back burner. I still have an aluminum case holding my 1/16th-size working prototype. Wind power blades of various sizes have been tested in a wind tunnel at the Tasmania University in Hobart. When I have time (if ever), I will make and test the new designs, which were a natural consequence of the earlier models.

Giving Your Helpers a Helping Hand

As previously related, an engineering workshop made the mushroom composting machine for me without formal drawings. I would go to the workshop, sometimes several times a day, to show the skilled workers what needed to be done and to help make decisions on exact locations of parts. Making chalk drawings on the workshop floor became the norm. I could visualize the concept in my mind, but making it work in a practical way was achieved only through much trial and error.

In each of the foregoing cases, I *always* received an exact or very close estimate of the final price I would pay for their help. Again, you should never get any outside work done unless you know what it is going to cost you. If the people you approach will not give you an exact or maximum price, go to someone else who will. Otherwise, you may find the costs are two or three times what you are prepared to pay. Don't accept their saying, "We will do it for the lowest price possible." That says more than you can afford.

Give and Get More

I like to use a "sprat to catch a mackerel" by offering a company an exclusive "local" manufacturing license if they will bear the costs of manufacturing my prototype, as opposed to a national or international license that will come later once the invention is off the ground. It's like walking first, then running later—you are less likely to stumble! If this does not work (as it won't for a very small company), then tell them you will pay for all material costs, but not labor, which usually represents the highest costs to you.

A manufacturer, especially a small one, might compromise and say, "If you will pay for the parts I will supply the labor." That's very satisfactory, but if they also want a license, the terms of the manufacturing license should be negotiated in your favor. You might offer them 2½ percent to 5 percent of your royalties within the territory or country, or offer them the state manufacturing license instead of the whole country. Only for exceptional assistance would you offer any percentages of your net world royalties. The problem is that most inventors

Presenting
Your Product
Without
"Bugs" Is
A Recipe For
Success!

(whether they know it or not) need help. You will need all you can get, and your helper needs to feel financially appreciated. The more he makes for himself, the more you make by a factor of 20 (if you give him 5 percent)!

There's a further advantage to this approach. Once I have really started—that is, patented the invention—I have found it is very important and helpful to get others involved. It helps the momentum and gives me a better perspective as I hear others' comments and enthusiasm. Also, it relieves my work load, enabling me to enjoy a less stressful lifestyle.

Do not be afraid to give (several) small percentages of your royalty to those people or companies who can materially help the success of your invention. Their deserved reward will help you be even more successful and, at the least, will reduce the risk of total failure. They get nothing without your success, so they will continue to help you along, and that is very good for your success and peace of mind. It's important too, not to be too greedy and not to try to keep all the financial success to yourself. I can assure you, you succeed more thoroughly when you bring others with you in your success!

When I was working on my wind-powered generator (a new type of windmill), I made a rough model out of tin and fiberglass. Then I tested it in a university wind tunnel, found technical faults, made another model, and tested it again. This time results looked promising from a cost/power perspective, so I approached a sheet metal workshop and said, "I have carried out trials at the local state university, and the results look promising. I now need a working model for field tests. I would like to make you a proposition. I will pay you your quoted price for the unit if you like, but if you will bear the full cost of it, I will be pleased to grant you an exclusive license to manufacture it for this state, which will also enable

you to export to other states." (You cannot legally restrict interstate commerce anyway.)

After the owner of the workshop phoned the university to confirm my work with them, he was glad to participate in my project at very little direct cost to me. He even went out of his way to help erect the unit on a high promontory and made some helpful changes to the unit for better operation!

Having a final working prototype to offer to a marketing company is essential for success. From a practical standpoint, you need it as soon as possible, after you have worked out the bugs and plan to proceed with marketing, or licensing. You may have only a limited time in which to clinch a licensing deal if you plan to minimize your out-of-pocket expenses or have plans to file overseas patents within the convention time of one year from your first filing date. (This is another reason why I later state, delayed filing effected by confidentiality agreements and possible strategic withdrawal and refiling of already filed patents can be so financially beneficial to you, as it delays premature, heavy overseas patenting costs until you are able or ready. A thorough examination of all circumstances and factors between you and your friendly patent attorney needs to be carried out as circumstances dictate.)

Asking Yourself Questions

Having developed your invention through to your prototype, take a good look at it. Ask yourself: Can I improve it by reducing parts? Reducing costs? Improving its operation and efficiency? Making it more aesthetic so people enjoy using it? If the answers to these questions are "no," be well satisfied. If the answer to any question is "yes," which is the usual case, change it now before it's too late. Attention to detail will be highly rewarding in sales, acceptability, and return to you.

Know When to Give Up

If despite your best efforts you find it impossible to get a deal with a manufacturer, the signs are not good for your invention's success. You have held out a carrot and it has not been taken! Your own confidence in your invention cannot bring success against all opposition even if your invention *is* good. It may just be ahead of its time. Talk it over with your patent attorney with a view to withdrawing your patent application from the patent office so that it will not be published and cited against you when and if you later decide to refile your patent application.

It is one of the rather sad quirks of patenting that in almost all countries of the world, any patent that has previously been applied for and then abandoned, for whatever reason, can subsequently be cited against any later (invention) patent application—this is because abandoned as well as granted patents are published by patent offices worldwide (except the United States, which keeps abandoned patents in an insecure location prior to destruction) and are available for subsequent viewing by the general public! Feel good that you dealt in confidence with those people you explained the details to. Put your idea on the shelf for a later airing. Remember that it is unreasonable to expect that every one of your inventions should be a financial success. The secret is to minimize your expenses on your "failures" so that you have adequate funds to expend on your subsequent inventions. Too many inventors "go for broke," especially on their early inventions, then suffer greatly accordingly.

You may be interested to know some of the things I have invented. Here they are:

My Better Inventions and What Happened to Them

Legend:

P = Patented	A = Abandoned or withdrawn
U = Used	F = Financially successful
I = Infringed	Y = Yes
M = Multicountry patented	N = No
O = On Hold	* Successfully used in business venture

Title	What It Did	P	U	I	M	O	A	F
An improved mixing machine	*Mixed mushroom spawn into compost	N	Y	N	N	–	–	Y
Improved heating device	*Controlled heating with very high humidity for mushroom growing	N	Y	N	N	–	–	Y
Interlocking mushroom tray	*Movable, stackable mushroom trays without machinery	N	Y	N	N	–	Y	Y
Seat belt safety deice	Motor vehicle seat belt positive reminder	Y	Y	Y	Y	–	Y	N
An improved composting machine	Thoroughly mixed and airated compost	Y	Y	Y	Y	–	–	Y
An improved pipe fitting	Versatile "Hand-tite" plastic pipe connector requiring no tools	Y	Y	N	N	–	Y	N
Plumber's universal pipe fitting	6,480 different pipe combinations (plastic and metal) from 6 basic parts	Y	N	N	N	–	Y	N
Motion transmission mechanism	Replaced tracks on heavy equipment vehicles	N	N	N	N	Y	–	N
Antitheft device for motor vehicle	Simple vehicle protection from easy theft	N	Y	N	N	–	Y	N
Automatic watering device	Operated in accordance with ground requirement—portable	N	N	N	N	Y	N	N
An improved composting machine	Developed to break my own first patent. Cross-mix action	Y	Y	Y	Y	–	N	Y
An improved tine	Special 4-pointed anticlogging fork for use in machinery	Y	Y	N	Y	–	–	Y
An improved conveyor device	For moving heavy material—did away with conveyor belts	N	N	N	N	Y	–	N
Solid-state solar collector	For supplemental heating/cooling	N	N	N	N	Y	–	N
An improved solar heating device	Designed to heat water for swimming pools—portable	N	Y	N	N	Y	–	N
An improved bed	A new type of bed (Relax-a-Flex) adjustable for comfort	Y	Y	Y	Y	–	–	Y
An improved tube design	A new type of functional tube for Relax-a-Flex	Y	Y	Y	Y	–	–	Y
Means for welding pockets in plastic	A method to reduce costs in the making of tubes for Relax-a-Flex mattress	Y	Y	Y	Y	–	N	Y
A new and improved mattress	Latest improvement in Relax-a-Flex, halving cost of mattress	Y	Y	Y	Y	–	N	Y
Registered name Relax-a-Flex	Restricts use of name to approved users	Y	Y	Y	Y	–	N	Y
Heat means for virus control in humans	Control of virus particles by heat-treating the body	Y	N	N	N	Y	Y	N

An improved wind power means	Low-tech, low-cost power from wind—ideal for pumping water from wells in Third World countries	Y	Y	N	N	Y	Y	N	
An improved windmill	Low-tech means for self-protective windmill (from storm damage)	N	N	N	N	Y	N	N	**Work Related Ideas Are**
An improved family game	Biography (A game of life) attempted to teach life's priorities in decision making	N	Y	N	N	Y	N	N	**Fairly Common, Though Rarely**
An improved valve	A flood irrigation valve for farmers	N	N	N	N	N	Y	N	**Patented**
Means for improved filtering	An automatic self-cleaning filter system designed primarily for precipitates in heavy industry	N	N	N	N	Y	–	N	
High speed boat stabilizer	Reduces side slipping while cornering at high speed. Boat racing circuit speed improvement	N	N	N	–	Y	–	N	

Inventing While Working for Someone Else

The great majority of applications for patents seem to come from individuals working for corporate entities; they are then concurrently assigned to the corporation. You may think that if you invent something, then you, the inventor, own the invention. Although this is most often true when you work for no one else, it can be totally different if you are employed by a corporation or anyone else. You need to first examine the total situation. Ask yourself the following:

Advice Too
Soon, Is Better
Than, Advice
Too Late!

1. What is your position in your workplace?
2. What is made by the corporation employing you?
3. Have you signed agreements with those you work for?
4. What have you invented?

Your Position in the Workplace

In general terms, your position within the employment structure is crucial. If you are a partner or senior executive, your problems are multiplied in obtaining an unchallenged patent—that is, a patent that is for your own benefit rather than your employer's. If, at the other end of the scale, you are employed as a washroom attendant or some other relatively lowly position, your chances of sailing through unchallenged by your employer are correspondingly improved.

I am reminded that the original inventor of the now very popular "Band Aid" was in a relatively low position in the corporation he worked for, but, possessing an inquisitive mind, he would take his company's sticky tape home. He and his wife would play around with it, attaching gauze and cotton wool onto the tape to fashion a handy protective bandage for cuts and abrasions (especially for children).

Eventually he obtained several major promotions for his contributions to his employer's profits, eventually even becoming a vice president of the corporation. No doubt he could have tried to patent his "Band Aid" and market the idea elsewhere, but he was smart enough and his corporation receptive enough to recognize the potential benefits to both. This demonstrates how it can benefit

employees to cooperate with their employers when their inventions are compatible with the products already being manufactured or marketed.

Your Invention
Is Best
Not Your
Employers
Business!

What Your Company Makes

What is being manufactured and your exposure to its manufacture is important. For example, if you are an on-line operator or come into contact with the manufacturing processes of, say, a television component part, and (because of this) you "invent" a better component part (that works better, is less expensive and more efficient, etc.) then your employer may have good grounds for claiming the rights to your patent if you refuse to cooperate with them.

But some form of compensation should be possible, depending on the invention's value to your employer. If problems were to develop (though they should not, because you have contributed to their business) and your employer were unwilling to use or compensate you for your invention or allow you to patent it personally (but want you to assign it to them to prevent others from using your ideas), then a friendly, private visit to a qualified patent attorney would be in order.

Fortunately, such a scenario would, I hope, be a rarity. If, on the other hand, you were working for that same corporation but independently invented something unrelated, such as a new type of efficient carburetor, then your employer would probably have little claim to your invention. It seems to me that what you have invented as opposed to what your employer makes (or markets) is the thing that may determine whether it's really your very own patent or becomes your employer's patent. But get legal advice to clarify your exact position.

Signed Agreements

Usually the most damaging situation for an inventor who works for someone else involves the existence of an employment agreement between the employee and the employer. Employment agreements usually are required when an employee works in an executive capacity or in research and development. The agreements usually have provisions that any discoveries (or inventions) become the property of the employer, without further remuneration. I have heard that the inventor of synthetic nylon thread was in just such a situation and did not receive commensurate financial reward, which, if true, would seem to be very ungenerous of the large company that employed him.

I was once put in a position of having to sign such an employee agreement. I had invented two types of mushroom composting machines, and the modern mushroom farm I had helped design and build was bought out by a very large corporation. One of the conditions of the purchase was that I worked for the corporation in an executive and advisory capacity. I was also required to sign an employment agreement that required me to sign over any new mushroom-related inventions I might later develop. The same agreement specifically excluded non-mushroom-related inventions, at my request! Corporate discipline and politics did not suit my temperament, however, so we parted company and I became a freelance consultant to them. It was a much better arrangement for us both, as well as more financially beneficial to me; it enabled me to carry on what I like to do most—inventing!

Being Reticent
Is Prudent,
Extreme
Reticence
Not So

What Have You Invented?

In general terms, the more your invention differs from your employer's product, service, or work, the more likely it is that you will have no trouble patenting it for your own eventual benefit. The normal, most beneficial approach would be to first get a general release from your employers for the general subject matter of your inventions (you may not need to explain the specifics of your invention to them in order to get it). In that case you would not necessarily need to file a patent immediately. (Early filing can be detrimental to your later financial benefit. See Chapter 9.)

If your employers firmly request a full, detailed disclosure before they will grant you an exemption, you can at least request that they sign a nondisclosure statement. As appropriate, you could also file a patent application and withdraw it, or not, later. There are so many computations on this whole subject that the foregoing can act only as a guideline for you. If you are in doubt about your specific situation but want to do something, then a visit to your friendly patent attorney can help you decide your best course of action.

The Problem with Over-Secretive Inventors

It may strike you as humorous, but it is a fact that some inventors (like gold miners) often will not reveal their "secrets." Quite understandable, you might say. However, I'm not just talking about secretiveness, which could be understood with

POT
OF
IDEAS

some inventions. I'm talking about outright refusal to discuss their inventions with anyone.

Tell The
"Doctor"
(Patent
Attorney) Your
"Symptoms"
(Ideas)

Such inventors do not understand the whole inventive process, from conception to ultimate financial success—even if success is possible. And they do not understand the very real hard work in between. They tend to think that they have the "ultimate mousetrap" and that disclosure to anyone will instantly propel that person to steal their invention, which will then rob them of the millions of dollars which should rightfully be theirs. Such a possibility is so very remote that I think no statistician would ever attempt to calculate the odds of such an occurrence.

Inventors who maintain such a position will almost inevitably cause themselves to fail, even if they have the very best of inventions! Such an inventor might draft out and submit a patent application, personally handwritten and delivered to the patent receiving office, but such a patent is extremely unlikely to adequately cover the invention, so any resulting patent would likely be circumvented by another due to its restricting, narrow clauses. And that's assuming that the basic invention is a good one!

Narrow, restrictive claims of the type defined are acceptable in the motor industry because they generally cover a specific type of part in a motor vehicle. Where there is a new concept involved, however, it is most important that claims are drafted that cover not only the embodiment of the actual invention but also the broader aspects of the overall concept. This is because inventions can almost always be improved upon or otherwise altered within the overall concept, so this wider spectrum needs to be covered fully. Such drafting of claims is a skill obtained

HOLD ON FIDO!
THIS IS THE
ULTIMATE
DOG FOOD.

only after much experience, as is found with people who have handled a wide range of patent applications. Usually patent examiners and patent attorneys (who may have cut their teeth as examiners first) obtain the skill only after considerable experience.

If you see any of your own inhibitions here, you will need to modify them and come to grips with reality. This book will, I hope, help you steer a straight path to possible success with your first invention, or at least enable you to save wasted time and money so that you can proceed to more inventions and eventual success. All your inventions may be successful, but remember, really financially successful inventions are more rare. One out of five would make you a millionaire; one out of ten would most likely give you financial security.

For goodness sake, don't be like the inventor who went to my patent attorney friend with an invention for a theft-proof bicycle. When my friend asked what the essentials were, so that he could draft the appropriate claims for the patent application, he was told it was a secret! My friend's wife commented that the inventor was like a sick patient going to a doctor and refusing to tell the doctor what the symptoms were! Further help is impossible, and the patient, like the invention, loses out.

Solicitations to Give You Help

You may have been approached with offers of help with your inventions and may wonder how your address was obtained. Or you may have seen impressive advertisements offering "free" help in papers or magazines, and you may have responded just to see if there was genuine help out there for you.

In business, where there is a perceived need someone will most certainly want to try to fulfill that need, and if it pays them, that business will continue until it is no longer profitable. I would suggest that where inventors are concerned, very many of the associated promotional companies are primarily interested in

making profits from the inventors rather than the inventions—though they are not averse to the latter if additional opportunities come their way.

Remember:
"A Fool And
His Money . . ."

The Semilegitimate Approach

I have been approached many times in Europe and the U.S. from companies congratulating me on my grant of a patent and asking if I would like to receive a framed copy with a "red ribbon" or some other visual enhancment. Such people offer a legitimate service and are obviously successful because they stay in business—even though the price for the service is a little steep. Patents no doubt look great framed and hung up.

Often the next level of solicitation is a small card in the mail advising me that it has come to the solicitor's attention that an already-granted patent of mine has been cited in the granting of another patent (somewhere) and for a fee I can obtain all the details of this other patent. The suggestion is that if I knew who the receiver of the new patent was, I could then contact them with a view to cooperation or some other beneficial happening. This too sounds reasonable and helpful. But if you think it through thoroughly, your fee would probably be wasted. After all, the other patent has been granted. The patent office examiners, having cited (examined and made known) several other patents (outdated or abandoned patents or applications), have decided they do not constitute a barrier to their granting of the new patent. Therefore, no infringement is likely, unless improvement relies on some of your patent material.

The person receiving the patent knows of your granted patent and can contact you, but he would consider his patent better than yours, partly because it is a new, more recent patent and partly because he does not think (like the examiner) that your patent is relevant to his invention. He is much more likely to contact you if he feels cooperation is necessary rather than face the risk later of you suing him for infringement. Almost all patents have other patents cited. The chances of your getting value out of your fee for such service are extremely remote. But the service is legitimate, and you may find a good reason for wanting such information. The foregoing types of services and others are usually generated from computers that scan the daily reports from various patent offices worldwide, which give the names and addresses of the interested parties. Once you respond you are likely to be placed on a priority sheet for more information or solicitation at a later date.

One Born Every Minute

It seems to me that the second area of business activity directed toward inventors usually operates on the premise that "there's a sucker born every minute." The promotional company places advertisements in appropriate media suggesting that "if you have an idea, we would like to help" or that they are "looking for ideas to promote." They give an address and usually a toll-free phone number, creating the idea that your invention or idea (no matter what stage you are at) is "urgently wanted" by them and by people they are in contact with.

Both these premises are true! They urgently want your invention or idea in order to stay in business for themselves! They are "in contact" with people through their (often junk mail) mass mailings to others or media advertisements paid for out of inventors' fees. The historical track record of success to the inventor from such companies is usually abysmal by any standard, which I suppose is to be expected, because the companies' appeal is to an inventor's vanity without regard to the invention or idea.

I would suppose that only about one out of a thousand original ideas can be developed into a viable, financially successful invention. Perhaps only about one in a hundred can make it from developed ideas, which is the basis for my contention that an inventor who has one (or more) out of ten of his or her inventions become financially viable can be counted as very successful indeed. You can see that if a promotional company were honest and rejected the more obviously way-out ideas that some people have, then they probably would go out of business fast. If you approach or are approached by a promotional company, you need to know or find out your chances of success relative to what they want you to give them, both in money and in any future rights, before you part with your own hard-earned money.

I must confess that I have had very little contact with promotional companies. I have always felt that any money I was able to put aside and risk for my inventions should be controlled by myself, not others. However, to give some substance to my opinions about invention-promoting companies, I decided recently to respond to one of those newspaper advertisements to see what happened.

The first thing I received was a thick envelope in the mail containing a printed letter and various pamphlets.

Next I got a phone call from a nice lady. She asked me if I had received a package from her company in regard to my invention. I said that I thought it had arrived, but if so, it had somehow been mislaid, possibly by my children. I apologized and said I would try to locate the package. She said, "No, don't worry . . . I'll send you another one." There seemed to be some urgency that I should have the information.

So within a few days I received another package, which I again looked at. My natural inclination was to throw it into the round file. But I resisted and put the package to one side. A few days later the same nice lady called to inquire first whether I had received the package and whether I had already responded to the printed disclosure form. I told her yes, I had the information, but no, I had been away and had not yet had time to fill out the details. She was very nice about it, obviously used to such procrastination from inventors. She said that their review committee met every Friday. Could I get it to her by a date three weeks later? I said I thought I could.

Ten days before the deadline she phoned again to remind me. I said I hoped to get it out shortly. She said I could do it all in about two hours. I said yes, but finding that two hours was difficult for me. But I would manage it somehow. Five days before the deadline the nice lady phoned again, a real professional:

Nice Lady: Have you already sent the submission that is scheduled for next Friday?
Me: I have it all ready to go. It's taken longer than I thought.
Nice Lady: Fine. I don't want to have to reschedule the review appointment. If you send it by tomorrow it should get here in time.

I did send it off with a photo of one of my many inventions, which did indeed need more work on it, even though I had already spent over $10,000 on a full working model! The invention has great potential for Third World countries. It's certainly not a fly-by-night idea.

In my response, I indicated the wide range of advantages and the multimillion-dollar market so as to give them some idea of the invention's far-reaching benefits. I noticed that the address was directed to a "grant center"—just what I wanted,

The More
Persistent
The Caller
The More
The Risk Of
A "Rip Off"!

a nice big grant of money to help me with further development! All indications had been that everything was free, so I stated my desire to apply for a grant. How naive could I be as a struggling inventor?

About eight weeks later, all my material was returned to me with a letter expressing their regret that I did not want to proceed with them anymore. Interesting, as I had had no other communication with them. Perhaps they smelled a rat or decided that I was a hopeless case to get money from!

On a recent six-hour drive to a bedding show I was surprised to hear on the radio five solicitations for people with new ideas and inventions. The Minnesota Inventors Congress (MIC) of Redwood Falls, Minnesota, was right when it recently warned of escalating activity by rip-off firms. The more a company resents your pertinent questions, the more you will know that you need to back off. Be warned that these companies are adept at relieving you of your money. When you are in doubt, the Minnesota Inventors Congress will be pleased to tell you what they know about a particular firm that you are in contact with. Write to them at MIC Inventors Resource Center, Redwood Falls, MN 56283, U.S.A., or phone (507) 637-2344.

Inspiration for Inventors

Once you become an inventor, you will not need to seek inspiration for new inventions, though you will almost certainly need inspiration for problem solving or devising improvements to the invention you are currently working on.

I find that I have too many invention ideas—so many I cannot possibly deal with them. Each one I get assumes a priority in my mind for future action. My wife has often heard me exclaim in an anguished voice, "Oh no, not another idea!"

As for primary thoughts for new inventions, my automatic self-cleaning pollution filter system came to me by way of a local steel works that periodically belches out quite large quantities of precipitates (by-product microsized particles). There had been some controversy in the local papers concerning the pollution problem the plant supposedly caused, and the idea just came to me late one evening while I was traveling back from my local airport and could see great clouds of smoke and steam coming from the steel works. I knew I had to try to help solve the problem.

The primary invention (the basic new approach) came quite quickly once I decided to tackle the problem. However, my mind soon found technical problems inherent in my basic approach. Each one of about six different problems had to be solved before I could go to anyone concerning my invention. In other words, I had to be able to answer fairly direct questions from experts in the field as to how to overcome certain inherent potential difficulties. In my process of exploration I was able to anticipate additional solutions for problems that would (or might) surface later. I devised flowcharts for the whole filtration system—it became a system because the original simple solutions required a whole system of operation and control outside the main control invention.

The inspiration for the various solutions came to me one part at a time while I was visualizing the whole, often late at night when I was relaxed. For a particular solution I sometimes took a pencil and pad to a quiet place (a park once, a library another time) so that I could draw rough sketches and concentrate on the particular difficulty. The preliminary development work had to be completed first before I could possibly approach the large corporations and experts in the field of pollution control.

Historically, The Greater The Invention, The Longer Until Success

This essential approach I can confidently recommend for refinement of your existing inventions. The key is to be as relaxed as you can, without distractions. A warm bath or jacuzzi can be a great place for solving problems if the problem is uppermost in your mind. A quiet walk in the country or lying down by yourself in a warm spot or on the beach can be great too. Do not expect the solution to come all at once; it's a painstaking procedure that will sometimes take months— the harder and more difficult the problem, usually the longer it takes. One such problem took me 18 months to solve—and the solution made me have to re-patent my original base invention.

If, however, you think you would like to invent something—anything—then you will need to have another approach. It is the approach of perceived need: what you feel to be a need in some area of human (or nonhuman) endeavor. Say you have been throwing your paper and household dry waste out with the garbage yet have been paying a hefty bill for winter heating. You think, "How can I solve both problems?" You perceive the problem and would like to solve it, but how? This is very often the seed of a new invention.

Having seen the need, you now must examine with pencil and paper how you can solve the problem. How do you use the inherent BTUs (heat units) in the material you are throwing away to help reduce your heating bills? This is where you need to have uninterrupted periods of time (one to two hours at the least) to cogitate on possible ways you can achieve this (no invention yet).

While in that relaxed state you may get and discard very many possibilities: (1) compaction of your dry waste, (2) a new type of boiler or furnace, (3) a specifically designed enclosed fireplace, (4) special packaging of your material for

easier handling, (5) special collection containers to collect other people's dry waste, or (6) breakdown of your dry waste into a burnable gas and additions and equipment to achieve same; and the list goes on.

Sometimes you may have to conclude that the solution to the perceived need is not possible, or if it is possible, it is not practical. But you have gained much valuable experience in the process. Your next try will be more successful. Don't expect each idea for an invention to be the big one. It may be, but more likely only about one out of ten inventions will ultimately be functionally viable in the marketplace.

Concluding Remarks

If you have a good invention, and you know it is a good one and is needed by others, then persevere with it. If it's a case of marketing it yourself, then do what is within your capacity, as outlined in subsequent chapters. Just remember, *do not overextend yourself physically, mentally, or financially.*

The inventor of the original game of Monopoly went the rounds of a great number of game-manufacturing firms and almost gave up, but he persevered and finally found a small, young game company that was willing to have a go. As you probably know, it turned out to be a blockbuster sales item and has proved to be one of the greatest games ever in terms of popularity and numbers sold. Consider the advice of your patent attorney or agent. He or she should have your welfare at heart.

There is one thing I have found out the hard way: Firms will mostly not help you, or will greatly resist you, if you try to introduce a product that threatens their existing marketable products. This is where any interest in your product by such allied product sellers should be examined for future problems very carefully. This is where a proper agreement comes in (see Chapter 7). Be prepared for failure, even though your invention is good, breaks new ground, or is revolutionary. Such inventions take time, *much* time and effort, to become accepted for marketing. Remember, the greatest of past inventions have invariably taken years to become really successful and a benefit to humanity.

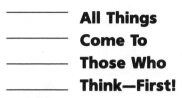

**All Things
Come To
Those Who
Think—First!**

2 The Inventor's Mind: Left Brain/Right Brain

You may well ask what this "left brain, right brain" business has to do with inventing. I hope I can convince you it has a great deal to do with it, although to make my point, I am going to simplify a complex subject. It can be fairly stated, however, that most (but not all) inventions have their origins in a right brain–dominant person.

Studies over the past few years by surgeons and psychologists have shown that the human brain has two separate (but normally connected) sides. Left and right have separate functions that enable each of us to operate on two planes. The dominant function of the left brain has been found to be analytical and symbolic—language, figures, and logic. This side of the brain enables people to communicate in symbols (as in legal documents) and make rational decisions (as in business deals). You could say that the left brain makes things happen!

The right brain is associated with visualization, intuition, and feelings. When we dream, we are right-brained. Right-brained, too, are conceptual ideas, imaginings, and the inner visualization of things as they are or may become.

Most of us possess a little of both logic and dreaming, but favor one or the other. It is clear, however, that both the right and left sides of the human brain are complementary to each other. Though it would seem that most humans have a bias, they don't always realize that an imbalance can be changed to enable each human being to understand the other complementary side.

I believe the knowledge of the two major hemispheres of our brain is of the greatest relevance to inventors who want to maximize the financial rewards of their inventions. Extensive and accelerated work over the past 30 years has confirmed previous theories that humans are unique in having complementary areas of the brain that serve specific functions. We deal here specifically with the right and left brain functions as they apply to two distinctly different attitudes in humans. The following is a list of their primary functions.

Left Brain Attributes

(dominant in so-called Western societies)

Critical
Positive
Logical
Efficient
Attentive to detail
Analytical
Verbal
Precise-speaking
Prefers sequential, logical order
Computer-like
Good with dates, putting thoughts into
    words, balancing checkbook, algebra,
    accounting, facts

Right Brain Attributes

(dominant in certain ethnic groups and
    so-called less developed countries)

Uncritical
Passive, accepting
Emotional
Prefers overviews and inventions
Mood music
Emotional response to music
Impressionist response to art
Creates pictorial scenes
Given to flights of Fancy, metaphor
Good at intuitive problem solving, art/
    music, whole body responses, motion
    skills, intuition and inspiration
Adopts a global philosophy

Can you recognize where you are dominant? Or perhaps you are one of the fortunate ones who have a good balance between both sides. If so, circumstances in your life have helped you achieve this balance, for in Western society usual circumstances favor left brain dominance. The early emphasis is on academics, with years of schooling devoted to the absorption of facts and figures, science and technology.

This training makes things happen and brings about prosperity. Those of us in the Western Hemisphere who have a dominant right brain have the advantage that all our ideas (such as inventions) have a large body of dominant left brains available who can capitalize on our ideas and make them commercially viable, thus our country's economic base continues to strengthen and advance.

To Dream Or Not To Dream Is The Question

Left/Right Dominance and Inventors

Certain ethnic groups are steeped in their past traditions and levels of mysticism and because of their right-brain orientation find economic progress as a group impossible. People decry the profit motive in the so-called Western societies, but without the profit motive we would soon sink back into a much lower standard of living, and humanity and progress would suffer. So-called "Third World" or disadvantaged countries are where they are not because they do not accept the profit motive, but because they cannot harness the correct internal forces to "get out from under." It's the old problem of the chicken and the egg—which came first? They need a good base of nationally trained (left-brain balanced) youth to make economic advancement begin to happen, and to take advantage of the inventions and solutions of their right-brain compatriots for there to be a significant lift in overall productivity. But when a country lacks the money for education (or misdirects the funds it has), then real progress is severely retarded, and the disparity between the haves and the have nots will continue and even increase.

It is very necessary in this world to have dreamers—that is, those who conceive of things that may be—but equally important are those whom we call practical individuals, such as bankers and successful businesspeople. Dreamers and sensitive people decry the success of the J. P. Morgans of this world, whereas the J. P. Morgans of this world sneer at the impractical dreamers who cannot make things

happen. The truth of the matter is that each is essential to the success of the other.

The dreamers, the sensitive right-brain–dominant individuals, can be happy all by themselves but unable to transmit their valuable ideas into end-product success (that is, success and value to the whole community); therefore they struggle for personal independence from want.

On the other hand, analytical and efficient left-brained people make their best forward progress when they use the ideas of the intuitive thinkers. Instead of being antagonistic, each type needs to recognize the other's strengths and benefits.

One of the problems in the past has been that so-called "cold-hearted" business people have found it difficult, if not impossible, to feel sympathetic toward the plight of intuitive thinkers. As clinical thinkers, they have been unable to put themselves in the others' place. They think how "stupid" the other is, and wonder why they don't do what a business person would do. They believe that the intuitive thinkers could make a killing if they'd only push ahead.

The left-brain–dominant person usually doesn't have the incentive to become like the inventor, but one of the purposes of this book is to try to get the inventor to move toward acquiring some of the skills of the left brain. (Otherwise it would be like asking a nonintuitive thinker to become an intuitive thinker—clearly a more difficult task.) Fortunately, the vast majority of us have some ability to transfer from left to right brain functions and vice versa. This can, I believe, be enhanced with a will and a way, as I will show.

Ironically, major advancements in human society have been made possible by right-brained people who can think three-dimensionally, "dreaming" of things and improvements as they could be but that have not yet been achieved. Left-brained people seldom contribute to original advancement, and even when they do, they tend to tread in the paths made previously by right-brained original thinkers.

Cooperation between the right-brain and left-brain people of this world is the key to the most progress for humankind. I believe if any country or society were totally left-brained, real general human progress would be as restricted as with right-brained societies. The real humanities, I suggest, are right-brain functions. On the other hand, so-called Third World countries might have many progressive ideas, but I believe it will avail them nothing without help from left-brain dominant people *to make it happen.*

I'm not saying that any one person is completely devoid of right- or left-brain functions. Though a person may be dramatically left- or right-brained, there will always be some chord that could be struck to bring into play the less-dominant one. For example, a left-brain–dominant stockbroker may well indulge the right-brain emotion of crying if he experienced a trauma like losing a lot of money! On the other hand, the most primitive of humans, say the jungle people of Borneo, have to do practical left-brain things in order to live and gain sustenance.

What I am postulating is that the mastery and balance of the left- and right-brain functions is the Western Hemisphere's "secret weapon" and is the reason for our comparatively higher standard of living. Our ability to "get up and go" and to make things happen is envied by many disadvantaged people of the world, and they want, rightly, to become like us.

The Balanced Brain Is The Western Hemisphere's Secret Weapon

I believe most inventors, from whatever country around the world, are (or become) right-brain–dominant people. They may have had limited academic exposure or ability in their earlier years and are often what I would designate late starters in life. Accountants, bankers, statisticians, and other left-brain–dominant people, on the other hand, by their very vocation have pursued a great deal of studying in their formative years, absorbing facts, figures, and "bookish" materials. They are sometimes so left-brain–focused that understanding the beauties of the arts, intuition, and human relationships can be difficult for them.

Balancing the Brain

Can either left-brain–dominant people or right-brain–dominant people learn to find a balance, developing or appreciating the other brain side? I think it is possible. But balancing the brain requires a wish to do so—less easy for the left-brain person who tends to look down on the dreamers of this world.

A book by Jacquelyn Wonder and Priscilla Donovan called *Whole Brain Thinking* discusses how to develop each side. Since inventors are usually (disadvantaged) right-brain people, I would encourage—even urge—you to *develop left-brain skills*. My advice to those of you who feel afraid of business or uncomfortable with activities that require analysis and use of precise details! Find books to read that require study of details! Such books could initially be quite boring for you, because they do not require any imagination on your part.

You might think a study of history, with all its details, would be just right. But if you are like me, history puts you into a nostalgic mood, and you start dreaming yourself back into the historical time—definitely a right-brain function. You will almost assuredly have to be bored with your first "efficiency" book. Pick one on self-education—the "how to" books work well. There are hundreds to choose from. It will be hard going at first; your left brain is not used to such hard work and activity and will tell you so in several ways, wanting you to go to sleep or giving you the occasional headache. These are actually good signs!

Keep at it. You will find it gets easier the more you try. I remember a book that helped me as a young person bridge the gap to my left brain (though I did not know it at the time)—that old standby, *How to Win Friends and Influence People* by Dale Carnegie. It was full of realistic, left-brain ideas on how to get ahead in business and make friends. Mixed with my right-brain humanity and imagination, it was a wonderful start to balancing my thought patterns for a well-rounded life in the future.

Education Needs

If you have had a limited educational upbringing, don't feel all is lost. Many of the most famous inventions in history have been made by people such as you. Think of Thomas Davenport, a lowly blacksmith in the 1830s in upstate New York—poor, uneducated, underprivileged in almost every way. He wasn't content to hammer out horseshoes and repair farm equipment. With sheer dogged perseverance he dreamed up and perfected the first electric motor, transferring static magnetism into rotary magnetism, in competition with all the academics of his day! The fact that he died in poverty cannot detract in the slightest from his great contribution to the essential progress of mankind. What would present-day humanity do without electric motors?

If you wish to succeed, eventually you must come to terms with reality. Read educational books on as many subjects as you can, and use that newly acquired knowledge to balance your mind. Do not be mistaken and think you can "luck it" through life unaided. I have friends who have told me how unlucky they have been, that things have not gone the way they had hoped, that next time they hope to be lucky. "Luck" thinking is self-defeating. If you are religious-minded, don't think God will give you success and do everything for you. God will help you. But of course God helps those who help themselves.

Inventing is the life blood of progress, but it needs to be balanced by left-brain thinking to make things happen. I believe underprivileged and Third World countries are unfortunately doomed to slip further and further behind the West in achievement and progress until they put more resources into truly educating the younger generations in order to develop and strengthen their left-brain functions.

I feel that it is self-evident that the natural and economic resources of any country eventually rely on the caliber and education of the people living in that country; the people of Switzerland and Japan are two notable examples. I feel that if they were forcibly transferred to the Sahara desert or the North or South Pole,

they would still, given time, become economically successful, molding their new environment to suit them because of their balanced-brain society.

Left-Brain Inventing

I have seemed to stress that only right-brained people can be inventors. This is true in general, but there are exceptions—for example, the Japanese approach to progress in more recent years. After World War II it became fashionable in Japan to find a product that was already selling well elsewhere, copy it in Japan, then export the product worldwide. This caused much severe criticism from Western businesses that had borne the major development work.

Fortunately the Japanese people are sensitive to criticism (to say nothing of expensive litigation costs and embarrassment to company officials), so there was a determined effort on their part to move away from copying. The manufacturing companies changed in a big way, moving to research and development—employing large numbers of people whose main purpose was to refine existing technologies, weeding out the bad features and keeping the good ones. This trial-and-error method proved very successful, to their great credit and financial success.

The new technologies became so different from the originals as to be patentable improvements! Many people with left-brain orientation were working together to bring about a new invention and were naturally very proud that their combined efforts resulted in their companies being granted one or more patents for the revised product or process. They usually started with another's earlier

THIS IS JUST TOO MUCH!

idea then improved upon it to make something better. But this sort of progress has been going on for generations, just like the present-day sophisticated electric motors that had their beginnings in Thomas Davenport's electric motor concept 170 years ago!

Taking Left-Brained Action

"This is all very interesting," you may say, "but I am left-brained. How can this talk benefit me?" Well, if you are truly a left-brain–dominant person, you may be involved in a technical field and know a great deal about a specific, well-defined subject. It is in the realm of your particular subject that you may be able to invent an improvement to a product or process.

For example, suppose you were in a supervisory position in a fast-food processing plant, making batter-covered vegetables and protein-filled rolls. The process is well established, and as an on-site supervisor you are confronted daily with breakdowns in the cumbersome machinery. You see that labor costs and machinery downtime result in waste and frustration to all. Through your familiarity with the process, you can pinpoint the bottleneck that is always responsible for the breakdowns and delays. If it could be changed or eliminated, your work life and that of others would be much more enjoyable, and there would be increased production and resulting profitability.

You know the problem is technical (left-brain oriented). You feel the necessity (right-brain emotion): Necessity is the mother of invention here. There has to be

a change in the process. You have concentrated, technical expertise in the subject and you come up with the answer. Your new machine will eliminate two processes and guarantee a smooth-running system! Not only will three people's jobs be eliminated, but your machine will halve the process time.

Negotiate Gently

What do you do? If you are mostly right-brained, you will probably go tell management. At best, they will thank you, give you a small bonus, and get you to sign away any rights you may have so the company, not you, will receive the patent benefits. At worst, your idea will be ignored, and you will be told to do your job and not interfere. Quite crushing to your ego!

If you are more left-brained, your approach will be more calculated. (A calculating person has to be thinking with the left brain!) If the company you work for has treated you well, you will perhaps make the machine (or a simulation of it) and date-stamp a photo of it with a witness (if it's in the USA), or even file a minimum patent application just before approaching management in confidence about your new invention. Then you will tell management that considering all savings (production space and costs drastically lowered per-end unit cost), your new machine or process will save the company $1 million each year ($1 million more profit!), besides generating many other logistical benefits. Their reaction might well be very generous to you, both money- and promotion-wise. Management usually appreciates the firm, forthright approach by employees, and conversely dislikes (or takes advantage of) the hesitant, "wishy-washy" approach.

If you are not so happy with management, then your best approach might be to show them the prototype (in confidence) anyway, to see their reaction—in a

low-key manner, so you aren't fired on the spot! If the response is negative, then approach directly other production companies in your fast-food area to see if they are interested in your machine. If it's a good machine and can be demonstrated to achieve the savings you claim, you may be able to work out a very good deal for yourself, like a higher-level position with a new company and added financial benefits!

For example, a bonus to you of ten percent of the company's total savings would in this case mean $100,000 a year to you in exchange for your allowing them exclusive use of your patent rights. Or you might be offered the chance to sell your patent rights. In this case, the correct figure might be in the region of $300,000 to $400,000, or about three to four years' worth of royalties you could expect to receive.

In any case, you must be left-brained enough to aim for a good deal! There's only one danger: don't overplay your hand or be too dominant in your approach. Go gently with your negotiations. Certainly the deal has to be good for you, but it also always has to be a good deal for the firm or firms you plan to license. Naturally I hope and expect that you would have kept in close communication with your friendly legal advisor through all this. If licensing becomes a problem, various ways to market your invention yourself are described in Chapter 4.

3 The Business Mind and Infringement

Many businesses view inventors as a necessary subspecies. Many inventors approach business with way-out, untried, unproven, uneconomic inventions, expecting to be welcomed with open arms and handed large sums of money. Businesses do know, however, that almost all major breakthroughs come from this type of inventor. They know that an inventor is usually quite helpless without them and that they can usually get the better of the inventor, which is in part why I am writing this book for you, the would-be private inventor or developer of a product you wish to see marketed.

Some new inventors seem to expect business to come knocking at their doors, offering them huge sums of money for their new inventions. This is a pipe dream, the achievement of which is very much the exception rather than the rule, except for that rare breed of inventor like Alexander Graham Bell (telecommunications) and George Washington Carver (food development).

Business Needs Versus Your Needs

The new inventor soon finds that industry is too concerned with making a profit to bother with seeking innovative products. It's the inventor who needs to beat a path to the industry, not vice versa. A company most likes new inventions that complement what it is already doing, making its existing product cheaper to manufacture and more profitable. (Note: I did not say better!) It will least like a new invention that makes its existing product obsolete, even if it is within its product range.

I had a product that the owner/manager of a factory freely admitted was superior to his. He said, "You tell me that I will need a fraction of my present machinery and less floor space?" "Yes," I said, thinking I was onto a winner. He said, "In order for us to take on your product, which would supersede what we are making now, we would have to get rid of all our existing machinery. It would become obsolete. Also, our engineering staff would have to go or be retrained, and our advertising and brand name would also have to go, as would half of our well-trained staff. The total upheaval of our present profitable operation would be unavoidable, and all for what? The knowledge of a better product and the hope for future greater profits in years to come. No, I'd rather keep running a smoothly profitable operation without hassle."

Notice he did not say he wished me success in my endeavors! He did not in the least wish me success. Why? He wanted to protect the status quo—his and that of the industry to which he belonged.

Licensing Large Companies

Interestingly, I have found that the larger the company, the more remote the possibility of a deal, unless you can get to the top management and really persuade them that your product will help their company to make greater profits within their existing operations and products. Showing your product to middle management (unless it's the research department) is usually fruitless because middle managers are entrenched in their positions and usually desirous of promotion and advancement. They generally prefer to make no radical decisions (and not stick their necks out) that may jeopardize their careers! It is most unlikely they will give you an instant response.

Usually several personal visits and sometimes forceful methods are needed. By forceful methods, I mean the implied threat of taking your product to a rival

company. This often gets attention. If the industry to which your invention is most suited is dominated by one company, sometimes the only way to get their attention is to test the market yourself, as did Ronald P. Hickman, the inventor of the Black & Decker WORKMATE, a multi-purpose work-bench. He tried to get Black & Decker and other companies interested early on but failed, so he contracted for the manufacture of the parts himself and began to make the Work Horse in his garage workshop in competition with Black & Decker and for sale to the traditional Black & Decker customer. After seeing the mushrooming popularity of this invention, Black & Decker decided to make a deal with Hickman and take it over. (It was just as well, as infringement actions increased in proportion to the Work Horse's popularity.) Legal agreements with a large company are usually faithfully adhered to, but royalties are generally lower, often by 25 percent. However, this could be deceptive because a large corporation might, and usually would, sell a great deal more of your product than a smaller firm.

Inventors Are Rarely Recognized As Prime Originators Of Success

Licensing Middle Sized Companies

The intermediate-sized company is more receptive than the large company to new products and ideas, if the products are within their general overall goals. Once interested, they pursue marketing with great vigor. Usually the key shareholders or top executives' staff have to be convinced first of the merits of the new product.

Soon, though, the inventor may get a feeling that he is no longer seen as important, that if it were not for the condescension of the company, he would get nothing at all. After all, it is pointed out, the inventor only put a little money into the product. It was the company that developed it for the commercial market and put all the risk capital into it.

Protect Your Interests

At this stage the value of the original agreement comes into focus. The licensed company finds loopholes and wants to renegotiate parts of the agreement, explaining the advantages (to the inventor) of doing so! You will also be left out of advancements and improvements in your original invention, but don't worry about it. Start putting your creative mind to a new invention! Feeling left out is inevitable, but do be very careful about any smooth talk from high-level executives or their attorneys as to "necessary" changes in agreements.

The line might go as follows: "You know, Mr. Inventor, your original invention was very primitive. We have had to put so much work and money into the product, much more than we expected, that the present product is hardly recognizable as your original. Also, we have had to go to great expense in patenting all of our improvements. We feel that as this is a type of partnership between us, you should help us be competitive, and with your help we can be! We believe much greater sales are possible, even four or five times greater than at present. We would like you to accept a change in our agreement reflecting what we have said."

You should look worried and ask what they suggest, being prepared to counter their request with a change of your own, such as their taking over all your patent protection commitments and renewals or buying your patent outright at a hand-

Agreement
Changes Can
Be Good For
Both Parties

some profit to you! In any case, mentally look at giving them no change or only one-half of what they request.

They then proceed to outline the maximum of what they want. Some ideas may be innocent and reasonable, but one might well be a change in your financial agreement. It may take the form of sharing your royalty 50/50 with them (now that they have doubled the expense and have their own patent of improvement) or (a softer approach), "You are now getting (a certain amount of money) for each unit we sell. We think that prices for the product may go down, and for us to properly plan our costs and safeguard your income, we propose guaranteeing your present royalty income of (that amount) for each unit sold, even if the price goes lower, for the life of your patent." Both proposals might seem reasonable—other approaches, too, are very subtle, cloaked in nice words! "There is no need for us both to incur legal expenses, so let's shake hands on it, and so there is no mis-understanding, perhaps you would be good enough to sign here, ratifying our mutually agreed-upon change."

You, in the meantime, have said almost nothing while facing one nice, impressive executive, or perhaps two or more of them. You may already have noticed in life that in any meeting, two (or more) against one in any discussion has the upper hand over one on one (that is why sales teams of two generally prove more effective). You feel overawed and slightly (or very) important because these important people are sitting down with you to explain their problems, wine and dine you.

You now have to ask for a copy of the proposed change in the agreement. With this in hand and with great self-control, you thank them for their time and helpful discussion (mostly one-sided!). You tell them you understand their concern for your future and understand and appreciate all they have done and are doing to promote your invention. As you get up from your seat, you say you must give proper thought to their suggestion and will be back in touch with them shortly. You may feel strong pressure to make an immediate decision, but resist it and make a beeline for the door and to your patent attorney (but not the one they deal with) for some very needed advice.

You have hurt your patentee's feelings by not making an immediate decision, and your relationship will never be quite the same again, but that's life! Be content to receive royalties as per the original agreement or some acceptable compromise and get on with some of your other inventions, if you have any ideas, or take a break until you do. If your original license agreement was not a good, tight one, now would be the time to strengthen your side by exchanging part of their wants with your wants.

What I have described here is by no means abnormal; rather, it is more the standard. It seems that the business person never feels the inventor deserves much money or recognition when it is the business person who is doing all the work, and you, the inventor, "only had the idea." You need (without being greedy or unreasonable) to be protective of yourself and, against your natural good nature, you need to be able to take a stance that matches the subtle rationalizations of the business mind.

But do not be rude or antagonize the other party. You at least should recognize their importance to you. They may need your patent, but you need their business expertise. Be reasonable. Give a little, compromise a little, but be firm. The more executives and the higher their positions, the more they want to impress (overawe) you. Otherwise, they would not give you their time—time is money and money is their business. You should think it through thoroughly. They will respect you more if you play their game, especially if you get a better deal than they wanted you to.

Left-Brain/Right-Brain Bargaining

It's all part of the general bargaining that so many of us like to do. I remember once in Hong Kong many years ago going into a private jewelry store where the manager tried to sell me a diamond engagement ring (my wife had lost her original one). I saw the one I wanted and very casually asked what its price was. "Five hundred dollars," he said. "My best price." I went on to several other nice-looking rings and had a roundabout discussion of many rings with many "best prices" for about an hour and a half.

The manager started coming alive with the excitement of the bargaining preamble, offering me drinks and privacy of discussion. I came back gently to several rings. Mine was offered at $460 this time, an extra-special price "just for me," and I went on to view other rings. I knew that his real bottom price was likely to be one-half to two-fifths of his first asking price, but you cannot rush these things in the Eastern style of bargaining. Nearly two hours after my first entry to his store, the owner asked me what I would offer for the ring of my choice. I then said, "I'll give you $260 for that ring," pointing to the ring I really wanted.

He looked at me, beamed, smiled, and said that because he had enjoyed talking to me and felt that I could direct more good business to his shop, he would ascribe his "loss" on the ring to promotion and let me have it for my offered price. Far from being sad about "losing" nearly $300, he was most happy to have had an enjoyable bargaining session! He respected me more for my bargaining ability, even though he made less (though you can be sure he did not take a loss). He would not have respected me if I had accepted his first two offers. He wanted me to visit him again. He had had such an enjoyable time!

The Individual Entrepreneur

Probably the best deal (but also one calling for the greatest carefulness in agreement) is with the individual entrepreneur who has money (or access to it), or the one-person business owner who sees a fortune in your invention and who plans to make it, all singlehandedly if possible. This person is nice, obviously successful, and praises your new invention, though pointing out to you the many pitfalls on the route to its success and the great amount of his personal expenses he or she will incur before success can be achieved. This person wants to shake hands on the deal with perhaps just a short handwritten agreement.

Ratification of Verbal Agreement to Written Agreement

As to your giving over the exclusive rights to your invention, you warm to the entrepreneur, you are flattered, and you want to concede to all these requests—but resist it. Entrepreneurs haven't gotten where they are by being Mr. Nice Guy. Say that you might be pleased to give an "exclusive" license but you feel that your agreement should be more formal and should incorporate in writing all that you have previously agreed to in verbal discussion. If the reply is, "Surely we need not go to all that legal expense," or "I thought we saw eye-to-eye on my role in promoting your invention," or "Don't you trust me?" then you need to be extremely careful. Having caught the fish on the hook, you don't want to let the line break, so you say, "Of course I trust you entirely and want you to have my invention, but if you or I were to be run over by a truck tomorrow, who would interpret the already agreed-upon terms of our agreement if it were not fully in writing?"

You should draw up the agreement or get it drawn up for you by a competent person, preferably a patent attorney. It's more costly to get legal advice now, but infinitely better than paying later! Be prepared later on after the agreement has been signed "because of changed circumstances" to get a request for a change in your agreement, and be prepared to be told that you are the "bad guy" for being "unreasonable" even if you have been and continue to be very reasonable in response to demands or requests.

You may detect a level of cynicism and mistrust on my part toward business people. Not so, it's just the way the business mind works, which is naturally to

get the best deal possible, the most profit, and the greatest success. That's what makes business people successful, and you do want them to be successful—the more the better, only not at your expense! They will like and respect you more if you can, to some extent, play their game. They least respect you when you're malleable and soft, even if they do make more money from you.

You don't have to change or become entirely like them in order to beat them. Your intention, on the contrary, is not to beat them, but to use their natural talents (which you do not have; otherwise you could do it all by yourself) to your own advantage, rather than disadvantage, so that mutual success flows in the right measure and is complementary to both of you.

The Importance of Attitude to Infringement

So your invention is a success! There is just one problem. The more successful it is, the more likely it is to be infringed. There is a saying that either no one wants your invention, so your patent expense is wasted, or everyone wants it and you are faced with numerous infringement court cases and legal fees. Actually, the best way to treat an infringement is to avoid going to court. Going to court should be only a last resort. It depends to a great deal on the circumstances.

It is possible the infringement was accidental. A small company would rather settle than incur court costs. A big company might not want the publicity. If the

infringement is accidental (that is, the infringer had no knowledge of your patent protection), then I have found that an attorney's letter to the infringer spelling out the gravity of this infringement and the possible action you could be entitled to take usually gets an apology and a promise not to carry on. Of course, if the "infringement" has taken place in a country in which you have no patent cover, then you can do nothing if they do not export to a country where you do have patent cover, but I will come back to that particular problem later.

An "accidental" infringer needs to be asked to give an accounting of the number of articles sold and a suitable amount of compensation to you, usually five to seven percent of their sales. However, even this action might turn out to be an opportunity for you if you are able to offer the infringer a license for their area— exclusive or non-exclusive. If they were keen enough to produce your product in the first place, they would be likely to be keen to make it legally with patent protection from you!

Once in my early days of inventing in Australia I had a report about an infringement and I handled it badly. I overreacted and sent the infringer a withering letter through my patent attorney with all sorts of accusations. I scolded him so much that he promptly stopped his infringement, replied with an apology (through his attorney) and refused even to discuss any possibility of an arrangement, supposing that I was too hard to do business with! A pity. I learned a sobering lesson— one of many over the years! I should have made a personal visit to him to try to work out a deal.

An Infringement Can Be A Good Opportunity

Unfortunately, more normally the company is deliberately infringing (that is, they have knowledge of your patent but have chosen to ignore it). By the way, remember that you can start the process of suing an infringer only after your patent has been granted—which may be several years after your filing date.

If you ever get into the foregoing situation, tread carefully; keep your cool and read Chapter 9 for ideas for your correct approach. And be sure to do it with your legal adviser's help.

Some Handy Tips for Inventors

These are not all-encompassing—nor all necessarily correct, in all situations.

1. Ask yourself: Why does a need exist?
2. What is the present state of art in your area of interest?
3. Brainstorm your area of interest.
4. What type of design do you want?
5. Remember, complex solutions are usually very easy to come by, but are usually of little commercial value due to their complexity and the cost of such factors as manufacture and breakdowns.
6. The simplest solutions to a problem are usually the most difficult to come by, and are often accomplished only by refining and re-refining the first complex solution!
7. Evaluate, then reevaluate.
8. Sketch and resketch your device, or write and rewrite your formula.
9. Satisfy all criteria necessary for its (your invention's) successful outcome.
10. Play the devil's advocate. Attack your invention from as many aspects as you can—costs, looks, functionality, maintenance, and so on.
11. Make or test the invention in minimum quantity or size, and refine as many times as needed.
12. Reevaluate all tested models; refine again as necessary.
13. Does it now meet all the criteria you want?
14. Low anticipated volume—market it yourself.
15. High anticipated volume—license others to manufacture and/or market it.
16. Learn how to handle inevitable disappointment. Nothing ever continues smoothly.
17. Identify market niches for your invention.
18. Avoid invention in areas of presently "hot" items—there's too much competition. By the time you got your product to market (probably two years minimum) the hot items will no longer be hot!
19. Use your local public library when things elude you; you'll be surprised at what you can find.
20. Usually try to avoid narrow-claimed patents; broadly claimed patents are best. Narrow-claimed patents can quite often be more easily infringed (broken). But circumstances will alter cases. (See Drafting your own claims can be hazardous to your patent Chapter 8).
21. Always try to break your own patent during its life—that is, finding new ways to do what you have done without infringing your existing patent. This will extend your invention life most likely. If you cannot, it is less likely that someone else can!

22. High-tech inventions often have a limited life before they are superseded by other high-tech inventions.

There's Always A Better Way

23. Low-tech inventions tend to have greater staying power.
24. Games and fad inventions, if they get off the ground at all, generally have explosive demand initially, then fizzle as others have done after their heyday.
25. Go to presentations of your invention well prepared to educate your potential licensee or customers about all the advantages.
26. Be able to answer *all* questions honestly and persuasively.
27. When licensing, try to get financial involvement of the licensee through a financial advance on an option, an advance on royalty, help from them with patenting costs, and so on.
28. Always ensure prior agreed performance by others such as minimum annual royalties, minimum escalating numbers performance each year. If not, the other party will walk all over you if they can. That's business.
29. Aim for a maximum "good deal" for yourself (this enables you to give some back as goodwill later); then make sure you give a good deal to helpers (licensees, etc.).
30. Know when to give up. This is the one essential lesson so hard for us all to learn.
31. If at first you do not succeed, which may well be nine times out of ten, don't waste your money flogging a dead horse. Try, try again with something different while you still have some cash!

4 Marketing

As we can see from the right-brain/left-brain dichotomy, it is a sad fact that most inventors do not make good marketers of their products or good managers of their businesses. They do best what they like to do, which is inventing. Nevertheless, a new invention must be marketed in order to be known. This chapter aims to outline key methods that will help you get your product off the ground, if it has a market.

Your Involvement in Marketing

The first thing you need to know is that however you rate yourself at marketing, you should avoid the easy way out of getting someone else to do it for an up-front fee. By this I mean that you should be personally involved at all times in doing your own selling of your invention, whether the actual marketing of the product itself or the selling or licensing of your product to another.

Individuals or groups that solicit you to take over from you all the responsibility for the promotion of your invention, for an up-front fee, should be avoided with few exceptions. This is not to say that at some time, now or in the future, some innovative person or group may be out there with some acceptable program to help inventors with their inventions in an overall statistically successful way. But so far, I have found no evidence to support any of the claims of such promotions. Your up-front money, subsequent fees, and relinquishment of certain percentages of your royalty, in the very unlikely event of success, ensures that you will only be considerably worse off going that route.

If there is no up-front fee, and the person or group thinks that your invention has enough merit for them to participate in helping you, then you might explore further—having, of course, first gotten the other party to sign a nondisclosure statement, if you have not yet gone ahead with your filing and feel very confident you will not need to withdraw your patent. This latter case would require an agreement setting out clearly the terms of such cooperation and the relative costs to be borne by each—and of course, the benefits! Of course, there are always exceptions.

What money you have available needs to be conserved in every way possible. Often you will be solicited when your patent has already been granted, which is too late to be of much help to you. Attention to marketing should begin to be paid as soon as you can safely do so—that is, either from the time of filing at the patent office, or earlier if it is a "hot" item and you first obtain a nondisclosure statement from your proposed licensee (see Chapter 10), which brings us to the subject of how to talk about your invention.

Dangers of Talking to Others

A good rule to follow is not to discuss the specifics of your invention with a proposed licensee or anyone unless you have appropriate cover. That is, you have applied for a patent and will not withdraw it. (See Chapter 8.) "Specifics" means the details: specifications of working parts or special measurements that make your invention unique and that might enable someone else actually to make it without any further help. You should, of course, be fully prepared to give this full information when the time is right. (I hope you have decided to use a patent attorney; he or she will gladly advise you.) You *must* request that the person or company to whom you need to reveal the exact nature of your invention sign a nondisclosure statement (see chapter 10, pages 370 through 377 for sample statements) or else you must have an application already filed at your country's patent office. But even in this case, you still need confidentiality—you always do. Confidentiality will always give you more options for future correct actions, whether you have a patent application on file or not!

Importance of Nondisclosure Agreements

The problem is that if you haven't already filed an application, a proposed licensee, to whom you have given only a preliminary, non-detailed idea of your invention, may inform you that they have research going on in an area related to your invention and that they are not prepared to sign any disclosure statement—or to treat any information you might give them as confidential—just in case they have already come up with the same basic invention that you have!

If this happens, it will be a standoff until you have filed your preliminary application. If you feel very confident about the uniqueness of your invention and its demand potential, do it right away, even with just a minimum outline of essentials. If you are not quite ready, then tell the potential licensee you will get back to them later. Another possibility is to suggest that your patent attorney and theirs communicate or, preferably, meet with each other to discuss confidentially each other's line of progress within the context of your own specific invention in order to see if a specific, perhaps restrictive or narrow nondisclosure agreement could be worked out between you.

There are many reasons why nondisclosure agreements can be beneficial to you and your proposed licensee. Do not leave anything with them or otherwise disclose anything to them. Be very suspicious if they suggest that, to save you the expense of filing unnecessarily, you could explain the full details of your invention to them, so they can to tell you if their research has anticipated your invention! If a potential licensee sees a way of using your ideas without paying royalties, or by paying less royalty, they will (sadly) do it—it's part of the makeup of the business mind. No matter how nice they are, they need to know whether you hold all the aces. If there is any chink in your armor, most business people will find it and make good use of it—and not to your benefit either!

Try To Hold As Many Aces As You Can

Dealing with Large Corporations

When approaching a very large corporation you need to be on especially solid ground. Certainly your invention needs to be in an advanced formative stage, not just an idea. A working model or even professionally drawn plans or designs would be good also, providing you have first ascertained the financial benefits and know you can answer all their legitimate questions as to why they need your invention! You have to convince them thoroughly—your dealings, to begin with, will be with middle management. At best, managers at this level are necessarily very protective of their individual positions in the corporation.

If you have, say, a unique motor vehicle invention that you wish to present to a large automobile manufacturing corporation, be prepared to receive instantly a waiver from them prior to their receiving or examining details. The waiver will state very clearly that the corporation will allow you only those rights you already have—that is, patent protection—and that all disclosures are on a nonconfidential basis.

Large
Corporations
Rarely Sign
Non-Disclosure
Statements

Large corporations (probably with good cause) want to distance themselves from the many solicitations from outside inventors, partly because of the fear of being sued later, when the product appears as one of their own models! Also, they have to protect their own research and development departments, which are always working on improvements of their models.

Once you submit your own invention to them, you can be sure that if they reject your proposal, there will be no further protection for you other than your patent application—no possibility of your stringing the patent life out by a strategic withdrawal procedure. At any later date you would have burnt your bridges thoroughly, except for any patent cover. (See Chapter 8.) Large corporations know that the individual inventor usually has very limited financial resources. Any necessary filing overseas just compounds the problems you may have.

Many years ago, I submitted one of my early inventions, a seat belt safety device, to a large automobile corporation. This was before it was mandatory or even popular to wear seat belts. But the evidence was mounting steadily that wearing a seat belt was good for one's health!

I had to sign such a waiver before the corporation would accept my proposal to even look at it. I had filed a patent application. I signed; then the corporation rejected my idea as not being acceptable to the public. It was a mechanical, electrical device—a solenoid that worked to prevent the starter motor from operating unless the seat belt or belts were secured. It was a fairly simple, safe method of ensuring the seat belts were done up. Not long afterward, legislation was proposed to make wearing seat belts mandatory. Still I was not contacted by the corporation

HOW CAN I GET MY PROPOSAL TO THE HEAD MAN?

I had approached. So I went ahead with a small motor parts company that made a retrofit model for interested customers who wished to install my device in their own vehicles.

Later still an executive order was issued in the United States requiring vehicles to be fitted with seat belts and drivers and passengers to wear them. I had filed in the United States, Australia, and the United Kingdom—all I could afford at the time. There then appeared a device that did the same function as mine but with a solid-state electrical circuitry. I was told by my then patent attorney that my U.S. patent employing a mechanical solenoid filed earlier would probably gain precedence over the new solid-state seat belt device.

However, before I could get into gear and gain financial support for my proposed legal action, the executive order was rescinded by Congress, thus eliminating the potential gain of any action I might take. The action even in those days would have cost at least $30,000, ample evidence that you must beware the costs and risks of litigation.

I know of at least one life my device saved, so that gives me some satisfaction. It was a case of its being a good invention slightly before its time, and it was, of course, a financial failure. I spent more on it than I got.

Third-Party Participation

I have found that the very best scenario for an invention is if you get financial participation by third parties. In other words, if you have an invention and try to do everything yourself, the going is usually tough. However, when you get someone

> **You Succeed More, When You Can Get Others To Help You**

Be Careful
Your
Inspirations Do
Not Lead To
Excess
Perspirations

else (preferably a licensee) to invest time and money in the project, then your chances of success are greatly improved.

When you can get others involved in your projects, there are benefits greater to you than trying to do it all yourself. Even if problems with the logistics of manufacturing and marketing develop along the way, your helpers will not willingly give up the effort and monetary expenditure they have invested. They have a stake in your product, and they do not want to guarantee a loss to themselves.

Premature Disclosures

As for disclosure to media reporters, this can be like fire; that is, a good friend or a bad enemy. Prior to filing, *any* written public detailing of your invention could prove catastrophic later. It depends on the nature of the disclosure—how much detail was printed. Published photos can be very dangerous. Such prior disclosure may actually prevent you from getting a valid patent, regardless of whether the publicity became known to the patent examiner. This is because the exposure could be used at a later date by another party who happens to find it to invalidate your patent by citing such publication (any publication) that is dated prior to your filing date and fully discloses the working and operation of your invention!

I once was involved with an infringement of one of my inventions (a mushroom-composting machine). The opposition pulled out every dirty trick they could, financial and otherwise. They managed to obtain copies of photos from obscure publications for composting machines built prior to my filing, trying to prove that my invention was anticipated by those earlier machines. Fortunately they were not on solid ground and their efforts failed, but it did serve to give me a lesson on premature publications.

Of course, there are photos, and there are photos. A photo of a distant object may disclose nothing that would enable anyone to understand how it worked, whereas a close-up, detailed photo or photos of an invention might disclose all essential details. Just be very careful.

On the other hand, as soon as you have finally filed, any and all publications concerning your new invention are to be encouraged, always providing that you do not find it necessary to stretch out your patent time by withdrawing and refiling the invention later. (See Chapters 8, and 9.) This free exposure for your invention could turn out to be worth a great deal of money to you. Also, it would be of the greatest help to you during that all-important first year after your filing, when you have the opportunity to file in other countries (see Chapter 8) where interest may have been generated through such exposure.

Stealing Inventions

Many inventors feel (especially with their first inventions) that someone might steal their inventions and make a fortune that rightfully belongs to them. The inventor who does what is necessary in the right sequence, such as is outlined in this book, need not unduly worry on this score or fear to lose his or her rights.

This feeling is counterproductive to the success of the invention and usually clouds the inventor's judgment, making him or her afraid to talk to *anyone* about even basic ideas, let alone specifics, which means that the invention cannot proceed in the proper manner to eventual success.

This is not to say that there are not those individuals (and remember that corporations are made up of individuals) who are always looking to take advantage in a given situation. But providing you take strict account of what you do and protect yourself appropriately as outlined in this book, such risk of another's blatant theft of your invention is minimized to the point of infinitesimal numbers.

The Very Best Inventions May Fail Financially

You can always recognize a potential problem developing when the other party declines or procrastinates signing any proposed letter of intent or nondisclosure, or other needed documents, or suggests that you should have a friendly handshake now and an agreement later. Make the other party put pen to paper, or back away from them. If they are genuine and do want to participate in your invention, they will come to see your position of strength and cooperate with you. Of course, your written demands on others must always be in the realm of reason and compromise, where necessary. It would not be reasonable for you to expect of others what you would not accept from them.

It is a truism, I'm afraid, that of the total time and effort needed for a successfully marketed invention, the original inventive process represents only a small fraction. Edison is reported to have said, "A good invention is 10 percent inspiration and 90 percent perspiration." Therefore, too much concern about someone stealing the first 10 percent of effort is too unrealistic to get worried about. Much more of a problem is persuading others that your invention is viable, cost-effective, and/or marketable.

It's the full disclosure of specific details to unauthorized persons that you, as an inventor, should avoid, not the general idea about what it can do. The very

Perfection
Like Perfect
Friendship Is
Ever Elusive

fact that you have a diary or journal and dated receipts for component parts of your invention will help you invalidate another's patent if someone were to steal yours. In the United States, such proof of being the first inventor could even be the means of obtaining a valid patent ahead of a person who has previously filed, but stealing is an unrealistic possibility if your disclosure has been in very general terms.

As I have said, limited nonspecific disclosures to close friends in confidence are, in fact, not only beneficial but essential in helping you to assess your possibilities for future success and to solidify your convictions as to the eventual value of your invention. However, caution and discernment are always needed as *detailed* disclosures to certain "friends" still have the potential to be troublesome if you are not properly covered.

I have never had an invention actually stolen in its formative or early stages. The stealing has come later because of the greediness of others who wanted to jump on the bandwagon of success. Some have been licensees trying to see if I was willing or capable enough to defend myself. Others have been individuals or companies that thought they could get away with it, or surmised that I could not withstand the financial strain of their legal maneuverings. I fought most of them and always won, but the legal costs were burdensome and mostly unrecoverable.

Facing the Problems of Marketing

Suppose, having gone through the steps detailed in Chapter 1, you find yourself with a workable unit ready to market. Marketing your own invention is fraught with all kinds of problems: (1) capital (money), (2) lack of expertise in selling, (3) distribution to a market you probably don't know too much about, (4) arranging your attendance at product shows, (5) preparation of brochures, (6) advertising, (7) time and expense of travel, and more.

If you have had no previous experience in these fields, life can be very tough for you and financial ruin or hardship can result. Not many inventors succeed in marketing their own products internationally, although there are some very notable exceptions, such as Thomas Edison with lighting (though I believe some of his patents were later invalidated in favor of Nikola Tesla), and George Westinghouse with his locomotive air brakes. But if you are satisfied with a local or country market, the following could help you be successful and financially secure. Even if you intend to "give it all" to a licensee, you will need to take some of these sequential steps to find interested parties to license.

But first you will need to evaluate the competition. You would be fortunate to have an invention with no competition whatsoever! Most inventions are seen by others as "being a better mousetrap." The old mousetrap then becomes the competition! If your product is no more complicated and no more costly than the item it supersedes or is in competition with, yet looks better or performs better, then you would again be most fortunate and have a much better chance of success. If there is some aesthetic merit, higher selling prices are warranted.

Price relative to performance is the best key to success. It's no good matching the opposition—you need either a price advantage or a performance advantage. If these are not present in your invention, STOP NOW and try to change it so it offers either advantage (or both of them). If you cannot do so, don't waste any more of your time and money. If you have aesthetic, price, and/or performance advantages, then proceed further.

I do not personally believe there are any real, lasting shortcuts to success. I believe all true success takes effort. Having lots of money just dumped in your lap isn't success. We have all heard the fate of those people who have come into sudden riches through little or no effort. Their eventual failure, financially and/or emotionally, is testament to the hollowness of mere instant wealth. Of course, we all want it, but it's probably just as well for our own and our loved ones' sake that it rarely happens. Wealth through effort and perseverance eventually gives the greatest satisfaction, hard though it may seem sometimes.

Merchandising Yourself

If you fancy merchandising your product yourself, consult with your trusted (not too costly) patent lawyer, who can help you understand the legal risks and potential pitfalls. Check with your attorney or another trusted adviser about requirements for selling in your state or others (or your country or another) where you intend to market, because certain types of products need state (or country) licenses before being sold in those states (or countries). For example, in the United States, the fees range from about $200 in California to no fee in Arizona. You also need to check whether your new invention falls under any state requirements, health or otherwise (such as whether it could pose a risk to children), prior to marketing it. The Small Business Administration can help too (see Chapter 10).

Know The
Parameters Of
Your Markets,
Then
Penetrate
Them

In my case, my Relax-a-Flex Comfort System beds were affected in each state by what is called law labels. A label showing the composition of the materials had to be attached to each mattress sold. Each state needed other legal codes and testing requirements (as do most countries) before the beds were legally allowed to be sold. While interstate commerce cannot normally be restricted, there are enough state laws to make it somewhat difficult sometimes.

In addition, you will be required to charge and collect state taxes on all retail sales in your state, if your state has such a tax. In Europe the countries of the so-called "common market" also have a number of health, safety, and other legal requirements you have to be aware of before you sell your product. I have great confidence that my Relax-a-Flex Comfort System or something like it will eventually supersede all present sleeping systems. Users are very dedicated. Though competitors and infringers are unforgiving, steady progress is still being made.

Capital

If you intend to market yourself, you will need capital (funds of money) to start; having too little capital is a recipe for disaster. Having about 20 percent more than your conservatively estimated needs is about right, but make a thorough examination of all your needs. Many businesses fail through undercapitalization—certainly as many as fail for other reasons.

If you have plenty of capital, more than is sufficient for your estimated needs, much of the following will be less problematic, but if money is restricted or you have to borrow it, then your risk of heartache and sorrow is greatly increased. It is my estimate that only about one in twenty succeed in marketing their own products successfully, and most of those with only marginal success. Only about one in a hundred succeed very well. With those odds, you have to wonder if these people might have done even better had they licensed their products to a larger specializing company.

Nevertheless, marketing in accordance with the following guidelines could be profitable for you and rewarding in many other ways. Don't start unless you can get, or until you have the funds to carry it through properly. However, as we saw at the end of Chapter 2, the marketing situation is different if you are a part of a well-funded company that has expertise in your new product area.

Selling

Do you have selling experience? Being a nice person who can talk to others is not good enough. There are techniques that are essential to learn. Unless you are very confident, you might want to hire salespeople with the attendant weekly salaries and various government regulations to comply with. Fortunately, this comes only when you have the product to sell; therefore, the decision as to whether to do it yourself or hire another can be delayed.

Market Experience

Are you familiar with the marketing of allied products to your invention? Do you know where the markets are and how to penetrate them in a hostile marketplace? I say hostile because almost all new products have great initial resistance to marketing, and you are entering them (perhaps) without a track record, making it harder for your invention to be accepted. Fortunately, though, your enthusiasm for and knowledge of your product helps overcome marketing inexperience, as long as you are not too shy or reserved in talking to others.

Be Especially Careful How Much You Spend

Shows

Attendance at some new-product shows to promote your product is almost always essential for its success eventually. Besides the minimum costs of a booth (generally $500 to $2,000 each in the U.S.), there is the staffing of the booth (two people minimum), plus travel, food, and hotel expenses for both of you, and don't forget follow-up time with an office, telephones, and secretary! Perhaps your new product lends itself to starting with mail order sales, which will help delay the costs of attending shows (see "Mail-Order Sales" later in this chapter).

Brochures

Many years ago I thought that I could design my own brochures and do a good job describing my own inventions. After all, I was the inventor and knew all about what I had invented. Now I look back at some of my primitive efforts with horror and disbelief. For just a small additional cost per brochure I could have increased their effectiveness so much more.

　　If your product is going to be presented at shows, or if you wish to impress a would-be licensee or customer, you will most often require some outside ex-

pertise. But don't just go to any advertising agency unless you have money to burn! In any case, you need to convince your chosen advertising agent that you really have something unique. Get the best you can afford. Try not to skimp in this area unnecessarily. In advertising, more than anywhere else, you get what you pay for, providing it is what you want and not just what your advertising agent wants. Advertising agents will often try to sell you what they think you can afford rather than what you really need! Be careful in your approach; tell them you have limited means (even if you don't!). The old saying "A fool and his money are soon parted" is very applicable here.

It is most important that you strive to obtain only that which is appropriate for your invention. Sometimes this is obvious. Sometimes you may first have to do your own testing or research by asking other people (such as friends) for their opinions. For example, if you intend to go to shows, you can be sure that you will need brochures, but what kind? Single-sheet, black-and-white, four-color glossy, single- or double-foldover, booklet, multipage? Is your proposed show open to the public or trade only?

In general terms with trade shows, the higher the sales price of your invention the fewer brochures you require, but you need increased quality (and therefore cost) of each brochure. With consumer shows open to the public, a two-tier approach is needed for brochures. The single-sheet photocopied flier type (lots of them) should be on hand to satisfy the children who will usually pick up anything and everything they can as they go by, or to give to casual passersby who are only marginally interested in your product.

You should also have a more expensive brochure for the really interested persons who stop and discuss with you the value and benefit of what you have to sell. This second-tier, more expensive brochure (at a cost suggested by the selling price of your product) is kept at the back of your stand, or even hidden away, to utilize its value to the fullest for the right type of customer or potential buyer.

Chart A gives you an idea of how many brochures you might need for the different types of shows you plan to attend. In conjunction with this, Chart B.1, B.2, and B.3 give you an idea concerning what you might pay for each brochure in relation to the unit sales price of your invention.

The purpose of these charts is to give you a guide as to where to start; the combinations are almost limitless. But by way of example, if I invent a road-making machine costing $100,000, then I would go only to highway construction shows. Knowing that I might sell only one or two units at each show, I would have a nice single-sheet, four-color brochure made, costing, say, about 30 cents each, for handing out to the anticipated 500 persons attending the show (although I would have to have at least 2,000 printed to keep the price down and to use at other shows) and a second brochure costing me perhaps $10 to $20 each for those perhaps 20 very interested potential buyers who really want to study the road-making machine in much more detail and want to use the brochures themselves to convince their business associates why such a machine would be good to purchase.

At the other end of the scale, if I invented, say, a molded plastic, nonspill, nonbreakable mug for children that could be sold for $2 each, I would first decide

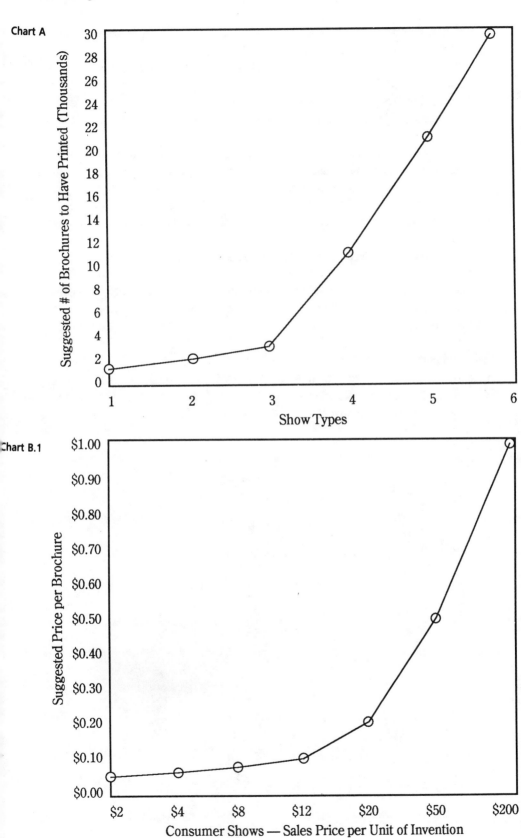

Chart A

Suggested # of Brochures to Have Printed (Thousands)

Show Types

Chart B.1

Suggested Price per Brochure

Consumer Shows — Sales Price per Unit of Invention

whether I wanted to sell wholesale to the trade by exhibiting at trade shows, or sell at full price at consumer shows open to the public.

At trade shows, I would consider giving some of my mugs away to convince would-be wholesale buyers of the value and the benefits of my children's mug. I would have a limited number of black-and-white or one- or two-color single-sheet (or perhaps single-fold) handouts costing up to 8 cents each—a print run of at least 4,000.

For the consumer shows, I would have only black-and-white or one- or two-color single-sheet handouts costing up to 4 cents each, which would mean that I would be looking at a print run of over 20,000.

If you have time and like to travel, and if you generate from each show enough money to pay all your expenses—hotel, airfare, and general out-of-pocket (as well as leaving a worthwhile profit for yourself)—marketing your invention yourself may be just the way to go. Selling your product at an allied product show can be very rewarding if your product has eye appeal or is what might be called an instant consumer-purchase item. If you have to do a lot of explaining as to how good it is or how it works, you may find that your considerable expenses might exceed your income!

Advertising

Advertising is a specialized profession. As I said, you usually get what you pay for: low costs, poor advertisements; high costs, high exposure (but not if the high cost goes into the wrong advertising slot or medium). It's costly any way you look

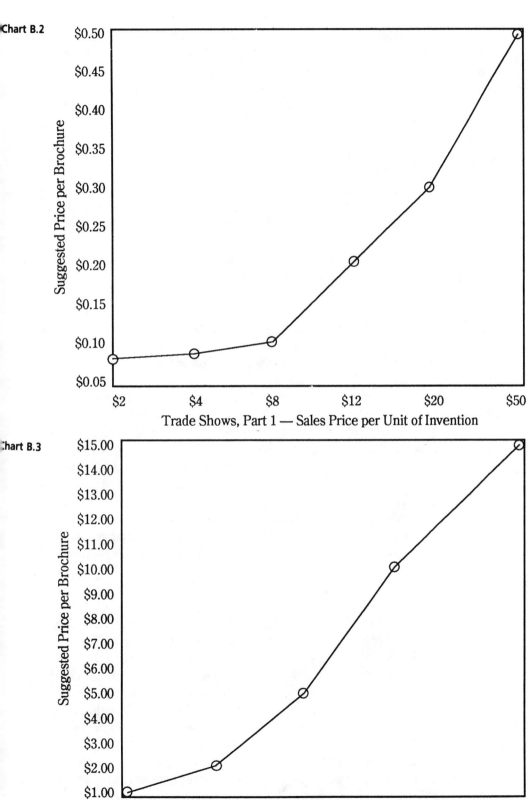

Chart B.2

Suggested Price per Brochure

$0.50
$0.45
$0.40
$0.35
$0.30
$0.25
$0.20
$0.15
$0.10
$0.05

$2 $4 $8 $12 $20 $50

Trade Shows, Part 1 — Sales Price per Unit of Invention

Chart B.3

Suggested Price per Brochure

$15.00
$14.00
$13.00
$12.00
$11.00
$10.00
$9.00
$8.00
$7.00
$6.00
$5.00
$4.00
$3.00
$2.00
$1.00

$200 $1,000 $5,000 $20,000 $50,000+

Trade Shows, Part 2 — Sales Price per Unit of Invention

at it. If you are already in advertising you can save some big money. Of course, if your invention is a small, improved, already-needed part for, say, a motor vehicle, then the mass advertising referred to here does not necessarily apply: A small advertisement placed in appropriate product magazines would be fine and generally is of good value for a limited but steady run of sales, which leads us to our next discussion.

Mail-Order Sales

If your sales at shows are not successful or if you find it too costly, be sure to try a mail-order service with advertising in appropriate papers or magazines and with nice brochures you can send to responders. Mail-order sales may be a shortcut to initial success, or they may be a relatively inexpensive way to get started and to build up funds for a more determined and longer attack on the market, shows, wholesalers, and so on. This will depend on your product and finances as well as your temperament.

You can send mail orders for appropriate products through parcel post at considerably less cost than what you'd spend attending shows. Your time is now your own and, should sales pick up beyond your physical capacity to handle all the incoming mail, packaging, addressing, and so forth, you will be able to involve your family first and then employ someone to help you. Many present-day successful businesses had their early beginnings with *both* of the approaches we've discussed— shows and/or mail order.

The big drawback to both is that your time and resources are tied up in your product, making it difficult, if not impossible, to have what I would call an inventor's lifestyle—one where you can let your fertile mind dwell on new ideas for future inventions. Your own personality will determine your best route (left-brain–dominant verbal and administrative skills or right-brain–dominant intuitive conceptual skills, or a balancing of both; see Chapter 2). If you like the idea of having total control of your own product and do not want to do further inventing outside the limits of your present invention, then go for the shows or mail orders—they will keep you very busy!

Know When to Give Up

"If at first you don't succeed, try, try again." So the saying goes. As far as inventing is concerned, I don't believe you should try again and again to flog a dead horse, but I believe you should try and try again, with a new invention! After all, inventors are generally regarded successful if they have only one really financially successful invention in ten. Who can tell which of your first ten is going to be the winner? You will at first always think, "This one is it," but if you go through all the correct procedures, you will almost certainly come to a different conclusion for most of your inventions.

If you do not subject each idea to proper scrutiny, you may get so stuck and bogged down with your first pet project that you'll never get the chance to reach your full financial potential with that real winner. There is no disgrace in admitting that your latest one is nonviable, for whatever reason. As I have said, your invention could be before its time!

My very first invention was a seat belt safety device that prevented a driver from starting the motor vehicle unless the seat belt was first fastened. It had the effect of disconnecting the starter solenoid when the seat belt was not secured, but it in no way affected the operation of the motor vehicle once the engine was running, even if the seat belt was later disconnected. This was in 1963, and seat belts were only just being fitted to passenger cars. Though there was ample evidence of their value, there was great resistance from the general public to using them. No laws were in effect as there are today making the wearing of seat belts mandatory. So my invention failed financially because it was before its time (but I still have the satisfaction of knowing it saved the life of one person, who had reluctantly fitted my device to his car and then saw its good effects after being in an accident!)

Division Of Effort And Resources Can Cause Both To Fail

Failure to succeed with any given invention must be accepted by all inventors as a matter of course. As in life in general, no decision is always guaranteed to be the right one. But to persevere against all opposing indications is a recipe not only for failure, but often financial disaster as well, which will have lasting effects on the inventor's ability to recover and have another go at it.

One more word of caution: Having two or more inventions is good only if you have them farmed out to licensees. To take more than one invention to market yourself, unless they are closely related, can have serious repercussions. Division of your effort and resources can cause both to fail. You are but one person, and there are just 24 hours in each day! Also, as the value of a patent extends only for up to 20 years (17 years after issue in the U.S.; 20 years from the date of

TOO LATE I FOUND OUT DEVELOPING OVERSEAS MARKETS CAN BE DANGEROUS.

If It's Worth Evaluating, It's Worth Evaluating Properly

filing in other countries), you will get older and more stressed as time goes on—the older you become, the more stress and strain you feel.

Then again, your whole business could be at risk with any setbacks to you personally, such as illness or death. You don't want to give up in this way! This is why I say having some company market your invention can save you a lot of strain and possibly ensure its life after death—yours and/or the patent's!

**Cost/Price
Is Very
Unforgiving In
The Marketplace**

5 Pricing

You should know after reading Chapter 4 whether your invention is appropriate to be marketed by you rather than to be licensed to another or sold outright. Then your next consideration is, "What am I going to sell it for?" A mistake here could be fatal and is generally the main area where products fail and individuals and corporations go bankrupt—because correct pricing has not been taken into account.

Pricing is part of marketing, but it is such an important part that it needs a chapter to itself. If you have not done any selling before, you might be at risk in wrongly calculating the price at which you need to sell your invention. You may have heard that retail prices should have 50 percent or even 100 percent markup on the wholesale price, or in other words, twice the product's cost. These are deceptive figures that could trip you up if used arbitrarily and without thought.

There are several approaches to pricing:
1. What your product is worth to others (uniqueness)
2. What others will pay (against competing products)
3. What it's worth to you (what it costs you to market it and make a profit)

If you see that numbers 1 and 2 are less than number 3, you had better start again with a new invention or refine your invention to make it worth more to others. Another approach is to take a closer look at number 3 to see if you can market your product at lower cost. Of course, if you license others who are already established in your product area, their marketing costs would be significantly lower due to their already-established manufacturing abilities and sales outlets. Now let us look at numbers 1, 2, and 3 in greater detail.
1. If your product is sufficiently unique and is of value to others, a price equal to 25 percent to 50 percent greater than the inferior, less-unique product might be in order.
2. If there is a limit to what others might pay, you would price your product at that limit and hope you can make a profit by proper attention to number 3.
3. A much safer approach than number 2 is the in-depth approach of fully costing your invention while keeping a watchful eye on numbers 1 and 2.

Do Not "Go
For Broke"
On Any
Invention—
Otherwise You
May!

If you are doing your own marketing, you will have to do the mathematics. If you are planning to license, it still helps to have a good idea of each step in pricing. As you try to see your product from a business point of view, you may be able to refine it, change it, and make it more cost-efficient.

The Cost Approach to Selling

Your Product

Let's start at the beginning and work through all costs as if you were a commercial business.

So you have a device or product and find out that you can get it manufactured in quantity at, say, $5 each at the factory. You might be tempted to put a price tag of $10 on it. Don't! As we shall see, there are many direct and indirect costs that have to be included before a profit is made, such as (1) delivery, (2) storage, (3) packaging, (4) interest on money, (5) advertising costs, (6) office expenses (rent, telephone, and so on), and (7) your time and/or an employee's time with vacation and sick-pay allowances. Then there are indirect costs (not money you have to pay out directly for your product, but things that still cost you). These could be (8) returned merchandise and damaged stock, (9) bad debts, (10) incoming shipping costs, (11) motor vehicle costs, and (12) contingencies. Some accountants might dispute the positioning of direct and indirect costs, but the end result will be the same. A friendly chat with your own accountant will help you cover everything you need in your particular costings. (See the actual projected costings of new [mythical] "boomerang" inventions later in this chapter.)

Let us now examine the costs. You need to truthfully assess each one. If you don't build in the costs now that would or might be applicable later when you are in full swing with your products, you might find yourself either paying additional expenses out of profits or raising prices later—both of which are to be avoided if at all possible. Of course, you can leave out those items not needed in your case and put in additional ones that you consider valid.

Delivery-In

This means your maximum but realistic delivery costs of all component parts to you or the licensee—that is, the total average delivery charges divided by the number of complete units so delivered.

Storage

This is all storage costs. Don't fall into the trap of saying, "It costs nothing because I will use my own home, workshop, or garage." Find out storage costs locally per square foot or the equivalent and assess a proper value to your own storage. After all, if you expand later you will then have to pay in hard cash for that needed extra storage. Cost of storage should be divided by the average number of units stored for a given time.

Packaging

If your product has to be individually packaged for your customers, there will be labor and materials involved—be realistic and don't skimp here. The way your product looks when customers receive it is very important. If the goods arrive in untidy, bashed-about packages, customers may return them as being damaged and request their money back! Add a per-unit cost.

Interest

This is interest on money used in the payment for operation, stocks, and supplies. If it is borrowed money, you should calculate the actual interest estimated to be charged. If it's your own money, calculate the interest you could prudently invest it for. Calculate total monthly costs divided by actual or projected monthly sales to arrive at a unit cost.

Advertising

This is all costs for advertisements and brochures, whether for television, radio, newspapers, magazines, or specialized publications; professional advertising fees; and/or shows and all associated costs. Put down your estimated first-year total anticipated costs for all of your planned advertising and divide by the total number of (conservatively) estimated unit sales. This will give you the cost per unit, which you will need to keep within reasonable bounds. It might equal 5 percent to 10 percent of your selling price! Too little advertising will not be good for sales, but too much advertising has broken many a good seller.

I knew an aggressive manufacturer and marketer of waterbeds in Tasmania, Australia. He set up a motivating, escalating profit-incentive scheme for his sales personnel and decided (without doing a forward sales balance sheet) that the more

Product's Eye-
Appeal Is
Often Crucial
To Sales

beds he sold, the more profit he would make! It turned out that the reverse was the case. He used television advertising to boost his sales, and it did. It also rose the escalating commission he had to pay out, thereby reducing his per-unit profit. As it turned out, he did not make enough per unit to cover the unit cost of his television commercials. The more he sold, the more he was losing. Within one year from the start of his great new marketing approach, he and his business went totally bankrupt! Yet his product was good. He did not fail because of his product but because he had failed to do his pricing properly with due regard to ALL his expenses, overheads, and projected profit margins. He also made no allowance for contingencies.

Office Expenses

Here again, do not fall into the trap that an office is free if you use your own home. Nothing is truly free, and if you outgrow your home office, you will soon find it costly to change to a new location with all its attendant costs: rent, equipment, supplies, and so on. Divide total projected costs of running your office, including rent, into total projected sales and arrive at a cost per unit. Be generous!

Labor

Count your own time as if you were unable to do the work yourself. You would, or might, have to employ and pay someone else if you become incapacitated. Anyway, you don't want to work for free, even if it is your own invention and business. Direct labor is that amount you have to pay out each week. Indirect labor is also a factor and often the downfall of small start-up businesses. Some of these indirect costs are employee taxes, insurance, and holiday and sick pay that you may or will be liable to pay at some time in the future—sooner or later! Some business concerns allow as much as 50 percent of employees' direct pay as an add-on cost because of retirement and other special benefits. Still, if you are not quite sure of the real figure to add on, 25 percent extra would be a good starting point. Add both together for the year's total labor expenses and divide by the number of estimated units to be sold in that year as before to come up with a unit cost.

Here, for a change, don't worry too much about a higher or lower sales rate. Labor per unit cost is much more stable than most of the previous factors. The fewer the sales, the less labor will be needed, and more sales usually means more labor, but the unit cost normally does not change dramatically, though greater efficiency may be possible. Remember, you can never expect hired help to work as efficiently or as fast as you do; it would be unreasonable for you to expect this (if it were otherwise, they might be in your position). Don't expect or calculate your hired help to give you eight hours of work for eight hours of pay. With start-up and finish, lunch, coffee breaks, and attendance at the washroom, a realistic figure might be only six and a half to seven hours of actual productive time daily. Take this also into account.

Returned Merchandise

Returned merchandise and damaged stock must be anticipated for the first year, at the end of which time more accurate figures will become available to you. It will, of course, depend on the invention you are marketing as to whether damage in storage or transit could make your invention totally irreparable. Only you can make this judgment. Of course, you don't expect any returned merchandise, but it would be quite exceptional for you not to get any. So be on the safe side and put a percentage down against costs. If the worst doesn't happen, you will be ahead financially, enabling further expansion or a reduction in price. If the worst happens, you are prepared. If you are not prepared, life could become tough for you, making recovery more difficult. Expect the worst and hope for the best—then you will not be disappointed!

Everything Costs Something

Bad Debts

Bad debts are to be expected to a greater or lesser degree. Insufficient allowance for these has sent many a business to bankruptcy. Don't let it happen to you. A purchaser's check could bounce; or someone may get his card-holding bank to reverse the charge entry within 30 days. Someone you trust may later be unwilling or unable to pay, and collecting could be expensive. Minimize your exposure to losses by getting payment from single sales before you send your product. Bulk sales to retailers and wholesalers are your biggest risk. Always get a credit report on all your retail and wholesale customers. Make sure they have a reliable payment record by phoning several of their other suppliers, as well as their bankers, to get a credit report. These outlets would like to sell your invention first and give you payment later—the later the better, so that they can "use" your money. This is fairly usual and is to be expected. This credit could kill your fledgling business,

however, unless you make provisions for it first. Your lowest and very best net selling price should not be less than 17 percent on top of your total unit cost price. The reason for this is that you need to put your whole operation on a business footing and get a good return for your sacrifice. You will be glad of good profits, especially if someone decides to infringe your product (see Chapter 9). Remember, too, that with less work and risk you might have been able to license another company and receive a 5 percent royalty.

Be prepared to offer a price, minus 2 percent for payment within ten days, net full invoice price in 21 days. You have to be strict from the beginning. Big chain stores are the worst. You might be happy to get such a large customer; you assume they are good for payment. But they may not tell you their "normal" terms are net (full payment) 90 days! You must first negotiate a written agreement for realistic terms you can handle, then insist your customers keep to it. If they insist on terms to suit them or else they will not take your product, don't let them have it. You don't need to guarantee your own demise! Tell them the terms could put you out of business. If they want to sell your product, they will come to terms.

You can be sure that if your product is unique and a good seller, the larger companies do not want you to go out of business, but they will squeeze you very hard with all kinds of arguments to get you to reduce your price. Buyers for large companies usually have a "game plan" for purchasing new products, which *always* involves saying your price is too high, then suggesting that your new product could sell for less, anywhere from 15 percent to 40 percent less. They will point out that you could make more by selling a larger volume (which is not necessarily

true). Your pre-game plan is to allow enough "fat" (profit) in your asking price so that you will be able to satisfy their request for a lower price and still end up with an amount that will satisfy you.

Allow Enough "Fat" In Your Asking Price

Whatever your asking price is, there will *always* be requests for a lower price, especially from a small company or entrepreneur. With smaller companies, you have to start with even higher prices and never go below a 20 percent markup. There is an inverse relationship between volume of sales and percentage markup. If you have an exclusive invention and it is salable, the demand will be there and wholesalers or large stores will want to handle it—they will pay to be exclusive marketers!

The buyers' job is to purchase your product at the best (lowest) price possible, so let them think they are earning their salaries by playing their game. Tie any reduction in price to increased sales, *but* do not let one large company take the majority of your production so as to make you completely dependent on them (unless you have a license agreement guaranteeing minimum sales and prices). To compute the bad-debt figure, add between 2 percent and 10 percent of your final cost per unit, depending on your exposure to bad debts—more if you have a limited number of outlets.

Shipping Out

Shipping costs are often forgotten when a product is priced. If you can get your customer to foot the bill, so much the better. More normally, but not always, customers expect the price you quote them to include delivery. Divide the total average delivery costs by the numbers to be sent to arrive at unit cost.

Motor Vehicle

You will have to run a motor vehicle for all sorts of expected and unexpected reasons aside from delivery. If you use your own private motor vehicle, then keep a log of the journeys and mileage attributable to your sales, and charge a mileage fee or percentage of use allowance. Divide total estimated annual costs by the annual anticipated sales of units. If the product is successful, you will be glad you have built in costs that will enable you to fund new motor vehicles.

Intangibles/Contingencies

Unlucky for some are those intangible costs and expenses, sometimes called contingencies. It's a catch-all term for those odd things that you haven't thought to charge to the invention or product but that are there or soon appear. A 5 percent to 10 percent charge for this item on *all* your listed expenses would be realistic, at least until after your first year's operation. I've known some people who have lost money (their supposed profit as well) even when they have included a 15 percent contingency allowance, but that's because they did a sloppy job of estimating their total costs and overheads in the first place.

Can you think of anything I have forgotten to include? Think a moment: What business are we talking about? Yes, the inventing business. Can we get protection for our patents without incurring costs? No! Each year we will have patent cost expenses— patent searches, examinations, patent attorney fees, annual maintenance fees, and so on. Had we in fact forgotten these items and neglected a contingency item in our costing, then these patent costs would have come out of our own profits. You should, of course, select only those costs that apply to your own invention. But if you think there are extenuating circumstances that create additional costs, then you should include them.

In any case, you should know that most inventions—and most small and one-person businesses—fail because insufficient allowance is made for total marketing costs. Don't be concerned initially at overallowance. You can always adjust your prices down or put your product "on special." But raising prices due to under-allowances is very bad for a product you are just launching. You do not want to be in a position of having your own royalties eroded because of underpricing.

Now you may begin to realize why I favor licensing others to market my inventions rather than taking the whole burden on myself. Nevertheless, I realize it's sometimes the only way to get started. By way of practical example, we will next explore a hypothetical invention that you wish to market yourself. Let's arbitrarily "invent" a new type of boomerang that is made out of plastic, is guaranteed to perform a figure eight, is safe for children, and cannot hurt anyone (we hope!). Here are the figures:

Pricing Our Boomerang

Conservatively estimated first year sales: 50,000 units
Overall size: 14 inches
Weight: 5 oz.

Plastic @ $1.80 per pound = unit cost of $.60

Manufacturing cost of boomerang ex factory (price as sold by the factory without shipping added) at twice raw material cost = $1.20
50,000 × $1.20 = $60,000

Two die molds: $12,500 each
Life of each: 25,000 units = $.50 per unit cost = 25,000 per annum (two)

Freight from factory to your packaging facility: $250
$.05 per unit × 50,000 = 2,500 per annum.

Pre-packaging—two-color printed shrinkwrap to go on cardboard packages:
$.20 per unit
$20/100 in 25,000-lot run × 2 = 10,000 per annum
Other packaging, shrinkwrapping, and labor: $.30 each × 50,000 = $15,000 per annum.

Note: With your own in-house labor, you may pay only $5 per hour for the unskilled job, but you have to allow twice what you pay because that is what it will probably cost you with all the present-day labor add-ons—downtime, sickness, holidays, insurance, taxes, and so on.

Advertising and brochures: allow 10% of sale price (including giveaways)
Average freight out: $.80 per unit = 40,000 per annum
Returns: 5% of sales—say $13,000

Telephone and office materials: $50 per week = $2,400 per annum but say $2,500

Office help: Two people for processing, returns, etc. @ $250 each = 500 total per week = $26,000 per annum

Depreciation on equipment, first year: $1,000

Office and storage rent: $500/month = $6,000 per annum

Supervising person (yourself or another): $20,000

Hazard and insurance: $2,000 per annum

Motor vehicle: $2,000 per annum

General overheads not already covered: $2,000

Contingency (for the unallowed and unexpected): $2,500

Patenting costs, first year: $3,000

Travel to sales promotions: 4 per year @ $750 = $3,000 per year

Show stand cost per show at $400 each: 5 per year (one local) = $2,000

Interest on borrowed money (start-up costs): $100,000 @ 13% per annum = $13,000

This borrowed amount should be ample for start-up even though first year costs are about 1/4 million, because you don't have to pay everything on day one.

Explanation	Unit Cost	Cost per Annum
Factory cost		**60,000**
Die amortizing		25,000
Freight in		2,500
Printed wrapping		10,000
Packaging		15,000
Freight out		40,000
Telephone/office materials		2,500
Office help		26,000
Depreciation		1,000
Rent		6,000
Supervisor		20,000
All insurance		2,000
Motor vehicle		2,000
Overhead		2,000
Contingency		2,500
Patenting costs		3,000
Travel		3,000
Show stands		2,000
Interest		13,000
		$237,500

Advertising say	25,000	Never Mix Your Profit With Your Royalty
Returned merchandise say	13,000	
Total	$275,500	

Total / 50,000 into $275,000 = $5.50
Add on your royalty say $.50 = $6.00 per-unit cost
Unit cost $6.00 × 200% add-on = $18.00 retail purchase price
Unit cost $6.00 × 60% add-on = $ 9.60 sale to retail outlets
Unit cost $6.00 × 25% add-on = $ 7.50 sale to wholesaler with retail outlets
(chain stores are the same as wholesaler)

On this basis, assume your allowed costs to be $6.00 for each unit. Each unit will be required to have a retail price of $18.00. If you are to get wholesalers interested, the preceding fairly represents your starting prices and gives you some flexibility in your individual selling negotiations. You might think that selling retail is the best. But this is not necessarily so, as you would have proportionately low volume to high expense and risk. Large chain stores or wholesalers will give you the best overall monetary return (if you are paid on time). There are also hidden profits, as some allowed for expenses would be greatly reduced.

After you've worked out your own costs and arrived at your total estimated markup costs per unit, the next crucial step is deciding what profit you require. I have just listed some arbitrary figures for the boomerang, but you may feel that your new inventive product might need more or less profit. Never mix your profit with your royalty—that is, the royalty you would have expected or negotiated if you had licensed your invention to someone else. Each should stand on its own merits. Your profit margin is important. Some influences on this figure will be whether you sell each unit with you as the sole marketer, whether you sell to retailers like the local gift shop as well, and whether you sell to wholesalers and major distributors. Possibly it would be best for you to plan for all three major outlets, but you will naturally expect a different profit from each.

The general principle is usually that smaller and lower-cost items require the greatest markup because you are required to sell more product for your monetary return. For example, a safety pin that costs 1 cent to manufacture might well end up retailing at 10 cents, which equals ten times the manufacturing cost or a 1,000 percent markup; whereas the manufacturing cost of an electric clothes dryer might be $100 and its retail price $225 (a 125% markup). Some of my original composting machines cost $83,000 (with my royalty) and sold for $95,000—a markup of only about 15 percent.

You will have to judge where you need to be with your own profit margin, but for the boomerang in our example, 200 percent on your total costs, or $18.00, would allow you to give approximately 60 percent off the recommended retail price (of $18.00) to a specific store wholesaler or major chain outlet (you would make only 25 percent but would sell a great many of them); and to sell to specific smaller stores, giving them 45 percent off of your recommended retail price; and finally to sell retail (which is always more costly) at the full recommended retail price.

**Don't
Undercut Your
Retailers**
Whatever you do, do not attempt to advertise your product below your retailer's selling price—it's very bad business. To do so would cause great ill will, and your retailer would be entitled to either cease buying your product or (if you've signed an agreement) to instigate a legal case for damages against you, by your action!

Personal Protection through a Corporation

The preceding should help you on your road to success, if the business life suits your fancy. Starting out can be stressful, but fun. However, your fun may be eroded if you have not taken certain protective measures against unforeseen events that are totally unconnected with your inventions. This has to do with your personal and business exposure to outside influences.

In this day and age of excessive litigation, it is clear that each of us should protect ourselves by whatever means possible. One of the best ways to separate our personal lives and activities from our outside business holdings is to place these nonpersonal pursuits in one or more corporations. Each corporation becomes a separate entity, like you and me.

The problem is that the more you are perceived as being successful, the more likely you are to be sued. In recent times, the legal system in the United States has tended to punish the innocent as well as the guilty by requiring that you defend yourself, usually at great expense—enough to make you or your business

fail! It is not right that a mistake made by someone else, perhaps an employee of yours, should jeopardize your own personal assets. But it happens. Making a corporation of your business might insulate you from such unknown personal risks, as long as you are not criminally negligent.

Form A Corporation Before You Need One

Generally, partnerships are, with very few exceptions, to be avoided for the same reason. For example, if your partner (or someone your partner instructs) injures another person, that person's legal adviser might be able to bring you into court as liable for damages. Of course, circumstances alter cases. The action eventually might fail, but the costs and worry of financial personal ruin aren't worth it. Recently I heard of a case that helps to illustrate my concerns for your financial well-being.

A child was seen to deliberately run into the road, obviously not noticing the approach of a truck, and the child was killed. All witnesses agreed that the truck could not have avoided the accident. It should have been regarded an open-and-shut accidental death. However, it was found that the truck driver did not have a valid driver's license. The child's parents sued the truck driver's employer, citing negligence. The employer lost his business and most of his assets, wiping out all his past years of effort. Unfortunately, so often all one gets in a court of law is an interpretation of the law, not necessarily true justice! Defending oneself can be very costly these days.

I have some well-established mining claims with a line of ownership going back over 50 years. About five years ago some claim jumpers instituted proceedings (presumably with a prior arrangement with an attorney) on a technicality. At one

Don't Let
People Think
You Will "Cave
In" Under
Stress

point it was suggested that I settle by giving some of the claims to the claim jumpers to save going through the long, drawn-out legal battle. It was all very stressful, even though I had the claims in a separate ownership of a corporation. We won after a five-year period, but it cost over $40,000 to defend the claims.

What had I done wrong? Nothing. I was perceived by their attorney as likely to cave in under his continuing legal pressure and expense. The protection and peace of mind afforded by the corporation enabled me to think properly and make intelligent, vital decisions. I was fortunate to have a good attorney of my own on a retainer basis—I paid him so much each month to defend me against legal assaults. He's been worth every penny. I can recommend that you do the same as soon as you are able to support it through the profits of your business.

A corporation is the way to go in all but the smallest of businesses, though you do not necessarily need to start out right away with one. Do not wait until you have trouble before you form one, because doing so would be more likely to work against you in a court of law. Naturally, seek further advice, especially from your accountant, before you form a corporation. Tax advantages could be significant, too. Get your legal adviser involved. I myself would never attempt to form a corporation without legal help.

So now you are beginning to see that having a good product with good demand and profits is only one area of success. Originally, before the large successful businesses of today were formed, individuals like you recognized the preceding

and took appropriate steps, thereby setting the foundation for their enterprises' future successes. I hope that you may establish the good foundation necessary to achieve your own goals by applying some of the essential principles in this book.

More Information Is Not Necessarily Better

**Know The
Other's Minimum
Performance—
Before
It's Too Late!**

6 The Importance of a Written (License) Agreement

So you have an individual or a company you want to license to make your new invention. Now you face even more important decisions that will make the difference between success and failure. Exclusive or nonexclusive? Royalty advance or outright selling of your patent right? How much to ask? Should you sell your patent outright in one country only? How long should you license it for? What minimum performance should you require? Supposing the licensee does not perform? And there are many more questions you probably did not know existed until you read this book.

Don't Rely on Trust Alone

One thing is sure, you must *not* accept the offer of your potential licensee to write up a contract. It might look good to you, but there are undoubtedly things the agreement does not say that, I can assure you, might have the effect of ruining your chances. If the licensee does submit an agreement for your signature, look at it very closely and compare it with one you would have given them. Also let your own patent attorney view it for his or her comments.

I would personally caution you against getting a nonspecialized attorney to work on your agreement. Besides the considerable expense, there is an unfortunate tendency for nonspecialist attorneys to look at the worst-case scenario and put in such restrictive wording that you may find your proposed licensee is prevented from signing such an agreement. Just make sure that your own essential needs are met.

Be Wary Of
Extra "Nice"
Businessmen
You should aim for an agreement that is not only good for you but also very good for your licensee because, once you license them, they must have the greatest motivation to succeed and make a worthwhile profit. If you are too greedy, you either won't conclude the agreement, or if you do, it won't be a good arrangement for either of you and it will not be adhered to.

Of course, you should and must avoid the "handshake" type of agreement that puts nothing or very little in writing—especially if there are a lot of verbal promises and the licensees "seem" like nice people. Companies as well as individuals can go back on their word and, regretfully, often do. My standard argument is, "Suppose you or I get run over by a truck? Who is to interpret our agreement?" A signed agreement is a safeguard for both the licensor (you) and the licensee (the others) and will protect both of you from the unexpected. It is my experience that the unexpected usually does happen.

I have a contractor friend who is good-hearted. He often conducts good business arrangements and sales agreements. But he has not thought it right to ask that such agreements be put down in a detailed written form. He is embarrassed to do so because he feels it might show that he distrusts the other person's word. The result is that he is constantly finding that these verbal, handshake agreements turn sour and he is left the loser, so much so that he and his family are constantly in financial difficulty and have to work out solutions to past agreements from a position of weakness and hardship.

Because of human nature, agreements not in writing are often changed later. Either party can claim a future need or supposed necessity, usually in an attempt to get a better deal. A good friend of mine told me that he had arranged to do some road works to upgrade a "nice" person's land in exchange for some other land he wanted. I recognized it as a bad, one-sided deal. However, he said he had agreed and that was that. When, however, it was time to exchange deeds and make the transfer, the "nice" person insisted that my friend's work only partly paid for the land he was to give him. He asked for another $20,000! The "nice" person ended up with a net gain in excess of $100,000. My friend, of course, lost money on the project. So much for the "nice" deal without a written agreement.

It matters not whether you trust someone, including—perhaps especially— relatives. In a business arrangement you should always have an agreement in writing and exchange signed copies so that there can be no mistake as to both parties' intentions. I once had a wealthy business associate who was recognized as a good church member and was well respected by a number of people for his good deeds and charitable contributions. We came to a verbal agreement for the work I was doing for him. I said I would write out our agreement to formalize it. He straightaway turned angrily toward me and said there was no need for anything in writing, that I should trust the word of a man in his position. He took some offense that I should even suggest his word was not good with my request that he sign some piece of paper.

My pleasant response was, "Certainly I trust you," though in this case I told a white lie, "but supposing you or I were to be run over tomorrow? Who would then be able to interpret or otherwise fulfill our verbal agreement, unless there were some signed agreement to back it up?" He said, "That wouldn't happen and you will have to accept my word because I never sign any agreement personally."

I told him that I thought our verbal agreement was financially good for both of us but that I on the contrary never went into any financial agreement unless it was properly signed by both parties. I told him I very much regretted that I could not proceed with our agreement and, therefore, the deal was off.

He signed the agreement. Ultimately, this man fulfilled exactly one-half of the promised amount and has never forgiven me for insisting on a written agreement, because then he would have given me nothing! Some people become wealthy by taking unfair advantage of others—a human trait that perhaps we all at one time or another run into during our travel through life. We should always try to protect ourselves from being taken advantage of, especially where our financial or emotional needs are at stake.

My contractor friend will continue to have financial and operational problems until he learns that written agreements are essential for smooth business success. I said to him once, "I will make an inspired statement. The people you have in the past made verbal agreements with, who have let you down the most and robbed you of the most money, originally seemed to you the nicest and most honorable people." "Yes," he said, "how did you know?" Be very wary of the nice people who refuse to sign or forget or procrastinate signing any agreement with you. Do not commit your own funds or efforts until you have such an agreement. It is essential to your ultimate long-term success.

You see, if you act on someone else's verbal promise before there is anything in writing, or even while it is being written, there are people who will use your

Legal Help
From Licensee
Is Like A Lion
Helping A
Baby

commitment, against you, to get a better deal. That's business. They are nice about it, too!

Unfortunately there are many people who will promise you things they have no real intention of carrying out, though they expect you to carry out your promises. Then, when you have already made some real commitment, you are in a poor position for negotiating.

I learned this lesson from a big company. The managing director and chief shareholder showed great interest in my inventions for the mushroom industry. I had made and trial-demonstrated a unique composting machine; it was my first major commercially viable invention. Several months earlier, I had made the mistake of applying for my patent before I had perfected its commercial design, which had in turn forced me to start work on applying for patent protection worldwide sooner than I now know was necessary (see Chapter 9).

At the time I met this nice managing director, I had completed the design and trials of my invention, and I had made a movie showing it in operation. I had also shipped a working model to England for a major industry showing. But I (and he) wanted to cover many major countries. This would be possible only within the one-year convention period allowed from my first filing application; time was running out. I had insufficient money to pay the filing costs. The managing director told me he definitely wanted a license agreement, and he asked me to cable instructions for the filing in nearly 20 new countries! I was so excited and pleased that I did the filing immediately.

He must have been pleased too, because he had maneuvered me into a position of no return. My very poor bargaining situation turned out to be a disaster on four counts, though I didn't know it at the time. (1) I had to pay for all the costs of all countries, even though the company had no intention of marketing in all the countries. (2) With the verbal promise of sales promotions worldwide, I gave the company an exclusive license with no minimum-performance clause. (3) The royalty was a fixed figure for each unit sold—a good amount then, but with inflation and time, the sales price went up and my relative return went down. (4) My very expensive trial model was taken by the firm as a manufacturing model and became a total financial loss to me.

Leaving Room For Error Is A Big Error

My (then) poor understanding of the business mind cost me very dearly over the whole life of the patent—probably not less than half a million dollars. I had to initiate constant infringement actions and would have started many more infringements had I the financial resources; generally two infringements were in some form of progress at any given time. The fact that I won them all was of no direct financial benefit to me, because of the loss of royalty and excessive delay in all legal systems associated with patents and the heavy costs involved.

This written agreement that we have talked so much about does not have to be in legal terms, but it must truthfully reflect what is wanted and expected on both sides. Be specific on what you want and expect, and give your licensee what they want and expect as well. If there is some discrepancy, try to compromise and meet their needs. You need their efforts and goodwill to succeed yourself.

Don't leave room for error or ambiguity. For example, to require a licensee to give the sale of your product their "best efforts" is meaningless—it sounds good, but "best efforts" as you understand it and as your licensee understands it may well be so far apart as to be unrecognizable! Such a phrase, by itself, is a fairly standard way for a licensee to avoid doing much at all. You may ask why a licensee would want a license agreement if they weren't keen on your invention. Of course they are interested in your invention, but that does not mean they want to manufacture and market it! Although it does not often happen, a licensee may see your product as a competitor to an existing product they are already selling, and they want either to eliminate some potential competition or to sit on the fence to see what happens. In either case, you are in trouble unless you have a provision for the licensee's minimum performance and a minimum escalating royalty (minimum monetary amount) to you. Also, the more the licensee perceives you as a threat, the more they are willing to look good to you, perhaps by guaranteeing certain minimum yearly payments. The foregoing, remote as it might be, should impress upon you the vital role of a properly executed agreement.

Finding Qualified Licensees

Finding qualified licensees is relatively easy. Finding one that has the time and motivation to discuss a license agreement with you is a great deal harder. You need to be persistent and persuasive. The old idea that industry will be clamoring at your door to offer you all kinds of deals for your invention is totally false. You have to put the effort into finding and convincing the right one to help you. Inventor

When Needs
Must, You
Should Try To
Meet Their
Needs

types are not generally good at this, having had little experience. But painful though it might be, you have to put forth the effort. You and only you can do it.

My experience has been that your best chance to find that licensee depends on your own needs. If you are prepared to invest additional time and money in your inventions, a capable and allied manufacturer is generally all too willing to be licensed if you will take on the major responsibility of marketing, either by yourself or through others. If, on the other hand, you are able to manufacture by yourself or arrange for others to do so, then finding a marketing organization that is willing to market another good product in their market range is relatively easy, price and quality being acceptable. Whether you market yourself or through an organization, both take a good deal of effort and involvement on the inventor's part.

If both approaches are outside your area of expertise and wishes, then you may be able to get another individual, small promotional company or business-development lawyer to take over your position by offering them some appropriate percentage of your royalty, even up to 50 percent or more in certain circumstances. They then do all the work and you reap a proportion of their successful efforts. The value of this approach is that by getting others to commit their time and resources to your invention, you better ensure a worthwhile return to you. They put effort—emotional, financial, or both—into your invention that you cannot. When you have to, do it. Better to have a piece of cake than none at all!

With a needed new technological development, approaching a larger allied corporation that already manufactures and markets their own products could prove

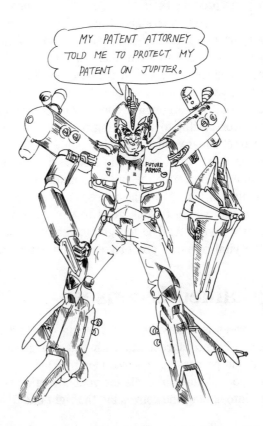

the best, especially if your product upgrades or otherwise improves their markets. But you must be wary to look out for the possibility of the firm's inclinations to go slow on your (competitive) invention.

Easy (Price, Quality, etc.), All Things Being Acceptable

Demonstrate A Working Model to Your Potential Licensee

Having a working prototype for demonstration is a distinct advantage in all the preceding. In general, you will be at a distinct disadvantage if all you have is an idea or a patent to present to a would-be licensee. This is because seeing is a much more potent force in convincing others of the viability of your new invention. For example, if you had an idea or even a drawing, for a new motor vehicle carburetor that you claimed increased efficiency by, say, 30 percent, you would probably get zero response from a motor vehicle manufacturer. And even if you did, any license agreement could not be as advantageous to you as if you had put a prototype model on one of their vehicles and demonstrated beyond a doubt that what you claim is in fact correct.

Seeing is believing, and believing gets others fired up with enthusiasm—to your own benefit. The single-most important persuader in any invention is its obvious demonstrated value in what is claimed, more so than its selling price (though price ultimately will prevail).

"Seeing Is
Believing" Is
True With New
Inventions

Having a great new invention that you know will work but that you have not been able to demonstrate *does* work is very unconvincing to a would-be licensee. Businesspeople are usually left brain–oriented. An inventor is usually right brain–oriented. They think that if you, the inventor, are unable to demonstrate your idea's workability, why should they have more faith? You should not expect others to make work what you cannot. The carburetor example is a good one. If you examined the granted patents of carburetors for gasoline engines, you would be amazed at the variety, many of which, however, are obviously nonviable. Patent examiners do not attempt to make any judgments as to the viability of a given invention. That is not their function. If you have worked out why your invention should theoretically work but have not demonstrated it, you are almost surely doomed to failure with it.

For example, I had an invention once for an antigravity device that worked on the theoretical utilization of centrifugal force. I went to great lengths to make it work, drawing and refining the parts needed. I thought it would be very good for outer space use if I could capture even a 10 percent bias of gravity in a given direction. It all looked good.

A retired Lockheed engineer assured me it had to work, but I knew I had to demonstrate it. I gathered the parts I needed and assembled them, then attached a 1/2 horsepower electric motor to the contraption and flipped the switch. Faster and faster the device rotated, with violent vibrations—and then it exploded! The forces involved in my antigravity device were too great to contain. I had not demonstrated that it would work (though it told me areas where I might get it to

do so). The additional work and technology were beyond my resources, so I gave up on it, and put it on the back burner. To this day, though I suspect that the counterbalancing forces may cancel out, I am not sure of it altogether. Certainly I had nothing I could convince a would-be licensee to take up. But imagine the response I would have received if I had been able to demonstrate a working antigravity device.

Industry Will Not Court You, You Must Court Industry

The more your invention resembles the final marketable product, the more potential success you will have at finding a good licensee. Licensees generally are least interested in doing further extensive work in refining for market your invention, though they will wish to refine and streamline it for acceptable retail or direct sales to customers.

Though I have outlined a more-defined "Near-Perfect License" in Chapter 7 to enable you to customize your own license agreement for your own attorney's approval, I thought you would like to view one of my own license agreements. It demonstrates how license agreements can be tailored to suit particular requirements. Pay special attention to my comments and the appendix at the end.

Sample License

The following license was different from the norm and reflects the three-tier royalty applicable to the Relax-a-Flex Comfort System, which gives me a cross-check on parts supplied versus product sold. It keeps the licensees psychologically honest!

This License is made the _____ day of _____ 19 _____

between Gordon Douglas Griffin _____ ,

("the Licensor") of the one part, and (name and address), having

its registered office at _____

("the Licensee") of the other part.

DEFINITIONS
In this License the following terms shall bear the meanings set against them:

The Patent Applications—the Design Applications particulars of which are set forth in the Second Schedule hereto;

The Authorized Tube Supplier—the person or entities identified in the Third Schedule attached hereto and any such further person or entities as the Licensor may specify in writing to the Licensee as an Authorized Tube Maker or Supplier or to be deleted as such for the purposes of this license;

The Authorized Stabilizer Supplier—the person or entities identified in the Third Schedule attached hereto and any such further person or entities as the Licensor may specify in writing to the Licensee as an Authorized Stabilizer Maker or Supplier or to be deleted as such for the purposes of this license;

Affiliate Company—any company which is or becomes a subsidiary;

Beds—any support means for furniture using the subject matter of the First and Second Schedule

Tubes—the actual support and stabilizing mechanism;

Health-related Markets—hospitals, nursing, geriatric, and convalescent homes, bad back and health centers, Chiropractic-Chemist Guild outlets;

Consumer markets—department stores, furniture stores, individual consumers, mail order houses selling to consumers and any other outlets designed to sell products for use by individuals;

Commercial Markets—hotels/motels, ships, armed forces, government nonmedical facilities, and other generally accepted commercial applications.

Definitions are important in that under certain legal conditions there can be no possibility of misinterpretation by your licensee when you make specific statements.

1. License

1.1. The Licensor hereby grants to the Licensee, from the date affixed above on the basis set out hereunder without any further steps or formalities having to be taken by the parties to this agreement, an exclusive license to manufacture and purchase for all markets in Europe (East and West) and sell to and through all European markets the Hybrid Relax-a-Flex Comfort System beds and all individual components for such beds, excluding the manufacture of Tubes and Stabilizers, under the Patent and Design Applications and Registrations in Schedules One and Two and made according to the invention protected thereby, in the Territory during

the period specified in clause 15 of this instrument. Without in any way derogating from the generality of the aforegoing all individual components of Relax-a-Flex Comfort System Beds manufactured and sold by the Licensee pursuant to the provisions of this License shall also be manufactured in accordance with the invention described in the Patent and Design Applications.

Defining What You Want Now Saves Misconceptions Later

1.1. Spells out what I was granting and limits of territory.

1.2. The Licensee shall purchase all Support Tubes and Stabilizers installed in the beds sold under this License from one or more of the Authorized Tube Suppliers and Authorized Stabilizer Suppliers listed on the Third Schedule attached hereto but may manufacture all other components of the beds or obtain manufacture and supply of such other components as the Licensee reasonably determines.

1.2. Makes sure that the licensee can purchase key component parts only from another licensed manufacturer of those specialized parts.

1.3. The Licensee shall not purchase Sensitive Foam from manufacturers other than those approved by the Licensor which approval should not be unreasonably withheld.

1.3. The foam quality must be approved (so far as is practicable).

1.4. The Licensee shall also be entitled to sell Relax-a-Flex Comfort System beds in other parts of the world, outside the Territory, upon written approval of the Licensor so to do, which approval shall not be unreasonably withheld.

1.4. If the licensee applies to sell elsewhere and has kept to the essential parts of the agreement, I must allow them to.

2. Royalty

2.1. The Licensee shall pay the Licensor _$ (an amount)_ in consideration of the grant of the License rights as an Advance Royalty, no later than _(date)_ .

2.1. I needed an advance on future royalty.

2.2. The Advance Royalty shall be accounted for to the Licensee by taking same into account against fifty percent (50%) of royalties payable by the Licensee to the Licensor as set out in sub-clause 2.3. so that fifty percent (50%) of the royalties to be paid pursuant to that sub-clause shall first be set off against the Advance Royalty. Accounting to the Licensee as described above shall continue until the full amount of Advance Royalty has been accounted for to the Licensee.

2.2. Fifty percent of royalties due will go to pay off the advance, after which I get 100 percent of the royalty payable.

2.3. The Licensee shall pay to the Licensor a royalty of _____ percent (___%) of the aggregate net invoice value from the European Factory, but excluding any sales or value added tax, of sales of Relax-a-Flex beds and components and for replacement parts of Relax-a-Flex beds by the Licensee under this License. Any sales of Relax-a-Flex beds by the Licensee to a related Company of the Licensee shall be subject to the payment of Royalties as herein provided to be

Aiming For
More Than
You Want
Enables You To
Give Some
Away

based upon prices to the said Related Company that will be in accordance with transactions at arm's length.

2.3. This tells that the percentage of royalty is agreed upon and there are to be no underhanded dealings to avoid it.

2.4. The Licensee shall keep at its registered office separate accounts and record of all sales of beds, together with all sub-license transactions under this License, giving true and clear particulars thereof whereby calculation of the aforementioned royalties payable can be made.

2.4. This requires my licensee to keep true and correct records.

2.5. Within thirty days of the end of each calendar month, the Licensee shall send to the Licensor a statement giving details of sales for that month together with total Tubes and Stabilizers purchased and showing the sum payable for royalties, together with payment thereof. The Licensee shall pay the royalties due directly to Relax-a-Flex account no. _____, or other as directed from time to time.

2.5. Spells out the necessity for statements and payments and where both should be sent.

2.6. The Licensor shall have the right to inspect the Licensee's books of account and records at the Licensee's registered office in relation to Relax-a-Flex bed's

sales at any reasonable time during business hours by his authorized representatives, who shall be entitled to take copies of or extracts from such books.

2.6. Being entitled to inspect books is essential in any agreement, even if this action is seldom carried out.

With Your Feet On The Ground, You Have Less Far To Fall

3. Marketing

3.1. The Licensee shall, on the request of the Licensor, ensure that all beds sold under this License are marked with the trademark Relax-a-Flex and with such references to applicable patent and design protection as may be reasonably specified by the Licensor.

3.1. All products have to be marked with the trademark Relax-a-Flex.

3.2. The Licensee agrees to become a registered user of the trademark Relax-a-Flex for so long as this License shall remain in effect and will, at the request of the Licensor, apply jointly with the Licensor for registration as a registered user of that mark.

3.2. My licensee agrees to use my trademark so that my product is standardized worldwide, no matter who is licensed.

3.3. The Licensor shall be entitled to call for inspection of samples of beds sold under this License for the purpose of satisfying himself that such beds meet with his approval in quality and finish and the Licensee shall observe any reasonable recommendations which he may make to ensure that the beds sold under this License are of a high standard of performance.

3.3. Again, this is a check against a substandard product being produced at any time.

4. Contrary Action

4.1. In the event the Licensee brings any legal action of any kind to invalidate or challenge the Patent or Design Registrations (of the Licensor), this agreement shall immediately terminate and the Licensee agrees to pay all sums due hereunder at least ten (10) days before litigating any legal action.

4.1. If my licensee decides to avoid paying further royalty and challenges my patent protection, he cannot expect to keep this license.

5. License Non-assignable

5.1. The benefits of this License shall be personal to the Licensee so as to be incapable of assignment by it. The Licensee acknowledges that the License is non-assignable and is personal to the Licensee and the Licensee shall not assign, mortgage, charge or grant any sub-license in respect of this License without the previous written consent of the Licensor which shall not be unreasonably withheld. The Licensor expects that the Licensee will need to grant sub-licenses in order to cover the markets.

5.1. This makes sure that I should be aware of anything my licensee does with his exclusive license.

5.2. The copyright in any drawings or photographs prepared in relation to beds sold under this License shall belong solely to the Licensor.

5.2. This keeps the copyright in my hands.

6. Advice

6.1. The Licensor will at all times during the continuance of this License give to the Licensee such advice, assistance, and information as the Licensee may reasonably require to enable it to manufacture and sell the said beds to the best advantage, but the Licensor shall not be required to incur any traveling expenses in or about so doing.

6.1. I will give all assistance possible, but not at my expense. This makes sure that I am not called upon weekly to travel somewhere, at my expense, at the licensee's whim.

7. Improvements

7.1. Each party hereto will, at all times during the continuance of this License, communicate to the other party any improvements it may make or acquire on the subject matter of the said patents, and will fully disclose to the other party the

nature and manner of performing the same and will permit the other party to use and vend the same during the subsistence of this License without payment of any further royalty, premium, or compensation other than such as is hereinbefore provided.

7.1. This mandates a free exchange of ideas between myself and all my licensees.

8. Infringements

8.1. The Licensee agrees, at all times during the continuance of this License, to promptly give notice in writing to the Licensor of any act of infringement or any threatened infringement of the said Patents or any of them of which the Licensee becomes aware. If the Licensor elects to institute legal proceedings to restrain such infringements the Licensee agrees to give the Licensor all information and assistance within its power to enable such proceedings to be instituted and prosecuted to a successful conclusion.

8.1. If the licensee becomes aware of any infringement, he is to advise me immediately and give me all information so that I can institute proceedings.

8.2. Alternatively, the Licensee will be at liberty (subject as hereinafter mentioned) to institute and prosecute such proceedings in the name of the Licensor but at its own expense and for its own sole benefit (providing due royalties on such infringements are met upon the successful outcome) upon keeping the Licensor effectually indemnified against all claims, costs, charges, and expenses of any kind which may be incurred thereby anything as shall or may be requisite or desirable and will give to the Licensee all information and assistance within its power to enable such proceedings to be instituted and prosecuted to a successful conclusion, provided always that the Licensor shall be at liberty at any time to instruct such separate counsel and to engage such expert assistance as the Licensor may think fit to represent the Licensor's interest in any such action paying all additional expense thereby incurred.

8.2. If for some reason I am unable to institute proceedings, or perhaps am incapacitated, then my licensee could start proceedings by himself to protect himself (and me), in his own name, if exclusive; otherwise in my name.

9. Royalty Cessation on Invalidity

9.1. If the Patents in any action for infringement of proceedings for revocation be declared to be invalid on any ground whatsoever, all Royalties payable hereunder shall forthwith cease to be payable but if the decision of the relevant court making such determination shall be reversed on appeal, the said Royalties shall forthwith again become payable together with all royalty which would have been payable but for the adverse decision.

9.1. If an infringer (or someone else) were to challenge and invalidate my patents, then the licensee would be under no further obligation to

If Your
Licensee
Attacks Your
Patent,
Withdraw Your
License

pay me anything; however, if my appeal were successful I would be entitled to collect all I would have been paid during that time, as well as a resumption of all royalty as if there had been no challenge.

10. Best Efforts and Performance

10.1. The Licensee agrees to use its best efforts, consistent with good business practices to make and market beds using the principles contained in the subject patent, and to maintain the exclusive manufacturing status the Licensee has to pay for product promptly according to the terms of the supplying manufacturer of tubes and stabilizers, and also be within six months of the program for sales of Relax-a-Flex product according to the attached schedule of marketing.

10.1. The term "best efforts" is given a bit more bite.

10.2. Any continuing help given by the Licensee to the Licensor which directly results in further licensees in other parts of the world not already covered by the Licensor, will attract a bonus of fifty percent (50%) of the royalty obtained from the licensed holder's selling price. This bonus to the Licensee will continue for a period of two years beyond such time as the Licensee furnishes meaningful help and assistance to the overseas license holder. The Licensor and Licensee agree to contribute fifty percent (50%) each of any stand direct cost which is mutually approved in order to facilitate such above license entry into an overseas market.

10.2. Should my licensee help me to obtain further licensees, I will give him half of my royalties and we would also share equally in the show stand costs.

10.3. It is further agreed that, where a market demand exists for beds using the Relax-a-Flex Comfort System principle in the territory covered by this exclusive license, such demand shall be met within six months either by the Licensee direct or by the Licensee granting a sub-license (which License shall incorporate the appropriate *provisions* of this License) to another entity in order to avoid an unsatisfied demand situation.

10.3. Any demand for the Relax-a-Flex Comfort System has to be satisfied by the licensee, somehow—or else!

10.4. The exclusive right given to _____
cannot be terminated in the first period of two years while the spirit of the terms of this agreement are adhered to.

10.4. My licensee wished to have this for his minimum protection. I had no objection.

11. Formal Licenses

11.1. The Licensor will, at the request and cost of the Licensee, execute such formal licenses in respect of the said Patents as the Licensee shall require for purposes of registration, such formal licenses being expressed to be granted subject to the covenant and conditions herein contained. The Licensor will, also at his own cost, use his best endeavors to obtain Letters Patent in respect of all the said applications more particularly specified in the said schedule attached hereto and when so soon as any such Letters Patent shall be obtained will, at the request and cost of the Licensee, execute similar formal licenses in respect thereof.

11.1. Formal licenses may be required by the licensor, especially if they require specialized bank or government assistance. I also agree to use my best endeavors to get all my patents allowed, which most of them have now been.

12. Successors

12.1. In this License, where the context permits the expression, "the Licensor" and "the Licensee" shall be deemed to include the successors and assigns of the Licensor and of the Licensee, respectively.

12.1. Self-explanatory.

13. Laws of (country)

13.1. This License shall be constructed in all respects in accordance with and shall be governed by the Laws of (country) . (Usually the Licensee's country or state)

13.1. I usually make it easy for the licensee to use the laws governing in their country or state.

Unlike Life,
Termination In
Agreements
Need Never Be
Final

14. Unenforceability

14.1. The provisions and paragraphs of this agreement are severable and a holding of unenforceability as to any such provision or paragraphs shall not affect the enforceability of the other provisions and paragraphs hereof.

14.1. Any unlawful clause will not affect the others.

15. Duration and Termination

15.1. This License shall, subject to the rights of termination herein contained, commence on the date hereof and shall continue for the life of the last to expire of any patent granted on the Patent Application and any design granted on the Design Application or such other Patents or Design Applications which may be granted in connection with the Relax-a-Flex Comfort System.

15.1. When my patent's cover finally runs out, my licensee and everyone else get my invention on a plate. It will help extend the life of this agreement if I can come up with a patent for a significant improvement! Before anyone else does!

15.2. The Licensor shall have the right to terminate or adjust this License if any royalty payable or payment to Tube or Stabilizer Suppliers is in arrear and the

Licensee fails to pay the same within fourteen (14) days of a written notice from the Licensor requiring payments; or if the Licensee fails to perform or observe any of the other terms hereof on its part to be performed and observed and fails to remedy the same within thirty (30) days of written notice; or if the Licensee has a receiver appointed or if an order is made or a resolution is passed for the winding-up of the Licensee, except where such winding-up is for the purpose of amalgamation or reconstruction, if a different legal entity shall effectively agree to be bound by or to assume the obligations of this Licensee and such company is a company to which the Licensor cannot reasonably object as a Licensee.

The Spirit Of The Agreement Makes It Easier To Swallow

15.2. If my licensee does not faithfully abide by the spirit and terms of this agreement (except by mutual agreement), then I will terminate this license.

15.3. On termination of this License, the Licensee shall be entitled to dispose of any stocks in its possession at the date of termination paying to the Licensor a royalty as aforesaid, calculated on the highest list price in force during the twelve months immediately preceding such termination.

15.3. This makes sure that I would get a full royalty and that the licensee could not just hold a "fire sale" with my product.

15.4. Within six (6) months of cumulative non-performance of minimum purchases as defined in sub-clause 10.1. above, the Licensor has the right to terminate the exclusive agreement (see sub-clause 10.1.) at his sole discretion.

15.4. I am given the right to terminate this exclusive license.

15.5. Any determination of this License from any cause shall be without prejudice to the remedy of the Licensor to sue for and recover royalty then due and to the remedy of either party hereto against the other party in respect of any previous breach of any of the covenants or conditions herein contained.

15.5. We can always sue each other.

16. Ancillary

16.1. Any notice required or permitted to be given hereunder may be given by sending the same by prepaid Registered or Certified mail to the last known address for the time being of the addressee and any notice so sent by prepaid Registered or Certified mail, return receipt requested, shall be deemed to have been given, ten days after the same was posted.

16.1. I certify all important correspondence.

APPENDIX TO LICENSE AGREEMENT

Performance of this appendix forms an integral part of the foregoing License Agreement.

The unusual nature of the new Comfort System in the industry is that it encompasses a new concept—giving a level of comfort not previously achieved. It can be

**Giving A Little
Can Often Get
Back A Lot**
applied in many varied ways and is not restricted to particular designs.

Because of the diverse uses to be made of the invention, we are reluctant to allow the application of the new concept in such a manner that its use will be applied only to a single design. There are, we believe, many individual applications for the subject invention.

In order to facilitate the growth of this concept for worldwide use, sub-licenses must be granted as follows:

> Upon the request by a third party for a license (the Licensee being unable to competitively supply the requested device), the exclusive license holder will allow a manufacturer a license on the following conditions:
>
> 1. A direct sub-license with terms substantially the same as granted in this License except that the percentage royalty, based on factory selling price, may be increased up to _____ percent (_____%), i.e., up to _____ percent (_____%) for the benefit of the exclusive license holder, plus an additional _____ percent (_____%) to cover administration.
> 2. The Licensor is always prepared to negotiate a reasonable and naturally fair solution to any future sub-license.

No sub-license will be granted that will result in the Licensor being in a less favorable relative financial position than he is with this license.

The spirit of this appendix is to be adhered to.

The appendix spells out, in plain English, what I expect and feel needs to be done for success. This appendix was initialed by both of us.

IN WITNESS whereof, the parties hereto have entered into the Agreement the day and year first above written.

Tying Up
Loose Ends
Ensures Less
Future
Unravelling

EXECUTED at _____ this _____ day _____ of 19 _____ .

GORDON D. GRIFFIN, LICENSOR

_____

Witnesses:

_____

_____

THE COMMON SEAL of (company/corporation)

was hereunto affixed in the presence of:

_____ , LICENSEE

_____

Witnesses:

_____

_____

THE FIRST SCHEDULE ABOVE REFERRED TO

THE SECOND SCHEDULE ABOVE REFERRED TO

THE THIRD SCHEDULE ABOVE REFERRED TO

Relax-a-Flex Inc

A layout for signature schedules gives a list of patent and design registration and authorized suppliers of key component parts.

You might think that the preceding license is fairly tight—that nothing can go wrong, especially when I tell you my licensee is a personal friend and a nice person (even though he's a left brain–dominant businessman); however, I began to see cracks in our business dealings when he requested that I help him reduce his costs by reducing my royalties! I told him my royalties need not be significant on an exclusive item.

**Say What You
Mean Now, So
You Won't Cry
Later**

If I reduce my royalties beyond a certain level, I will have no possibility to recover my total costs to date, let alone make a profit. I understand my licensee's thinking and even sympathize, but my feeling is that either my invention is a goer, or it isn't. I have no intention of guaranteeing a loss to me, in either case.

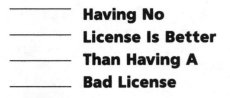
7 The Near-Perfect License

The pitfalls that inventors have encountered in trying to license others are legion. Spelling out in exact detail what you expect from your licensee is vital. To help you get your license agreement refined somewhat, prior to your patent attorney's review, (though do not expect him to give you commercial advice; he is not normally equipped to do so). I present the following "master" license agreement, though strictly speaking there is no such thing as a master license. The idea is that you pick out what you want, so as to customize your own license for negotiation with your prospective licensee. But please, during this phase, constantly run it by your legal advisor— someone who is expert in patent licenses. More wording is not necessarily better. Some sections *must* be included in any license agreement. Other sections are optional, depending on your own preferences and needs. But the relevance and importance of each is explained so that you can make an intelligent decision. With the aid of this chapter, you need not fall into that terrible position of having a good invention that fails as a result of a bad license. With a bad license you will be locked into any errors you have made, and it will be difficult, if not impossible, to extricate yourself. Believe it or not, having no license is better than having a bad license!

No Patent "Know-How"

If you have no patent, then a proper license agreement is even more important. This would be the case if you came up with a new superior recipe for, say, Coca Cola. If you patented your new, unique feature, then you would lose substantial control, due to its general availability to the public. Your potential licensee would not want this because they would wish to protect their markets worldwide. The resulting "know-how" agreement (you know how the formula or method is achieved; your licensee does not) would be even more important to you because you would not have any independent patent to fall back on should your licensee become difficult later. Key areas that would be most vital to you would be royalty—how much and on what percentage basis (do not, except under exceptional circumstances, agree to a monetary amount). Then you would need to be able to verify the sale (or manufacture) of the product; that is, verify the amounts as routinely reported to you (monthly, quarterly, and so on).

Then there would be your remedy in case of failure of your licensee to perform, as well as your licensee's minimum escalating performance and minimum royalty. This latter is often overlooked in the flush of getting a licensee. The licensee will tell you many good things about what they are going to do, but they may be considerably more reluctant to put it down in writing! The more unwilling your potential licensees are to spell things out, the more you must question their statements and suspect that they are looking for a way out later. As mentioned earlier, they may already be intending to sit on your new product (patented or not). It matters not how much better your product is than theirs or the competition's! They may be trying to tie up your new invention or know-how so that it will not interfere with their established markets and production procedures. Your product or process may be great, but they may not want to use it. They may not want to jeopardize inventory, past capital expenditures, staff training, and existing specialized dies and machinery they already use! Your agreement has to make them pay for the luxury of doing nothing or very little with your invention.

If you have a protected invention or process and no license, you are still in control—you can still get a license down the road. With a bad license, with or without a patent, you lose all control. The following may help you have the best of both worlds, though you must remember that almost all good agreements rely to a great extent on the goodwill of both parties; without it the very best of agreements will run afoul. It is as much your responsibility as theirs (if not more so) to see that harmony and goodwill prevail. It takes two to tango.

I urge you to remember that the following is not meant to be an instant, off-the-rack legal agreement ready to be copied and used. Rather, the following is my personal experience as to what may (and I stress, *may*) be needed. The idea is to stimulate you to look at what may be applicable to your own situation. When you have found what you think you want (and anything else you know you want included), then take it to your own attorney for proper incorporation into your country's legal system. You will have helped greatly your attorney's work. Your patent attorney or agent will suggest additions and modifications to strengthen your agreement against possible problems later on. *Do not try to finalize legal work that is outside your own expertise.* We all have levels of expertise in one area or another, but none of us can know all things in all situations, so allow your own patent attorney or agent to help you in *their* area of expertise! You'll sleep better, too!

Here is a checklist of possible ingredients for a license agreement:
1. Names of the parties entering into the agreement
2. Starting dates for the agreement
3. Monetary amounts to be paid in advance
4. Whether the agreement is to be exclusive or not
5. The territory that the agreement covers

6. The keeping of good accounts and records
7. Are the accounts to be audited?
8. What currency is to be used?
9. What percentage of royalty is agreed?
10. When do royalties become payable?
11. Do you give any grace period for payments?
12. Are there other royalty advance payments?
13. Is there a minimum royalty; if so, when is it payable?
14. If the licensee does not perform financially, will you cancel or modify the license?
15. Must you require your licensee to mark the goods?
16. Are your licensees to manufacture only under your patents?
17. Can you inspect your licensees' accounts?
18. Are you going to object if your licensee tries to invalidate your patent later?
19. What, if any, assistance are you going to give your licensee?
20. Who is going to pay patent renewal fees?
21. What happens when there is an infringement of your patent?
22. Are you going to defend your patent against revocation?
23. What happens to your royalties if your patent is found to be invalid?
24. Will you allow amendments to your invention by the licensee?
25. Can you grant another license while you have already granted an exclusive license to another somewhere else in the world?

Licensees Strangely Resist Help (Interference) By Licensors

Tie Down
Percent
Royalty/
Verification
And Minimum
Performance

26. When a nonexclusive license is granted to one party, can you give a better deal to another licensee?
27. What about cross-selling from one licensee's territory to another's territory?
28. If you or your licensees make any improvements, should they be confidential or open for use by other licensees?
29. What about granting formal (registered) licenses?
30. How about your licensee granting sublicenses to others? Do you think it's okay? Under what terms?
31. Supposing your licensee amalgamates or changes its name; what is your position to be?
32. Can your licensee assign their rights?
33. What about canceling your licensee's agreement, and under what circumstances if your licensees do not keep to your agreement?
34. How many days do you wish to give them to right any wrongs?
35. If you do cancel, do you or they have any rights left?
36. What about communication between you—how is it to be legally binding?
37. Do you like the idea of arbitrating any disputes?
38. Supposing your licensee tries to invalidate your agreement, What do you do? What happens?
39. What happens if a court of law finds any clause to be invalid? What happens to the rest of the agreement?
40. Who is going to sign your agreement to make it binding in law?

41. Are there any other specific points you wish to have incorporated into your license agreement? If so, now is the time to list them for your attorney to incorporate.

Exclusive Products Usually Command The Highest Prices

A Basic License Agreement

BASIC WORDING

In pursuance of the said Agreement and in consideration of the [sum of * now paid by the Licensees to the Patentees (the receipt whereof the Patentees do hereby acknowledge) and of the] royalties hereinafter reserved or made payable and of the covenants on the part of the Licensees and conditions hereinafter contained, the Patentees do hereby grant unto the Licensees FULL AND EXCLUSIVE LICENSE AND AUTHORITY (so far as the Patentees can lawfully grant an exclusive license) to make use, exercise, and vend the several inventions the subject matter of the said patents and each of them throughout * (all which said countries are hereinafter collectively referred to as "the Licensees' territory") and during the residue now unexpired of the respective terms for which the said Patents were or shall be granted and during any prolongations or extensions of such terms AND IT IS HEREBY MUTUALLY COVENANTED AND AGREED by and between the said parties hereto as follows:

1. THE Licensees will at all times during the continuance of this License keep full, true, and particular accounts of all * manufactured or sold by them or by their sub-licensees hereunder and of all matters relating thereto and will within thirty (30) days after the last day of the previous calendar month (hereinafter referred to as "the said account days") in every year during such continuance as aforesaid render to the Patentees an account in writing (certified by the auditors for the time being of the Licensees to be a true account) showing the number of * manufactured and/or sold by the Licensees or their sub-licensees here-

MY COMMENTS

*Monetary Amount. Include this material in brackets if you want or have agreed on an amount of money you are to be paid in addition to regular royalties.

Or nonexclusive or sole license (in case the patent is proved invalid or other unknown problems arise).
Exclude *several* if there is only one patent.

*Insert the country or countries this license covers. If it is for a state, local area, or part of a country, then so state.

You are the "Licensor" and the others are the "Licensees."

*Insert the name of your invention.

Auditor's Certificate is generally not needed if you personally plan to audit them annually; it's only needed in a very large company.

*Insert the name of your invention.

under during the period of each calendar month ending on the last of the said account days immediately preceding the delivery of the account and an account of all, for the time being in stock or in hand and will at the time or rendering each such account, pay to the Patentees in currency of * a royalty at the rate of ** shown by such account to have been sold by the Licensees or their sub-licensees. The first of such accounts shall be rendered and the first payment of royalty made within * days from the last day of the previous account period and shall be in respect of the period between the date of this License and the said * day of ** next.

*Insert your preferred currency.
**Insert the wanted or agreed percentage of royalty based on sales that have been made.

*Number of days grace you will give them—generally 15 to 30 days.

*The day (** or month) that the first account period goes to.

Payment in Advance on Account of Royalty

2. THE said sum of * paid to the Patentees on the execution hereof shall be deemed to have been paid on account of the royalty due from the Licensees to the Patentees hereunder.
[THE Licensees shall on the execution hereof pay to the Patentees the sum of *.]

*Insert the amount agreed.

Minimum Royalty

3. IN the event of the royalties due from the Licensees to the Patentees hereunder during the period from the date hereof to the end of the [? year] not having amounted to the sum of * at the least or during the period of twelve calendar months thence next ensuing to [date] or during any consecutive period of twelve calendar months thereafter and of the Licensees failing before the expiration of thirty days from the end of any of the said periods to pay to the Patentees such a sum as with the royalty actually due for that period shall amount to the minimum total for that period hereinbefore provided.

*Alternative agreed amount if the money to be paid is a lump sum *not* to be deducted from future royalty payments.

? Insert appropriate future dates.
*Put in the amount of minimum royalty you require each year, which amount should equal at least twice your annual expenses. But also ensure that your licensee does not find it more financially advantageous to "sit" on your invention. First, chart your minimum royalty over each of the first, say, three to five years, allowing for inflation and your yearly increased costs. Average them for the first year figure then escalate minimum royalty requirements by a compound percentage requirement each year thereafter. Be reasonable with your li-

Written Agreements Often Keep People Honest, You Too!

censee; you should both be happy with any arrangement. Another approach is to ask your licensee what their estimate for sale is during the first five years of the Agreement, then make their minimum royalty 1/3 to 1/4 of their figures. Licensees will promise a lot, but when it comes down to the final nitty-gritty of paying a minimum royalty, they may refuse, promising to do their very best! *Do not license a licensee without a minimum royalty, unless you have a minimum-performance clause.* If your licensee does not do what you expect, you need to be free to negotiate from strength, or to find a new licensee.

DETERMINE LICENSE

In the event of non-compliance with the minimum royalty or failure to meet quantity or financial obligations:
[THE Patentee shall be at liberty by notice in writing addressed to the Licen-

This clause is the harshest action you could take and keeps your licensee on

BYE THEN! I'M OFF TO PAY MY RENEWAL FEES.

sees forthwith to determine this License.]

or

[THE rights hereby granted to the Licensees shall forthwith cease to be exclusive but without prejudice to their continuance as non-exclusive rights or to any of the other provisions hereof.]

their toes. *Determine* is the legal term for "decide what to do with"—usually terminate.

This alternate clause would allow your licensee to continue, but allows you to license another or several other licensees nonexclusively. If you feel it is very important to have your invention handled exclusively, then you have to keep with the first clause; otherwise you will find it more difficult to find another licensee. Licensees almost always are attracted by an exclusive license for a given area. It gives them power to set prices higher and gives them more profits!

Often Not Appreciated! But Constructive Help Can Enhance Royalties!

Marking

4. THE Licensees shall mark or cause to be marked on every licensed product hereunder the words "Patent Nos." followed by the number or numbers of such of the said patents as shall, for the time being, be in force in that part of the

This is a very important clause and must *always* be put into your license agreement. If it is left out and your licensee does not have your product so marked, then any infringer could plead that though he may have seen your invention, he had no idea that it was patented because there was no patent number to be found, and therefore he may not be required to pay back damages (that is, damages for past infringement) in a patent infringement action. Most countries have a requirement that patent numbers be shown on patented products.

Licensees' territory in which the * is manufactured or sold and relate to the * so manufactured or sold or to any part or parts thereof.

*Insert the name of your product.

Licenses to Manufacture Under These Patents Only

5. THE Licensees will not at any time during the continuance of this License manufacture or sell or cause to be manufactured or sold any * except under the said Patents and in accordance with the inventions or one or some of them protected thereby by embodying any such improvement or further invention as is hereinafter referred to.

*Insert the name of your product.
Clause #5 is an important, though not essential. It keeps your licensee from manufacturing or selling your product or an allied product under another name or packaging type. It keeps them honest.

**Payment Of
Renewal Fees
Is A Real Trap,
For Unwary
Inventors!**

Inspection of Accounts

6. THE Licensees will permit the Patentees or their Accountants, Solicitors, or agents at all reasonable times to inspect and takes copies of, or extracts from, any books, accounts, receipts, papers, and documents in the possession or under the control of the Licensees and relating in whole or in part to the manufacture, sale, or use of * hereunder and to inspect and take an account of all * for the time being in stock or in hand.

An important clause that you should always include, not that you will necessarily need to carry it through, but the ability to be able to do so at any time in the future is essential.

*Insert the name of your product.

*Insert the name of your product.

Validity

7. THE Licensees will not raise or cause to be raised any question concerning or any objection to the validity of the said patents or any of them on any ground whatsoever.

This clause reminds your licensee that they should not attempt to take any action that might hurt your invention or your patent. This is thought to be generally the most difficult clause to enforce, because the courts do not generally prevent anyone from taking

HONESTLY! I DIDN'T KNOW YOU WERE COPYRIGHTED!

JUPITER

action that may be appropriate in any given situation. Though probably invalid under the European Economic Community law, this clause tends to dampen your licensee's endeavors in any contrary action. He has after all signed the agreement with this clause in it.

Assistance

8. THE Patentees will at all times during the continuance of this License give to the Licensees such advice, assistance, and information as the Licensees may reasonably require to enable them

to manufacture the said * to the best advantage, but the Patentees shall not be required to incur any expense in or about so doing.

This assures your licensees that you will continue to give them all assistance in your power but cannot be responsible for all the expenses (such as travel, accommodations) associated with such on-site advice.

*Insert the name of your product.

Renewal Fees

9. THE Patentors will duly and punctually pay all renewal fees necessary to maintain and keep the said patents on foot and will, on demand, produce the renewal certificate to the Licensees not less than 21 days before the last day for payment of the renewal fee and in default it shall be lawful for, but not obligatory upon, the Licensee to pay such renewal fee, in which event they may deduct the amount thereof from the royalties thereafter due from them.

[THE Licensees will pay all renewal fees necessary to maintain and keep on foot the said patents and will produce each renewal certificate to the Patentees not less than 21 days before the last day for payment of the renewal fee and in default it shall be lawful for, but not obligatory upon, the Patentors, themselves, to pay such renewal fees, in which event they shall thereafter be at liberty to recover the amount thereof from the Licensees as royalty in arrears.]

The *Patentor* is you, and the *Patentees* are you, too, as you both make and receive the patent.

Clause #9 is if you pay renewal fees, which is best if you do not want to see your patent lapse through some mistake on the part of your licensees.

OR

This clause should replace Clause #9 if you are assured that all due fees will be paid. This assurance could be given if you were to require your licensee to employ a specialized renewal company (your patent attorney will be able to give you such a list of reputable companies) to make such payments and to advise you directly in the event of a problem in so doing. Do not rely on a single person (patent attorney or agent) to do the renewal. The risks of their nonperformance is too great.)

Actually,
Taking Legal
Action Against
Another, Is
"The Pits"

Infringement

10. A. THE Licensees will at all times during the continuance of this License forthwith, upon any act of infringement or any threatened infringement of the said patents or any of them coming to their knowledge, give notice thereof in writing to the Patentees.

B. [AND if the Patentees shall be desirous of instituting legal proceedings to restrain such infringement, they, the Licensees, will give to the Patentees all information and assistance within their power (but without being compelled to incur any expense in so doing) to enable such proceedings to be instituted and prosecuted to a successful conclusion.]

C. [IF the Licensees shall require the Patentees to institute legal proceedings to restrain such infringement and the

Generally Necessary

A. It is my experience that the people you have licensed are the most likely to know of, or find out about, any infringement by a third party. This makes sure they advise you promptly (which they generally do).

Optional—add onto A

B. This says that your licensees will give you all assistance possible without expense to them. Clauses 10.A and 10.B are normally used with smaller companies.

Alternatives to 10.A and 10.B
Optional—add onto A
in Licensee's favor

C. This requires you to take legal action against any infringer but if you cannot then D. or E. will come into effect.

Patentees make default for a period of three calendar months in instituting or thereafter in prosecuting such proceedings]

D. [THE Licensees shall be at liberty by notice in writing in that behalf addressed to the Patentees forthwith to determine this License.]

E. [THE Licensees shall be at liberty (subject as hereinafter mentioned) to institute and prosecute such proceedings in the name of the Patentees, but at their own expense, and for their own, sole benefit, upon keeping the Patentees effectually indemnified against all claims, costs, charges, and expenses of any kind or description which may be incurred thereby and the Patentees will execute and do all such instruments, acts, and things as shall or may be requisite or desirable and will give to the Licensees (but without being required to incur any expense in or about so doing) all information and assistance within their power to enable such proceedings to be instituted and prosecuted to a successful conclusion PROVIDED ALWAYS that the Patentees shall be at liberty at any time to instruct such separate solicitors and counsel and to engage such expert assistance as they may think fit to represent their interest in any such action upon paying all additional expenses thereby incurred PROVIDED FURTHER that notwithstanding any refusal or default of the Patentees to institute or prosecute any such proceedings as aforesaid the Licensees shall not be at liberty to institute or prosecute any such proceedings unless and until there shall have been obtained, upon the joint instructions of the Patentees and of the Licensees, an opinion from Counsel practicing in Patent Matters (to be se-

E. This option allows your licensees to prosecute any infringers. C. or D. or E. is usually included when licensing a large company. Normally only *exclusive* licensees can actually sue in their own name. Although a patentee could sue, the licensee controls the action and pays; that is, they rarely use the patentee's name, in which case they should indemnify the patentee against all possible costs.

**Royalties
Should Be
Seen
(Received)
And Not Heard
(Promised)**

lected by both parties hereto, or if they are unable to agree, by an arbitrator) that such contemplated litigation affords a reasonable prospect of success.]

Revocation

11. THE Patentees shall defend, at their own cost, every action or proceeding instituted (otherwise than by way of counterclaim in an action for infringement) for the revocation of the said patents or any of them.

Royalties to Cease
if Patent Invalid

12. IF the said patents shall in any action for infringement or proceeding for revocation be revoked or declared invalid on any ground whatsoever all royalties payable hereunder shall forthwith cease to be payable but if the decision of the Court revoking the said patents or declaring the same invalid shall be reversed on appeal the said royalties

This requires you to defend your patents in any lawsuit against them, as opposed to an infringement. This is a normal provision for inclusion in any agreement; otherwise your licenses could refuse to continue payment of royalties to you!

If your patent were to be declared invalid by a court of law, then your licensees will not have to pay you any more royalties. However, you might be able to persuade them if you could establish *copyright* for the plans and drawings previously supplied (see Chapter 8, "Patents and Patent Attorneys").

WHY IS IT THESE INTERSTELAR GUYS KEEP CHECKING ON MY PERFORMANCE ?

shall forthwith again become payable, together with all royalties which would have been payable, but for the adverse decision. If one or some only of the said patents shall be so revoked or declared invalid royalty shall cease to be payable only in respect of those patents which embody exclusively, the invention or inventions, the subject matter of the patent or patents so revoked or declared invalid and do not embody any of the inventions the subject matter of the remaining patents or patents or any of them.

It Is Usually Hard To Prevent Cross-Selling Between Territories

Amendment of Specification

13. THE Patentees shall not amend the specification of any of the said patents without the written consent of the Licensees first obtained, but such consent shall not be unreasonably withheld.

Optional. If you grant an early license and then, before final acceptance or issue of your patent, you have to change or amend the claims, you would need to get approval from your licensee. Only rarely applicable.

License to be Exclusive

14. THE Patentees will not at any time during the continuance of this License, without the written consent of the Licensees first obtained, make use, exercise, or vend any * embodying any of the inventions protected by the said patents or any such improvement or further invention as is hereinafter referred to within any part of the Licensees' territory and will not, without the like consent, grant any license to any other person, firm, or company to make, use,

*Insert the name of your invention. This is not needed if the license given is nonexclusive.

This protects your licensee from your contrary actions if you should attempt to sell privately in their exclusive area, though if you were to become an agent of your licensee, you would be enabled to sell some product made by them—at their prices.

*Insert the name of your invention.

exercise, or vend such * within the same territory. The Patentees further will not at any time during such continuance as aforesaid knowingly sell or permit to be sold any such for resale within the Licensees' territory or any part thereof and will at all times during such continuance as aforesaid take all reasonable steps and precautions by marking goods and by the making and imposing of ap-

A Good
Invention
Always Lends
Itself To
Improvement

propriate stipulations and restrictions in their contract with and on the occasion of sales to their distributors and purchasers to prevent any sales by such distributors or purchasers or any sub-distributors or sub-purchasers which would be a breach of this clause if made by the Patentees.

No License to Be Granted
at Less Royalty

15.   THE Patentees will not at any time during the continuance of this License grant to any person, firm, or company, other than the Licensees, any license to make, use, exercise, or vend under the said patents or any of them or embodying any such improvement or further invention as is hereinafter referred to at a lower royalty than that hereinbefore made payable or otherwise on terms more favorable to the Licensees thereunder than those herein con-

Optional—licensee's protection.
This protects your licensee from your granting another license in another territory (or country) on more favorable terms than theirs. With more or less free trade worldwide nowadays, your licensee does not want to find themselves undercut by competing with license-holders elsewhere.

tained without making a corresponding reduction in the royalty hereinbefore made payable or making such other modifications in the terms of this License as shall make it equally favorable to the Licensees.

Licensees Not Import into Patentee's Territory

16. A. THE Licensees will not at any time during the continuance of this License knowingly sell or permit to be sold any * embodying any of the inventions protected by the said patents or any such improvement or further invention as is hereinafter referred to in, or for resale in, any part of the world outside the Licensees' territory.

B. [except at such prices as shall not be lower than the prices at which the Patentees shall, for the time being, be selling similar products in that part of the world]

C. [and further the Licensees will not sell such in such manner as to make it appear that such are the products of the Patentees or are in any respect identical with or similar to such products or are made according to the formula or processes of or supplied or disclosed by the Patentees]

D. [and the Licensees will take all reasonable steps and precautions by marking goods and by the making and imposing of appropriate stipulations and restrictions in contracts with and on the occasion of sales to their distributors and purchasers or any sub-distributors or sub-purchasers which would be a breach of this clause if made by the Licensees.]

Having The Legal Right To Take Legal Action, Is Always Necessary

A. Optional—protects other licensees' and patentees' territory.

*Insert the name of your invention.

This is another clause that may be found to be invalid if it were to be challenged in a court of law because of free trade practices encouraged by most countries.

B. Optional inclusion. However, licensees generally favor this clause as it gives them some feeling of security from imports of your invention into their exclusive territory, so they are quite happy not to undercut you or your other licensees.

C. Optional inclusion.

D. Optional. Tie into A. where your licensees have sub-licensees, sub-purchasers, etc.

Improvements

Sublicensees
Need To Be
Controlled, No
Less Than
Licensees

17. EACH party hereto will at all times during the continuance of this License communicate to the other party any improvement it may make or acquire on the subject matter of the said patents or any of them or any further invention it may discover or acquire with reference to * (whether such improvement or further invention shall be patented or not) and will fully disclose to the other party the nature and manner of performing the same and will permit the other party to make use, exercise, and vend the same in its own territories during the subsistence of this License without payment of any further royalty premium or compensation than such as is hereinbefore provided and further each party will, at the request and cost of the other party, execute and do all such instruments, acts, and things as

Necessary inclusion if appropriate.

*Insert the name of your invention.
If you or one or more of your licensees makes an improvement on your invention (which I have found is highly likely to happen), then this clause ensures that you and all your licensees will have access to the improvement (resulting in more sales and royalties), which will be highly beneficial to you in the long run. Everyone benefits without further expense.

shall or may be requisite or desirable in order to obtain Letters Patent in respect of such improvement or further invention in any or all countries of the territory of the other party which that other party shall desire, and to enable that other party to become registered licensees under such Letters Patent when obtained upon the terms of this License. Such Licenses to determine upon the expiration or sooner determination of this License.

Some Favors Turn Out To Be Too Painful

Formal Licenses

18. THE Patentees will, at the request and cost of the Licensees, execute such formal licenses in respect of the said patents as the Licensees shall require for purposes of registration such formal licenses being expressed to be granted subject to the covenant and conditions herein contained. The Patentees will also, at their own cost, use their best

Optional. If your invention is licensed to a sufficiently large company, it may require a formal license to be registered. If you have licensed a company prior to getting a patent granted, then this also assures your licensee that you will do your best to obtain it.

endeavors to obtain Letters Patent in
respect of all the said applications more
particularly specified in the said Schedule hereto and when so soon as any such
Letters Patent shall be obtained will, at
the request and cost of the Licensees,
execute similar formal licenses in respect thereof.

Assignments and Sub-licenses

19. THE License hereby granted is
non-exclusive and non-assignable and
the Licensees shall not assign, mortgage, charge, grant, sub-license in respect of, or otherwise dispose of or deal
with the rights hereby granted to them
without the consent in writing of the
Patentees first obtained, but such consent shall not be required to an assignment of this License together with the
whole undertaking and assets of the Licensees to any company which may
carry on business in succession to the
Licensees.

Necessary if you grant a nonexclusive
license.

This tells your licensee that they cannot
assign or mortgage what you have given
them unless you agree in writing, or unless your licensee and their whole operation is amalgamated or taken over by
another for continuing business purposes.

[THE Licensees shall be at liberty to
grant sub-licenses hereunder to make *
PROVIDED that all sub-licenses shall
contain covenants by the sub-licensee
with the Licensees and conditions identical (Mutatis mutandis) with those
herein contained and shall further contain a provision enabling the Patentees
upon the determination from any cause
of this License to assume the position
of the Licensees with reference to the
sub-licensee in the same manner as if
the Patentees had been the original
grantors of the sub-license.]

Licensee's Favor
*Insert the name of your invention.

If you will allow your licensees to sub-
license, then add this to the previous
paragraph.

Proviso for Determination

20. IF any royalties hereinbefore covenanted to be paid shall be in arrears
and unpaid for a period of thirty * days
after the same shall have become payable or if the Licensees shall commit or
allow to be committed a breach of any

Your Favor

*You may vary the number of days to
suit you.

of the covenants on their part or conditions herein contained and shall not remedy such breach within fifteen * days after notice is given to them by the Patentees requiring such remedy or if the Licensees shall [become bankrupt or commit any act of bankruptcy or enter into any arrangement or composition with their creditors] go into liquidation whether voluntary or compulsory (other than a voluntary liquidation for the purpose of amalgamation or reconstruction) or suffer the appointment of a Receiver of their assets or any part thereof, then and in every such case it shall be lawful for the Patentees by notice in writing addressed to the Licensees forthwith to determine this License and thereupon the License hereby granted and all rights, privileges, and advantages of the Licensees hereunder shall forthwith cease and determine.

Determination to Be without Prejudice to Accrued Rights

21. ANY determination of this License from any cause shall be without prejudice to the remedy of the Patentees to sue for and recover any royalty then due and to the remedy of either party hereto against the other party in respect of any previous breach of any of the covenants or conditions herein contained.

Notices

22. ANY notice required or authorized to be given by either party hereto to the other party may be served by prepaid letter sent through the post to the last known address or place of business of the other party and it shall operate and be deemed to have been served at the expiration of fourteen days from the time of being put into the Post Office and proof that the letter was properly addressed and posted shall be sufficient evidence of service.

*You may vary the number of days to suit you.

This enables you to extricate yourself from a difficult situation in the event of serious problems with your licensee.

What's Good For The Goose, Is Good For The Gander

Equal Favor

This allows both you and your licensee to take legal action if either feels it is warranted.

This is an important proviso for both parties. Certified or registered mail is the normal method of posting important communication.

Arbitration

23. ALL questions or differences whatsoever which may at any time hereafter arise between the parties hereto touching this License or the subject matter thereof or arising out of or in relation thereto respectively and whether as to construction or otherwise shall be referred to a single arbitrator in case the parties can agree upon one, but otherwise two arbitrators (one to be appointed by each party hereto) or their umpire and, in either case, in accordance with and subject to the provisions of the Arbitration Proceedings for * or any statutory modification thereof for the time being in force. All proceedings, notice of proceedings, and other notices in connection with or to give effect to the arbitration shall be deemed to have been served seven days after certified postage to the last known address of the party being notified.

An optional inclusion. Arbitration can have many benefits, not the least of which is a considerable saving in legal costs. Each party may not get all they want, but the end result can be fairer overall.

*Insert country or territory.

24. ANY attempt to invalidate any part of this agreement or the underlying patents or any patents applications associated with the subject invention will immediately determine this License and require the Licensee to give a full accounting and pay all royalties due.

This would cancel your license if your licensee took action against either your patents or this license. The laws generally do not uphold too-restrictive clauses in licenses, but this lets the licensee know that they cannot "have their cake and eat it too." European Common Market law may have some negative reaction to this clause, but it's best to put it in anyway.

25. ANY clause deemed to be invalid in a court of law shall not affect the validity of any other clause.

Your licensee cannot claim this license is invalid just because any individual clause is found to be unlawful.

**Patent
Attorneys And
Agents Are A
Special Breed**

8 Patents and Patent Attorneys

The following is a somewhat generic publication on the nature and duration of patents in the United States that I felt would be helpful for the inventor's under-standing and is generally applicable on a worldwide basis to all inventors. For further specific information, please write to your own country's patent office, or the address listed for the United States or of course to your own patent attorney. (NOTE: Most of the following questions are based on the needs of right-brained conceptual thinkers but the answers rely on the facts and figures of left-brained thinkers!) The original,helpful Nature and Duration of Patents was printed for the Superintendent of Documents, Washington, D.C. 20402, for which I gratefully acknowledge its format and concise wording for United States residents.

The Nature and Duration of Patents

1. Q. What is a patent?
   A. A patent is a grant issued by the government giving an inventor the right to exclude all others from making, using, or selling his or her invention within the country's countries, territories, and possessions.
2. Q. For how long is a patent granted?
   A. In the United States, 17 years *from the date on which it is issued* (granted); except for patents on ornamental designs, which are granted for terms of 3-1/2, 7, or 14 years. Practically all other countries grant patents for 20 years—but from the date of filing.
3. Q. Can the term of a patent be extended?
   A. Yes, but only by a special act. This occurs very rarely and only in most exceptional circumstances.
4. Q. Does the patentee continue to have any control over use of the invention after the patent expires?
   A. No. Anyone may use an invention covered in an expired patent. This does not apply to features covered by other unexpired patents.

5. Q. On what subject matter can a patent be granted?

   A. A patent can be granted to the inventor or discoverer of any new and useful process, machine, manufacture, or composition of matter, or any new and useful improvement of these items. A patent also can be granted on any distinct and new variety of plant, other than a tuber-propagated plant, which is asexually reproduced, or on any new, original, and ornamental design for an article of manufacture.

6. Q. On what subject matter can a patent not be granted?

   A. A patent will not be granted on a useless device, on printed matter, or on a method of doing business. A patent will not be granted on a device that would be obvious to a person skilled in the art, or on a machine that serves no useful purpose.

The Meaning of the Words "Patent Pending"

7. Q. What do the terms "patent pending" and "patent applied for" mean?

   A. They are used by a manufacturer or seller of an article to inform the public that an application for patent on that article is on file in the Patent and Trademark Office. The law may impose a fine on those who use these terms falsely to deceive the public.

Patent Applications

8. Q. I have made some changes and improvements in my invention after my patent application was filed in the Patent and Trademark Office. May I amend my patent application by adding description or illustration of these features?

A. No. The law specifically provides that *new matter* shall not be introduced into the disclosure of a patent application. However, you may include the new matter in another patent application. You should notify your attorney or agent promptly of any such changes you may make or plan to make so that he or she may take or recommend any steps that may be necessary for your protection.

9. Q. How do I apply for a patent?

A. In the United States, by making the proper application to the Commissioner of Patents and Trademarks, Washington, DC 20231.

10. Q. What is the best way to prepare an application?

A. Because the preparation and prosecution of an application are highly complex proceedings, they should preferably be conducted by an attorney trained in this specialized practice. The Patent and Trademark Office therefore advises inventors to employ a patent attorney or agent who is registered in the Patent and Trademark Office. No attorney or agent not registered in the Patent and Trademark Office may prosecute applications. The publication *Attorneys and Agents Registered to Practice Before the U.S. Patent and Trademark Office* contains an alphabetical and geographical list of persons on the Patent and Trademark Office Register. See Question 40 for source.

11. Q. What does a patent application consist of?

A. An application fee, a specification and claims describing and defining the invention, an oath or declaration, and a drawing if the invention can be illustrated.

12. Q. What are the Patent and Trademark Office fees in connection with the filing of an application for a patent and issuance of the patent?

A. A filing fee plus certain additional charges for claims depending on their number and the manner of their presentation are required when the application is filed. A final or issue fee plus certain printing charges also are required if the patent is to be granted. This final fee is not required until your application is allowed by the Patent and Trademark Office. Note: The fees charged by the Office for its various services can vary. Consult the Patent and Trademark Office for the correct fee to be applied.

13. Q. Are models required as part of the application?

A. Only in the most exceptional cases. The Office has the power to require that a model be furnished but rarely exercises it.

14. Q. Is it necessary to go to the Patent and Trademark Office to transact business concerning patent matters?

A. No; most business with the Patent and Trademark Office is conducted by correspondence. Interviews regarding pending applications can be arranged with examiners if necessary, however, and are often helpful.

Time Is Usually
Allowed For
Extrenuating
Circumstances

15. Q. Can the Patent and Trademark Office give advice as to whether an inventor should apply for a patent?

A. No. It can only consider the patentability of an invention when this question comes before it in the form of a patent application.

16. Q. Is there any danger that the Patent and Trademark Office will give others information contained in my application while it is pending?

A. No. All patent applications are maintained in the strictest secrecy until the patent is issued. After the patent is issued, however, the Patent and Trademark Office file containing the application and all correspondence leading up to the issuance of the patent is made available in the Public Search Room for inspection by anyone, and copies of these files may be purchased from the Patent and Trademark Office.

17. Q. May I write to the Patent and Trademark Office directly about my application after it is filed?

A. The Patent and Trademark Office will answer an applicant's inquiries as to the status of the application and inform the applicant whether his or her application has been rejected or allowed, or is awaiting action by the Patent and Trademark Office. However, if you have a patent attorney or agent, the Patent and Trademark Office cannot correspond with both you and the attorney concerning the merits of your application. All comments concerning your application should be forwarded through your patent attorney or agent.

18. Q. What happens when two inventors apply separately for a patent for the same invention?

Wait, Or Apply Privately When The Chips Are Down

   A. In the United States, an *interference* is declared and testimony may be submitted to the Patent and Trademark Office to determine which inventor is entitled to the patent. The patent is awarded to the first inventor. Your attorney or agent can give you further information. (Note: Identical, somewhat simultaneously filed patent applications are extremely rare.)

19. Q. Can the period allowed by the Patent and Trademark Office for response to an office action in a pending application be extended?

   A. Yes, if the period allowed is less than the statutory period. The application will become abandoned unless proper response is received in the Patent and Trademark Office within the time allowed.

20. Q. Can applications be examined out of their regular order?

   A. Normally not; all applications are examined in the order in which they are filed, except under certain very special conditions.

When to Apply for a Patent

21. Q. I have been making and selling my invention for the past 13 months and have not filed any patent application. Is it too late for me to apply for a patent?

   A. Yes. A valid patent may not be obtained if the invention was in public use or on sale in the country for more than one year prior to the filing of your

You Pay
"Searchers"
For The Skills
You Do Not
Have Yourself

patent application. Your own use and sale of the invention for more than a year before your application is filed will bar your right to a patent just as effectively as though this use and sale had been done by someone else.

22. Q. I published an article describing my invention in a magazine 13 months ago. Is it too late to apply for a patent?

A. Yes. The fact that you are the author of the article will not save your patent application. The law provides that the inventor is not entitled to a patent if the invention has been described in a printed publication *anywhere in the world* more than a year before the patent application is filed.

Who May Obtain a Patent

23. Q. Is there any restriction as to persons who can obtain a patent?

A. No. Any inventor can obtain a patent, regardless of age or sex, by complying with the provisions of the law. A foreign citizen may obtain a patent under exactly the same conditions as would a United States citizen but must have a local address (in this country) for service.

24. Q. If two or more persons work together to make an invention, to whom will the patent be granted?

A. If each had a share in the ideas forming the invention, they are joint inventors, and a patent will be issued to them jointly. If, on the other hand, one of these persons has provided all of the ideas for the invention, and the other has only followed instructions in making it, the person who contributed the ideas is the sole inventor and the patent application and patent should be in his or her name alone.

25. Q. If one person furnishes all of the ideas to make an invention and someone else employs that person or furnishes the money for building and testing the invention, should the patent application be filed by them jointly?

A. No. The application must be signed, executed, sworn to, and filed in the Patent and Trademark Office in the name of the true inventor. This is the person who furnishes the ideas, not the employer or the person who furnishes the money. Of course, the employer may be entitled by contract or by law to have the application assigned by the inventor to him or her.

26. Q. Can a patent be granted if an inventor dies before filing an application?

A. Yes; the application can be filed by the inventor's executor or administrator.

27. Q. While in England this summer, I found an article for sale that was very ingenious and has not been introduced into my country or patented or described. Can I obtain a patent on this invention in my country?

A. No. A patent can be obtained only by the true inventor, not by someone who learns of an invention of another.

Ownership and Sale of Patent Rights

28. Q. May the inventor sell or otherwise transfer the right to his or her patent or patent application to someone else?

A. Yes. An inventor can sell all or any part of the interest in the patent application or patent to anyone by a properly worded assignment. The application must still be filed in the Patent and Trademark Office by the true inventor, however, and not by someone who has purchased the invention from the inventor.

29. Q. Is it advisable to conduct a search of patents and other records before applying for a patent?

A. Yes; if it is found that the device is shown in some prior patent (prior art) it is useless to make application. By making a search beforehand, an inventor often saves the expense involved in filing a needless application.

Your Approach
Will Determine
The Quality Of
Your Patent

Patent Searching

30. Q. Where can a search be conducted?

A. In the United States, in the Public Search Room of the Patent and Trademark Office at Crystal Plaza, 2021 Jefferson Davis Hwy., Arlington, Virginia. A complete set of United States and foreign patents, arranged or classified according to the technology described, and numerically arranged sets of both U.S. and foreign patents are available for public use.

31. Q. Will the Patent and Trademark Office make searches for individuals to help them decide whether to file patent applications?

A. No. But it will assist inventors who come to the Patent and Trademark Office by helping them find the proper patent classes in which to make their searches. For a reasonable fee it will furnish lists of patents in any class and subclass.

Technical Knowledge Available from Patents

32. Q. I have not made an invention but have encountered a problem. Can I obtain knowledge through patents of what has been done by others to solve the problem?

A. In the United States, the patents in the Patent Search Room contain a vast wealth of technical information and suggestions, organized in a manner that will enable you to review those most closely related to your field of interest. You can go to Arlington and review these patents, or you can engage a patent practitioner to do this for you and to send you copies of the patents most closely related to your problem.

33. Q. Can I make a search of or obtain technical information from patents at locations other than the Patent Search Room?

A. Yes. Many libraries now have paper or microfilm sets of patent copies numerically arranged that can be used for searches or other information purposes as discussed in the answer to Question 34.

34. Q. How can technical information be found in a library collection of patents arranged in bound volumes in numerical order?

A. You must first find out from the *Manual of Classification* in the library the patent classes and subclasses that cover the field of your invention or interest. By referring to the *Index of Patents* in the library, you can identify the patents in these subclasses and look at them in the numerical sets. Further information on this subject can be found in the leaflet *Obtaining Information from Patents*, which you can obtain from the Patent and Trademark Office.

Patent
Searching Can
Help
Determine
Patent
Wording

Infringement of Others' Patents

35. Q. If I obtain a patent on my invention, will that protect me against the claims
of others who assert that I am infringing their patents when I make, use,
or sell my own invention?

    A. No. There may be a patent covering a basic feature on your invention. If
your invention includes such a protected invention, you cannot use it without the consent of the patentee, just as no one will have the right to use
your patented improvement without your consent. You should seek legal
advice before starting to make, or sell, or use your invention commercially,
even though it is protected by a patent granted to you.

Enforcement of Patent Rights

36. Q. Will the Patent and Trademark Office help me to prosecute others if they
infringe the rights granted to me by my patent?

    A. No. The Patent and Trademark Office has no jurisdiction over infringement
of patent rights. If your patent is infringed, you can sue the infringer in
the appropriate court at your own expense.

Patent Protection in Foreign Countries

37. Q. Does a granted patent give protection in foreign countries?

    A. No. The patent protects your invention only in the country granting your
patent. If you wish to protect your invention in foreign countries, you must

file an application in the Patent Office of each country in which you seek protection. You can do this may be done by filing in each country, or by using a multinational or regional treaty to effect filings in the desired countries. This is quite expensive, both because of the cost of filing and prosecuting the individual patent applications, and because most foreign countries require payment of fees to maintain the patents in force. You should ask your patent attorney or agent about these before you decide to file in foreign countries.

Get A Patent Attorney Who Knows What You Are Talking About!

How to Obtain Further Information

38. Q. How do I obtain information as to patent applications, fees, and other details concerning patents?

   A. By ordering a pamphlet entitled *General Information Concerning Patents.* See Question 40 for source.

39. Q. How can I obtain information about the steps I should take in deciding whether to try to obtain a patent, in securing the best possible patent protection, and in developing and marketing my invention successfully?

   A. By ordering a pamphlet entitled *Patents and Inventions—An Information Aid to Investors.* See Question 40 for source.

40. Q. How can I obtain copies of the pamphlets mentioned in the answers to Questions 10, 38, and 39?

   A. You can purchase these pamphlets from the Superintendent of Documents, Washington, DC 20402, or through any District Office of the U.S. Department of Commerce. The prices are subject to change without notice, so please write for the latest costs and a list of any new pamphlets available.

• Attorneys and Agents Registered to Practice Before the U.S. Patent and Trademark Office
• General Information Concerning Patents
• Patents and Inventions—An Information Aid to Inventors

Patent Attorneys

Patent attorneys are a special breed of people who generally have unique qualifications for their vocations. Seldom do they even consider participating in the financial rewards of inventions; I have heard of only one patent attorney who was also an inventor. This would indicate that they are predominantly left-brain dominant (having verbal and analytical bias). My experience has been that many patent attorneys start their careers as patent examiners working for the government after obtaining degrees in such fields as law, science, engineering, or even languages.

The lone patent attorney is becoming a rarity. That's a shame, but I suppose it's inevitable due to the ever-widening spectrum of new inventions. The recent tendency is toward groups of patent attorneys working together, so that a specialist within their organization can more thoroughly deal with a given subject. For example, if you were to invent a new type of computer chip, a specialist in your attorney group would understand the exact nature of your invention and would be able to formulate the correct wording ("patent-ese") and guide your patent ap-

Patent
Attorneys And
Agents Are A
Special Breed
In Themselves

plication through to the successful granting of a valid patent. The same would happen with different specialists if you developed, say, an unburnable plastic, a new type of electric light, a new chemical, a new type of combustion engine, or even a new type of engineered growing organism.

Such multiple-specialist patent firms have a needed place in society, especially for large development companies. I believe the one- or two-person patent firms have a place, too. These can give great personalized help with the utilitarian inventions that do not fall within a highly technical realm. The danger, as I see it, is that inventors, if not given the choice between the large or small patent firms, may find themselves at a disadvantage with more consumer-oriented inventions—the so-called nonspecialized inventions usually associated with impulse buying by individuals.

For my part, I have used and currently use both large and small firms on an equal basis. In Australia I use a large firm to cover Southeast Asian countries, except China. In Hong Kong I use a smaller firm that specializes in Chinese patents only. In the United Kingdom I use a large group of patent attorneys who specialize in all European countries. And in the U.S. and Canada I have used a one-man patent company whose principal was a former U.S. patent examiner. Now I use another one-man patent attorney because my first one overextended himself to my nonbenefit!

When my inventions are covered worldwide, I have the best of all positions: (1) access to each firm's specialized locale; (2) cross-references to the best wording for each invention application; (3) more economical costs, because each firm deals with its country's patent office directly or has such volume of business with its area that processing and translation costs are kept within acceptable bounds; (4) cross-reference help, because the processing of the same patent is being dealt with in various countries more or less concurrently. For example, one patent firm came across a particularly difficult government patent examiner who wanted to refuse or water down some of my claims. Confronted with arguments previously made in other countries, the examiner changed his mind and accepted the claims.

Remember that a patent attorney is not all-knowing in every patent situation. The attorney is almost certainly not as knowledgeable about your invention as you are, so your patent attorney should not be blamed for inadequacy on your behalf. You must fully explain every facet of your invention. You need to educate your attorney gently about its full ramifications and value. You must convince him or her thoroughly—get your attorney on your side. If you find that your patent attorney is too remote, too clinically business-like, and not particularly open to or understanding of your invention, find another!

It's important to be clear about costs. Make sure that once you have discussed your invention with your attorney that you ask immediately what the costs might be for patenting your invention—how much payment now and how much estimated cost until the actual granting of the patent. Also, ask what the costs might be to patent your invention in other countries of your choice. Don't be afraid to shop around, especially in the United States, where fees range widely depending on where the patent firm is located and whether or not you are perceived as having a lot of money.

The United States has the widest range of patent attorney fees. In large cities, particularly New York and Philadelphia, fees are probably the highest; smaller cities under one million in population are generally the most reasonable. If you find yourself in an expensive area that is beyond your financial resources, then send a letter to your state law society asking for a list of qualified practicing patent attorneys; they'll give you a long list to work from. You do not need to have an attorney who lives close to you, though that is always an advantage. Sending letters to several patent attorneys telling them that you are an individual inventor wishing to use their services and that you have limited financial resources can be rewarding. Here is a sample format for such a letter.

A Good Patent Attorney/ Agent Is Worth His Weight In Gold

Sample Letter to a Patent Attorney

(Address To:)   (Address From:)

(Date)

Dear (attorney's name):

I believe that I have an invention worth patenting but am concerned at the possible total cash involved.

I would appreciate it if you would advise me as to the basis for your charges in helping me with my patent application—that is, the cost of a single [or multi-] country search; the range of cost for a patent application (per page),

**Patent
Attorneys
Often Have
Soft Spots For
Inventors**

bearing in mind your present charges for such services; and also your estimated range of total final costs to granting (if the patent is granted), bearing in mind your present figures.

Do you require up-front money and if so, what amount would you require to start?

[IF APPROPRIATE] Also, could you give me an idea as to the range of costs for filing overseas in Japan, Germany, the United Kingdom, and Canada [or any other countries you, the inventor, may be interested in]?

I look forward to your early reply.

Sincerely,

(SIGN)

If you sent out ten such letters, the responses (of those attorneys who replied) would give you some idea as to whom to arrange an interview with. Those who gave you their specific scale of fees and charges would at least give you some basis for what you would have to pay. Those that replied in the least specific way or with extreme fluctuations in their possible charges may be more difficult to assess. Those who also offered to give you a free interview in order to assess the possible charges and terms under which they might help you might prove the best ones to start with. You would be able to assess how you liked their personalities.

Fortunately, I have found that individual inventors are generally treated well by the majority of patent attorneys and will strive to keep costs down for the individual inventor who is perceived to be financially disadvantaged over their corporate clients. Sometimes some extended credit (perhaps 50 percent) is available if the attorney knows that you are good for the money eventually. Here, a good name and a good credit rating is essential. Always keep your word in such financial matters. Always let your attorney know of your difficulties as they occur. Attorneys are humans, too. Sometimes a good patent agent, knowing your overall financial situation, will decline to extend help to you financially, realizing that it will put added strain on you and your family. He or she may already understand that your chances of success are infinitesimal and would be trying to do the best

by you. If this ever happens to you, think twice about going off in a huff to a more accommodating agent.

In other countries, attorneys also have a wide range of costs for the same apparent work. My advice is to avoid the two extremes—both the cheapest and the most costly and prestigious. Your aim is to get the best cover possible for the money, not a patent with holes in it. The final costs of a patent will, to a great extent, depend on several factors.

Searching for Other Related Patents

Does your patent need to be searched for novelty? A professional, single-country search could cost you $500 to $1,000 if you get it professionally done (I will later in this chapter outline the risks of doing your own search unless you have—or get— some level of skill).

However, always get a quote as to the range of fees to be charged. In Europe a multicountry search could cost as much as U.K. 1,200 pounds (US $2,000). There are also other ways of getting patent search work done that could be significantly less expensive for you. Chapter 10 will detail these other possibilities that include various access to specific data banks.

Having a search done can be like fire—a good friend or a bad enemy. Not all patents necessarily need it, though I have always found a search to be of help in correctly formulating my patent applications; that is, avoiding or getting around the claims in other granted patents.

The other major cost relates to the number of pages of preamble, or explanations of your invention, and the number of claims and drawings. If your invention is complex and needs lots of explanation, resulting in a great number of claims (ten or more) and drawings, then you must expect your costs to be higher because of the extra work, fees, and, if you are filing overseas, translations. Bigger is not better, so keep an eye on your patent attorney's proposed filing. A good attorney will normally point things out to you and be receptive to your questions. Do not be afraid to edit the filing for unwanted preamble. Take a good look at the claims. Usually the first three claims are the key and the most important. Extras may be superfluous. If in doubt, ask your patent attorney for reasons and explanations for things you do not agree with or understand. If you intend to file in only one country, the final cost may be $2,000 to $5,000 (UK 500 to 3,000 pounds), but these figures escalate when additional filings are made in foreign countries.

You need to know personally about your chosen patent attorney: How long has he been practicing? If for only a short while (qualified for less than a year), does he get his work reviewed by a senior associate? How do you rate his grasp of your invention? Can you feel he is your friend, able to fully argue with the government patent examiners on your behalf? Ask what his relations are with examiners. Do you feel he might be easily browbeaten with the first objections to your patent? What is his percentage of final rejections to patent applications?

A government examiner's job should be to help you obtain a patent. But realistically, examiners almost always respond initially by pointing out that your invention is obvious—not novel—and cite (bring to your attention) previous patents going back to the "Dark Ages." At first their arguments might seem to preclude

**When In
Doubt, Consult
An Expert**

any possibility of patent cover, and you might be inclined to despondently give up if you applied personally. But you need to know how the system works. Persevere energetically. A good patent attorney will fight for you and often will even point out how, with differently worded claims, your patent can be broadened to cover a wider spectrum and enhance its value and salability.

Drafting Your Own Claims Can Be Hazardous to Your Patent

If you have not had some experience in drafting patent claims, do not attempt it for submission to the patent examiner without getting some advice from someone who has. Even if your claims are honest in relation to your particular invention, you will be most unlikely to have the range of claimed cover you need, even if the patent examiner grants your claims. Remember, the examiners can give you no more than you ask for, whereas a skilled person will claim the maximum depth and width of claims possible around your central invention and make the examiners whittle them down if they can. In other words, with a professionally prepared filing, the onus is now on the examiners to justify through their searches (not yours) any refusal to any of your claims.

Suppose that door bolts do not exist, and you have just invented the first ever door bolt and it works beautifully. If you drafted a claim yourself, it might read as follows:

Claim 1. A round piece of metal, sliding along inside a restrictive metal holder to engage into a separate restrictive holder on an aperture to be secured.

Claim 2. A claim as in Claim 1 with means for attaching a handle to said round piece of sliding metal for the purpose of moving said piece of metal in and out of said secured aperture.

Sounds okay to you, and it covers quite well the revolutionary bolt you have invented. But you left out a square bolt or a curved bolt, or a plastic or wood bolt, or a curving centrally hinged closing mechanism. Once your bolt hits the market, its success will instantly generate a flood of inventions for improved closing fixtures or the like. You would have done all the work and taken all the risk, but others would have reaped the rewards, at best. Or, worse, as you progressed, you would have to file more and more patent applications, perhaps worldwide, to try to cover all your improvements in bolt and fixing devices at very considerable cost to you, as well as ward off would-be infringers. How much better to have gone first to a skilled patent attorney and gotten everything in one go. A patent attorney might have drafted a claim such as the following:

Claim directed to a sliding bolt fastener

Claim 1. A fastener for releasably connecting a hingedly mounted member to a fixed member, said fastener comprising a first member slidably mounted in guide means fixed to said hinged member and which permits linear movement relative to said hinged member, and a second member fixedly mounted on said fixed member, and forming a bore into which said first member is slidably received to effect fastening of the hinged member to said fixed member.

Note that this claim, which includes the sliding bolt fastener mentioned in the previous example, also includes and covers a hingedly mounted latch. The wording of this claim is also broad enough to include the releasable fastening of slidably mounted members.

Claim Drafting Is A Specialized Art

Claim 2. A fastener for releasably connecting two relatively movable members, said fastener comprising a first member mounted on one of the relatively movable members and a second member mounted on the other of said relatively movable members, said fastener members, in use, engaging one with the other to effect fastening of said relatively movable members.

This claim closes the door on those circular fastenings such as those found in some windows.

Such broad claims, if granted, would now give you a very broad coverage. Anyone rushing to make a related product (such as fasteners) would have to deal with you and your patent first and would now be reluctant to deliberately infringe, preferring to negotiate a license agreement for their own type of improved closing or lock device. In such a case as this one, claims thus worded could be worth hundreds of thousands of dollars in saved additional patenting and attorney's fees— not to mention a few additional years to your life in which to spend your royalties in physical and mental health.

Applying for a Patent Yourself

I believe that only under extreme and special financial circumstances should you initiate applying for a patent yourself. Applying by yourself to your country's patent office is a relatively simple matter. If you have insufficient money to get the services of a patent attorney, then you will just have to do it, or else wait until you can afford help. But there are inescapable problems you will most certainly encounter if you go ahead. There are three main areas of difficulty:

1. You will be unskilled at making a patent search yourself.
2. You will be unskilled in wording an application—you can be granted only what you apply for.
3. If you wish to apply in a foreign country, you will need to conform to that country's full requirements (translation of the texts, and so on), which include providing a local address (in that country) for the correspondence.

Actually, if money is a problem, you would do well to wait until you have an interested party who could finance the patent for you through an advance on your royalties. Premature filing can only cause you much heartache later. But let us deal with each of the preceding problems to see how you might best cope.

The Patent Attorney's Skill

A patent attorney will almost always have a search made, at a cost of anywhere from $500 to $1,000 depending on the complexity of the subject matter. You might wonder if you could do this yourself. You could, but you would need to go to the appropriate patent library. In the United States the main office is in Washington, D.C. The search would entail long hours of tedious looking through cross-referenced files, and you may still miss some relevant material.

Patent attorneys generally do not do search work themselves, though I have known some who do. Their time is too valuable. They normally employ regular full-time searchers who are skilled in looking for the correct subject matter and assessing, to some extent, its relevance to your search area. Usually they will find several prior patents, though the searchers do not make any legal determinations as to what they may have found. Your patent attorney makes the assessment as to how the prior art (found material) might affect your ability to get a valid patent, though it is good to give him or her your input, too.

If you can get to a patent library (in the United States, the one in Washington is by far the best), you may be able to get some help and direction from one of the librarians about doing your own search and making your own assessments, especially if your invention is a breakthrough in a new field of endeavor. But your assessment is very likely to be biased in your favor, or, conversely, after looking at "the opposition" you may (wrongly) give up. A good patent attorney, however, will usually give you an unbiased opinion. Practically speaking, I have found that at some stage you will almost certainly have to get a patent attorney involved to be sure that you have a good chance to get a valid or worthwhile patent.

The reasons are these: Doing your search by yourself and writing your own patent application will normally give you, even optimistically, only a 60 to 80 percent–value patent, often less, compared to that prepared by a professional patent attorney. And your homemade patent will not be acceptable in a foreign country, where it has to be done all over again according to that country's legal system and in its language.

Wording

The wording of the claim is crucial. If you claim too much, the patent examiners will reject it, almost as a matter of course. And they will not let you know the limit of what they would have granted you. Most private applicants ask too little. They make a narrow and specific main claim, which the examiners initially reject from force of habit but, upon a personal appeal, later allow! Then you have a good invention for which you believe you have a good patent, but because of your too-restricted claim, an improvement by you (or another) on the invention may fall outside your first patent coverage. That puts you in a position where you must either go through the whole process of making a new patent application, or risk having someone else come up with the new improvement.

Someone else may be able to develop and market improvements on your invention with impunity if your claims are too restricted. It doesn't matter that you may have indicated some possible unspecified improvements in your description, prior to your specific claims. Patent examiners never give more than you ask for. If you claim too little you are the loser, either because you leave the door open to competitors, or because you are unable to get a valid patent on the improvement, or perhaps because someone else exposed it prior to any new filing you could make. But if you claim too much, your patent will be rejected.

Correct Claims Become Very Important With Invention's Success

I wish I could advise you to save money by doing your patent work yourself. But this would create conditions for possible failure and heartache, and even for further work and expense due to later changes in your application. At this point, especially, I urge you to process your patent through "the system" as soon as you are able to. The wording and processing will cost you, but without professional expertise you may well find you have a nice piece of paper (a granted patent) with little monetary value. Any potential licensees will also quickly become aware of the holes or weaknesses in your patent.

Foreign Applications

If your invention is likely to be produced in other countries, then you may want to patent it there. You have a maximum of one year from the filing in your first or home country to file in other countries. (You may usually claim priority in those countries back to your first filing date.) In general terms, the key to obtaining a patent in any country is the absence of prior art, any prior publication, or specific public knowledge prior to the date of your application. If none of the preceding have taken place, then the date of foreign filing is of less importance up to the time just before such public knowledge, generally anywhere in the world. You need to approach a patent attorney by at least the ninth month if you are at risk of public knowledge and need the protection of your priority filing date. (Publication of your patent anywhere constitutes start of public knowledge.)

Your attorney needs a few months' time to take certain sequential steps:

1. Tidying up your original application (particularly if you filed yourself initially) and making sure that your foreign application has claims that properly cover the broadest possible area.
2. Corresponding with your designated country's patent agents (all countries require resident addresses in that country for correspondence).
3. Preparing an exact translation of your typed patent application into the designated country's language.
4. Filing (sometimes after clarifying correspondence) at the appropriate government patent office before your 12-month deadline.

In some countries, eight weeks is on the short side for doing all these steps, and allowing such a short time may ultimately cost you significantly extra for priority handling. So approach your patent attorney for foreign cover as soon as you are able. If finances are a problem, as they generally are with individual inventors, then weigh all your pluses and minuses and discuss these with your attorney. Costs vary widely from country to country. My experience is that patent attorneys are quite human, friendly people who will work with you on any financing problem you may have. They incur considerable expense in processing your patent, especially in foreign applications, and naturally they want to be certain that they will be reimbursed for these expenses and their work time.

I recommend taking these steps, especially if you are short of funds:

1. File personally in your own country if you must, giving comprehensive details, including the advantages of your invention.
2. If you can interest a would-be licensee who will financially support you, so much the better.

3. Within nine months of your filing date, if you have licensees, see a patent attorney. If he or she unreasonably refuses to accommodate your reasonable financial needs, you may wish to look for another patent attorney (or funding from others—for example, your licensees or investors). Back off from your attempts if you cannot get any help or financial support. It's not worth the later risks to you, or the disappointments.

4. Study the market for potential need for your invention in other countries and try to find would-be foreign licensees (using nondisclosure agreements) so you will know in which countries to patent.

Instruct your patent attorney to file in at least three key countries that you consider essential to your invention's success to prevent the possibility of imitation in other countries. Presently, I consider the four key industrial countries to be the United States, Japan, Germany, and the United Kingdom, in that order. If your invention is of general acceptability, minimum first-level countries would be these four. Second-level countries would be the balance of the European countries, but would probably exclude Belgium, Spain, Portugal, Italy, Greece, and Turkey. Third-level countries would be Canada, Australia, Israel, and Taiwan. But this will always depend on what you have invented. It may have applications in only specific countries—for example, a new rubber tree extractor might be good to patent only in Malaysia. Patenting it in other rubber-processing countries such as the United States, Japan, Germany, and Great Britain would be a total waste of money, as they do not have commercial rubber trees. Be aware of each country's possible acceptance of your invention.

> **Patents Are Primarily Granted For The Benefit Of The Country**

**Inventions
Before Their
Time Have
Difficulty
Hatching**

The scope of your invention will determine the areas you need to cover. If you must or want to cover the world but do not have the money to finance the patent costs, discuss it fully with your patent attorney and get his or her advice. If all else fails, try to file for cover in the four key industrial countries—the United States, Germany, Japan, and the United Kingdom, in that order—always providing you have positive knowledge of getting foreign licensees to cover sales or manufacturing in those designated countries. Get firm written (financial) commitments from your proposed overseas licensees, or back off from sticking your own neck out!

The decision for legal patent coverage always requires a careful balance between your expenses now and the possible future return to you. When the chips are down—you have run out of money or possible licensees (providing you have not made your invention public knowledge but have dealt with everyone confidentially)—go back to square one. Get your patent application withdrawn (not abandoned) and look at filing again immediately, if you have hot prospects, or later if you don't. It's better to have possibilities for good prospects in the future than to guarantee none by shooting yourself in the foot now.

The latter is more likely to happen if you have prematurely applied for a patent—that is, before you have enough convincing evidence to satisfy a would-be licensee or buyer. Some people might think that getting a patent is of top priority. I have found that a good, or not so good, licensee is better for financial success. Don't be in too much of a rush to apply. Be prepared to play the waiting game so

as to maximize your potential profits and minimize your early expenses. Too many inventors prematurely drive themselves into financial distress needlessly.

A Patent Examiners Most Frequently Used Phrase: "It's Obvious!!"

Examiner's Response to Your Patent Application

I need to reemphasize: Do not be put off by an examiner's first response to you or to your patent attorney's application. It is my experience that the most common initial response by examiners for the rejection of a patent is "obviousness." They will cite (put before you) patents that, acording to them, make it obvious that anyone "skilled in the trade" could have come up with your invention. Personally, I have yet to hear of anyone looking at old, sometimes very old, patents (there have been over ten million worldwide this century) and being able to come up with a new, present-day usable invention. I remember that when I was in the process of patenting my first composting machine—a high-speed specialist machine, the concept of which has revolutionized the composting process in the mushroom industry in America and Europe—the patent examiner cited a late 1800s farm muck spreader as being relevant to obviousness. Fortunately for the mushroom industry, I, through my patent attorney, was able to convince him he was quite mistaken!

If you are interested in helping your patent attorney (educating him or her about your inventions) to draft a good, economical patent application, I suggest that you draft out a preliminary outline as best you can. This will save you money and give your patent attorney more background information to strengthen the application on your behalf. I always supply the maximum background information I can before the attorney's drafting. The following will give you an idea as to what is needed—first, a preamble background on my wind power generator, and then another on my Relax-a-Flex Comfort System beds. Both these preambles are now used by my patent attorney in patent applications and could not have been drafted by him without his expending great additional time and costs.

Sample Preamble #1

Wind Power Generator

Attempts to harness the wind for power have continued over the past centuries using many designs and devices. Many of the wind power devices have failed altogether, and those that are viably successful have limited specific use and applications. Most of the wind power devices either do not work or have uneconomic performances at low wind speeds: This is especially true with wind-driven devices for pumping water for agricultural and remote-area use.

All of the present wind power devices employ a system of gathering a limited amount of the available wind power output, and moreover are only marginally cost-effective on a work/power ratio for financial investment and maintenance costs.

For example, the cost of KW, or power produced by the wind, is usually found to be uneconomic against other forms of power production such as grid or hydro. Where this is not a factor for consideration, such as remote-area bore holes to supply water for livestock, such wind power devices are expensive relative to the power and water produced, prone to high-wind damage, severely limited as to the depth and amount of water recovered, and effectively nonoperable at low wind speeds.

Sample Preamble #2

Description: This invention relates to support systems for mattresses or cushions in beds, chairs, sofas, settees, stretchers, and other body-support appliances. Such support systems will be referred to as systems "of the kind defined."

The invention is particularly applicable to support systems of the kind defined in which a mattress or cushion rests on slats extending between supporting air springs. My European Patent Application publication No. 0.0 38155 discloses mattress support systems of this kind in which the air springs are in the form of long inflatable tubes on which the ends of mattress supporting slats are rested. Such beds have been successful, but one problem has been the tendency for the slats to move on the tubes and the consequent need to provide some holding means that will not interfere with the flexure of the springs or the slats and that is not unduly complex and expensive. The present invention enables economical manufacture of air springs fitted with appropriate slat restraining means.

DE-B-2621803 (Eggenweiler) discloses a bed having spaced, longitudinally extending rigid members each accommodating a closed elongate resilient tube that is filled with a medium capable of flowing and pressurized to meet the requirements of the person using the bed. The upper surface of each tube has a plurality of spaced pockets vulcanized thereto with the pockets of one tube all facing toward the pockets of the other tube. The body support surface of the bed is formed by a plurality of transversely extending, laminated slots arranged parallel to each other with their ends fixedly mounted in the tube pockets.

> If You Do All The Work You May End Up With A 60% Patent

This prior art arrangement is complicated and costly due to the vulcanizing of the pockets to the tubes, which, in addition, increases the possibility of failure at the seams of each pocket.

According to the invention, there is provided a support system for mattresses in beds or the like comprising spaced elongate air springs formed by inflatable tubular bladders, each provided with a series of longitudinal spaced pockets, having open mouths, a plurality of transversely extending slats, having their respective end accommodated in the pockets of said air springs, characterized in that stabilizer means are provided, interconnecting said air springs to provide lateral stability of the support system, the stabilizer means comprising a transversely extending member accommodating, without clearance, the air springs. (Author's Note: The immediate foregoing is pure legalese patent language beloved of patent examiners for clarity!)

Preferably the pockets are formed in a tangential flap connected to the tubular bladder along a longitudinal connection line at the surface of the tubular bladder such that the open mouths of the pockets are spaced along a longitudinal edge of the flap.

The invention also provides a method of making an air spring, comprising forming two tubes of heat-weldable sheet plastics material with a longitudinal heat-welded seam and so as to leave a longitudinal strip of said sheet material projecting beyond the seam exteriorly of the tube, and folding and welding said strip of material to form a tangential flap with longitudinally spaced pockets having open mouths spaced along a longitudinal edge of the flap, so as to form two air springs, interconnecting the two air springs by means of a plurality of transversely extending slats having their respective ends accommodated in the pockets, and providing stabilizer means interconnecting said air springs to provide lateral stability of the support system, the stabilizer means comprising a transversely extending member accommodating, without clearance, the air springs.

In order that the invention may be more fully explained, some particular embodiments and methods of manufacture will be described with reference to the accompanying drawings in which:

Life After
Premature
Filing: Less
Long

Figure 1 is a perspective view of part of a bed comprised of mattress support slats extending between a pair of air springs;

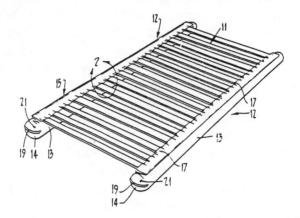

Figure 2 is an enlarged scrap view taken in the region 2 in Figure 1;

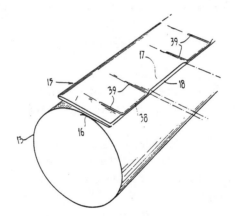

Figure 3 is a transverse cross-section through an upper part of one of the air springs;

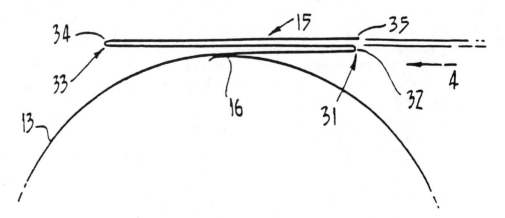

Figure 4 is a side view of the upper part of the air spring in the direction of arrow 4 in Figure 3;

Patent Size:
Bigger Is Not
Always Better

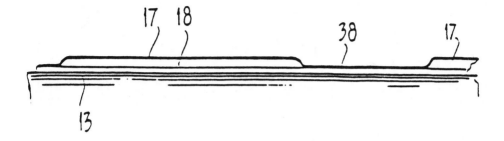

Figure 5 is a perspective view of a heat-welding apparatus used in the forming of the air spring illustrated in Figures 1 to 4 and shows a partly formed spring in the process of manufacture;

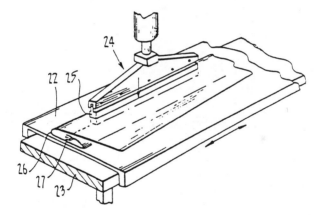

Figure 6 illustrates a specially shaped heat-welding bar that is fitted to the apparatus during a later stage of the forming process;

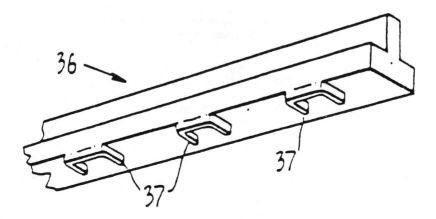

Figure 7 is a vertical cross-section through the apparatus of the partly formed tube at the stage of the forming process illustrated in Figure 5;

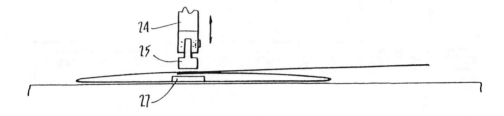

Figure 8 is a vertical cross-section through the apparatus at a later stage of the forming process;

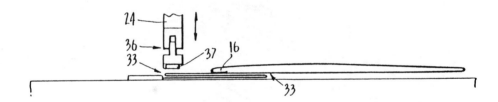

Figures 9 to 11 diagrammatically illustrate alternative types of air springs constructed in accordance with the invention;

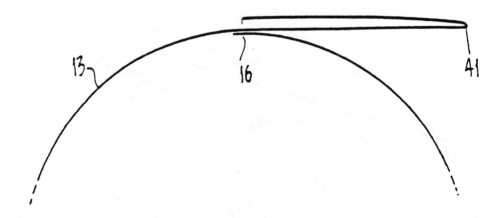

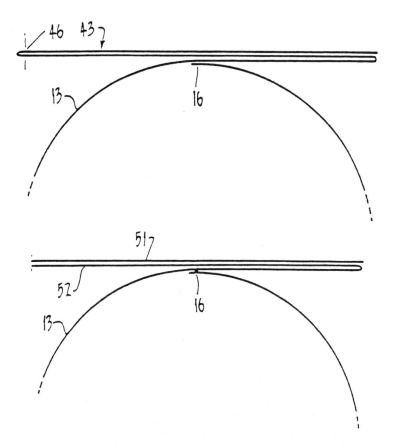

Glitter Is Claim
Wording Costs
Gold; Worth
Less

Figure 12 is a perspective view of part of an air spring of the general kind shown in Figure 2;

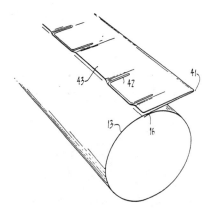

The Patent
Examiner Does
His Job, You
Should Do
Yours

Figure 13 is a perspective view of an air spring of the general kind shown in Figure 10;

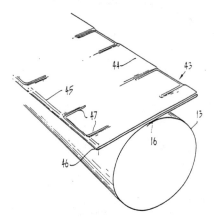

Figure 14 is a perspective view of a stabilizer for use with a bed according to the present invention;

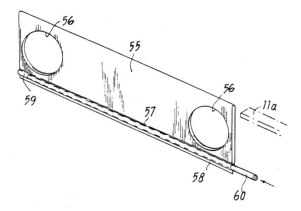

Figure 15 is a perspective view of part of the bed shown in Figure 1, including the stabilizer shown in Figure 14 mounted thereon; and

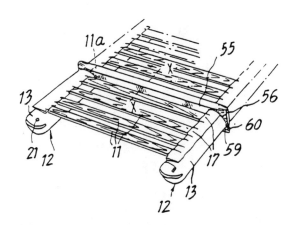

Figure 16 is a cross-section taken on the line X-X of Figure 15.

Superfluous
Words Are A
Costly Liability

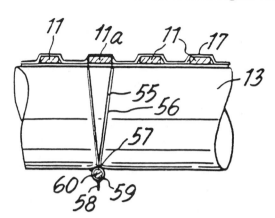

Figure 1 illustrates a mattress support system for a bed comprising a series of parallel wooden slats (11) extending between a pair of elongate inflatable air springs (12). The air springs (12) can be mounted in any convenient frame (not shown). Each air spring (12) comprises an elongate tube (13) formed with closed ends (14) and with a tangential flap (15), which is connected to the tube along a longitudinal connection line (16) at the surface of the tube and has a series of longitudinally spaced pockets (17) with open mouths (18) located along one longitudinal edge of the flap to receive the respective ends of the slats (11).

Each tubular bladder is formed of heat-welded sheet plastics material, the tube being closed by a longitudinal welded seam defining the connection line (16), and the flap is formed by a continuation of the sheet material of the bladder, which is folded and welded to form the pockets so that the flap is integrally connected with the bladder at the seam. The ends of the tubes are closed by heat welds (19), and one end of each tube is fitted with an inflation valve (21).

As referred to above, in order to maintain lateral stability, the air springs (12) can be mounted in any convenient frame (not shown), which is usually of U-shaped cross-section for at least a portion of its length. However, for certain applications, such as the provision of a portable bed or a design application where lateral stability is required without any constraint at the sides, the support system shown in Figure 1 incorporates a stabilizer arrangement as shown in Figures 14 to 16 and now to be described.

As shown in Figure 14, before fitting on the bed, the stabilizer comprises an open-ended, flattened tubular member (55) of sheet plastics material similar to the tubular bladders (13). The member (55) is of a length slightly greater than the overall width of the bed and is provided with spaced apertures (56) whose axes correspond, respectively, with the axes of the tubular bladders (13). The diameter of the apertures (56) is slightly less than the diameter of the tubes (13) to provide a gripping action when the stabilizer is mounted on the tubes. One edge (58) of the tubular member (55) has a seam (57) formed by heat welding extending parallel to, but spaced slightly from, the edge (58) to provide an elongate chamber (59) extending the length of the member.

In use, a predetermined slat (11a) is removed from the bed and a rod (60) is accommodated in the chamber (59). The stabilizer is then positioned on the bed

Your Fees Help
Pay For The
Patenting
System

after removing slats (11) as necessary, by passing the tubular bladders (13), respectively, through the apertures (56) in the tubular member (55) until it reaches the location at which the predetermined slat (11a) has been removed. The slat 11a is then passed into the upper portion of the tubular member (55) (see Figure 14) and its ends respectively reinserted into the pockets (17) formed in the tubular bladders (13) so that the cross-section of the stabilizer adopts a triangular configuration (see Figure 16).

Any desired number of stabilizers may be used, but in general, from one to five are sufficient to provide lateral stability of the bed depending on the use and manufacturing design.

It will be readily appreciated the stabilizers may take other forms. For example, the lower rod (60) may be replaced by a slat (11) similar to the slat forming the support surface. In this arrangement, when positioned on the tubular bladders (13), the stabilizer cross-section is of rectangular configuration.

Alternatively, the upper slat (11) may be replaced by a rod similar to the lower rod (60). In this arrangement the stabilizer is positioned between adjacent slat (11). In a further embodiment, the stabilizer comprises a single membrane of plastics material having rod-accommodating chambers formed along its upper and lower edges.

The method of manufacturing the air springs, and the heat-welding apparatus employed, will now be described with particular reference to Figures 5 to 8.

Figure 5 shows a heat-welding apparatus comprising a sliding table (22) slidable along a bench (23) beneath a vertically movable welding head (24) fitted with an elongate heat-welding bar (25). A sheet (26) of heat-weldable plastics material is wrapped around a backing bar (27) on table (22) to form a tube, and this tube is closed by heat welding a longitudinal seam by bringing the welding head downwardly so that the overlapping layers of material between the welding bar (25) and the backing bar (27) are welded together. This stop in the process is shown in cross-section in Figure 7.

As shown in Figures 5 and 7, a wide strip of the plastics material is allowed to project beyond the heat-welded longitudinal seam exteriorly of the tube. This strip is subsequently folded and welded to form the pocketed flap. More specifically, the strip is double-folded in the manner that will be apparent from Figure 3. Thus the sheet material extends from the seam to a first longitudinal side edge (31) of the flap where it is folded back at (32) to extend to the second longitudinal side edge (33) of the flap, and it is there folded at (34) to extend to a free edge (35) at the first side edge (31). The thus folded strip is then laid flat on the table (22) as illustrated in Figure 8 for welding of the pockets. In order to weld the pockets, the welding bar (25) is replaced by the specially shaped welding bar (36) illustrated in Figure 6. This bar is formed with U-shaped projections (37) at intervals along its length, and when the welding head is brought downward, these projections weld the three layers of the sheet material between the longitudinal seam and the side edge (31) of the flap together to define the pockets. More particularly, the sliding bar produces U-shaped heat welds having limbs (38) sealing the edge of the flap between the pocket mouths and legs (39) extending from one another. The pockets are not completely sealed from one another since the welds do not extend across the full width of the flap, but they do serve effectively as individual pockets to hold the slats apart. The flap can move about the longitudinal seam and can flex so as to permit free flexure of the slats while the pockets provide the necessary restraints against shifting of slats.

An Original
Patent Must
Have The
Actual
Inventor(s)
Name On It

After formation of the tube with the pocketed flap from a single sheet of plastics material in the manner described above, the ends of the tube can be closed by simple heat welding and inflation valves also heat welded in place to complete the air spring.

Figures 9 and 12 illustrate an alternative construction in which a pocketed flap is formed by a single fold and welding operation rather than by double folding as described above. In this case the tube is again formed by producing a longitudinal seam with a strip of the plastics material projecting beyond the seam. The strip is folded with a single fold at (41) so as to form a flap having only two layers of material and extending only to one side of the longitudinal seam. In this case the U-shaped welds (42) defining pockets may be produced by gripping the material to be welded between the welding bar (36) and the backing bar (27).

Figures 10 and 13 illustrate the manner in which a flap may be formed so as to have pockets along both of its longitudinal edges. An air spring with such a double-pocketed flap may be used to support the ends of two adjacent sets of mattress support slats, either as a central support spring in a double bed or, in some cases, as an additional central support in a single bed. In this case the flap (43) is initially formed in the same manner as the flap (15) of the construction illustrated in Figures 1 to 4, and the flap thus has a series of pockets (44) along one edge corresponding to the pockets (17) of the previous construction. However, an additional series of pockets (45) is formed along the other side of the flap by trimming off the folded edge of the flap at the line (46) and applying additional U-shaped welds (47).

Figure 11 shows an alternative manner of producing a flap with pockets along both sides. In this case a separate sheet strip (51) of weldable material is laid over the folded strip (52) and the two welded together at the seam line and around the pockets.

The illustrated constructions are exemplary only, and they can be modified or varied considerably. For example, the pockets could be formed by welding a strip of material to the surface of the tubular bladder so that the pockets are formed directly at the exterior surface of the tube. The pocket-forming strip could be connected integrally with the tube and be folded back against the tube after the longitudinal seam has been welded, or it could be a separate strip welded to the tube. The pockets are formed in a tangential flap to avoid direct contact between the slats and the wall of the inflatable tube, and the welding of the pockets directly to the tube wall entails the risk of pinholes and localized thinning of the tube wall, which could give rise to blowouts. However, the alternatives are feasible.

Claims:

1. A support system for mattresses in beds or the like, comprising spaced elongate air springs (12) formed by inflatable tubular bladders (13), each provided with a series of longitudinal spaced pockets (17, 44) having open mouths (18), a plurality of transversely extending slats (11) having their respective ends accommodated in the pockets (17, 44) of said air springs (12), characterized

Your Patent
Agent Will
Normally Deal
With The
Patent Office

in that stabilizer means (55) are provided interconnecting said air springs (12) to provide lateral stability of the support system, the stabilizer means comprising a transversely extending member (55) accommodating, without clearance, the air springs (12).

2. A support system as claimed in claim 1, characterized in that said member (55) is tubular and has one of said slats (11a) extending lengthwise along its upper portion and a rod (60) extending lengthwise along its lower portion so that the cross-section of the stabilizer, in use, is of triangular configuration.

3. A support system as claimed in claim 1, characterized in that said member (55) is tubular and has one of said slats (11) extending lengthwise along its upper portion and a further slat (11), not forming part of the support surface, extending lengthwise along its lower portion so that the cross-section of the stabilizer, in use, is of rectangular configuration.

4. A support system as claimed in claim 1, characterized in that said member (55) has spaced rods (60) extending lengthwise, respectively, along its upper and lower portions, said member (55) being positioned between adjacent slats.

5. A support system as claimed in claim 2, characterized in that said member (55) comprises a single membrane having rod-accommodating chambers formed along its upper and lower edges.

6. A support system as claimed in any of the preceding claims, characterized in that the pockets (17) are formed in a tangential flap (15, 43) connected to the tubular bladder (13) along a longitudinal connection line (16) at the surface of the tubular bladder (13) such that the open mouths (18) of the pockets (17) are spaced along a longitudinal edge of the flap (15).

7. A support system as claimed in claim 6, characterized in that said bladder (13) and the flap (15) are formed of heat-welded sheet plastics material.

8. A support system as claimed in claim 7, characterized in that bladder (13) has a longitudinal welded seam and the flap (15) is formed by a continuation of the sheet material of the bladder beyond the seam, which is folded and heat welded to form the pockets (17) so that the flap (15) is integrally connected with the bladder (13) at said seam.

9. A support system as claimed in any one of claims 6 to 8, characterized in that the flap (43) has an additional series of longitudinally spaced pockets (45) with open mouths spaced along the other longitudinal edge of the flap.

10. A method of making a support system as claimed in any of claims 6 to 9, comprising forming two tubes (13) of heat-weldable sheet plastics material with a longitudinal heat-welded seam (16) and so as to leave a longitudinal strip of said sheet material projecting beyond the seam (16) exteriorly of the tube (13), and folding and welding said strip of material to form a tangential flap (15, 43) with longitudinally spaced pockets (17) having open mouths (18) spaced along a longitudinal edge of the flap (15, 43) so as to form two air springs (12), interconnecting the two air springs (12) by means of a plurality of transversely extending slats (11) having their respective ends accommodated in the pockets (17), and providing stabilizer means interconnecting said air springs (12) to provide lateral stability of the support system, the stabilizer means comprising a transversely extending member (55) accommodating, without clearance, the air springs (12).

**Like Dying—
Do Not
File Before
Your Time**

9 When to File for a Patent and Taking Action Against Infringers

Many people, including many patent attorneys, advise you to file for a patent as soon as you can. It sounds like good advice, and it can be for "hot" items. But my experience indicates otherwise. The standard argument for filing early is that there may be someone else in the world working on an identical invention and therefore the sooner you file, the earlier the priority date.

The fact is that parallel identical inventions by people remote from each other is so rare that any statistician would hardly find it worth documenting, except perhaps in the pharmaceutical industry. Some problems or subjects are being worked on by many research groups at the same time, and in these areas you occasionally hear of parallel breakthroughs, but for the individual thinker, the chances of this happening are very unlikely. You might say there is a risk, but risks are all around us anyway—life itself is a risk, so why emphasize one risk above another? Life is too short.

I know from experience the mistake of filing prematurely as soon as you get an idea, because I have often done so, to my regret. My argument against filing prematurely is that so often an invention can be significantly improved from its first conception. I cannot remember any of my inventions that I have not improved with later inventive steps, thus necessitating a patent change that caused me considerably more effort and expense than I might have had if I'd waited.

Strictly speaking, patents do not *do* anything. A patent has no intrinsic value unless it is used to good effect by the holder. It gives the holder the exclusive right to effectively stop or delay other parties from making and marketing products based on the patent. This has been taken advantage of in the past, when a competing company has found it prudent to buy, or otherwise acquire, patent rights and to stifle or delay their development in order to prevent a rival (even a better product) from competing with their existing profitable line too soon—quite a natural business approach, if you think about it!

Not many people know that in some countries it is possible to petition a court of law for a license (under court terms) to manufacture (use) and sell products covered by a current patent that is not being or intended to be used. This requires the patent owner to grant a license for a patent (that is not being exploited) under reasonable terms. But in practice it is seldom done, and even when it is, due to the high cost and time constraints, it is only by large or well-financed entities. It is self-evident that countries, of course, always want the patents they grant to be exploited for their own country's benefit of trade.

The granting of a patent by a country or kingdom is meant to give the inventor or owner of the patent exclusive rights to the new product or process for a set period of time. However, with over 140,000 patents being granted worldwide each year, it is easy to imagine that only a small percentage of them become successful in their own right. Many are taken out in order to upgrade existing inventions (sometimes called *patents of improvements*) where a new patent is subject, in part, to a past-granted patent. Many are taken out for small improvements to larger machinery in order to stop competing companies from copying a product—a quite normal practice in the motor vehicle industry. Then there are a host of design patents that rely entirely on the shape and design of the article rather than on inventive steps or new principles.

Individual inventors are probably the least represented in overall numbers of patents granted, yet they have supplied a disproportionate number of the world's greatest breakthroughs in the so-called industrial era. (See the story of the electric motor later in this chapter.)

Patents usually have a great many prior arts—that is, previously granted patents—cited against them. An examiner once cited one against me that was a hundred years old! My experience is that an invention is more likely to be financially successful if it is an improvement on something already in use or marketed, or is perceived as a need by any sector of the public or by the government. Breakthroughs in new technology often take so long to refine for commercial use that the original conceptual inventor gains relatively little financially. What would we do today without xerography? Yet it took over 20 years and much heartache for that technology to be commercially viable.

Breakthrough Inventions Are Usually Before Their Time

One of the problems with an individual inventor inventing some breakthrough product or technology is that it will probably be "before its time." By this I mean that there is often insufficient backup technology to support the new invention, and the invention fails because of it. The inventor has to search diligently just to find ways of getting the invention to work, even in a rudimentary way. I have had this happen to me several times and have myself had to take out so many patent improvements that my first set of patents became obsolete and were abandoned. Look at the evolution of the hydrofoil, which began about 90 years ago (see p. 175). (see p. 175)

It might seem that governments are generous in granting up to 20-year exclusive patent protections. But it is my opinion that for the individual inventor with really original material, 20 years is not nearly enough. The preliminary stages of application often take two to four years from the original filing date (the filing date is usually considered the first of the protective years). The filing of a license and preliminary start-up takes perhaps six years from the original application. Then bugs (problems) are found and have to be rectified.

Finally, after about ten years, the inventor finds that the annual royalty returns only then begin to exceed patenting and maintenance expenses. Real, substantial income return may begin (if the inventor is lucky) to mature only during the last five years, if all has gone well. No wonder most individual inventors have a hard financial existence and often fail or just give up. Of course, this does not always have to be the case and can be alleviated by the inventor's better understanding of all the processes for success. However, I personally believe there is a good argument for the patent protective time to be extended for up to another five years for the original individual inventor (or personal corporations) and be nonassignable.

In several cases, I have filed and have had to withdraw my patent application prior to examination or publication because of peculiar circumstances of different

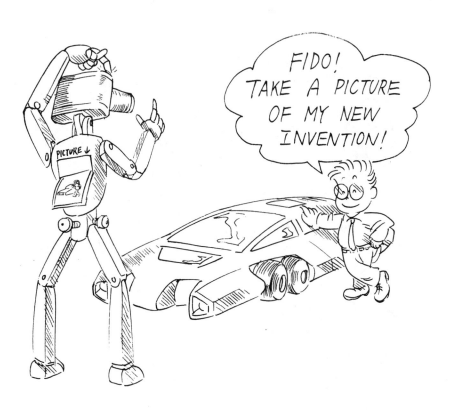

patent offices. On one occasion I filed a preliminary first patent application in a country that was not my resident country. Each country has its own little peculiarities as to patents, even if they are broadly linked to the patent cooperation treaty. Your patent attorney will tell you what you can and cannot do in your particular circumstance. However, in my opinion—and in general terms, providing you have not exposed your invention to public scrutiny—the longer you can delay or extend your primary filing date, the greater will be your financial reward, given that your invention is financially viable. The main thrust of this maneuver is in the area of the necessary development and refinement time to bring your invention to commercial viability.

Publication of Your Patent

In many countries, publication of your original filing takes place within 18 months. (United States publication takes place only after granting.) This does not mean that your patent has been or will be granted. Patent offices do this so that future searchers can use the published specifications against a future patent application. Also, the patent might be challenged by another who feels that you should not get the patent granted.

In my case, my patent application for a virus inhibitor for the treatment of virus particles in humans seemed so good, especially in light of the AIDS virus epidemic, that, though I could get no positive response from research organizations (they were too busy with their own research programs), I felt it sufficiently worth-

while to withdraw the application prior to the 12-month convention time and refile (since withdrawn again). To do this, I just instructed my patent agent (in London, where I had filed a provisional patent) to request the return of all relevant papers from the patent office. In this way I avoided the possibility of my own invention being prematurely published (within a further nine months) and later cited against me!

Trading Future
Success For
Today's Money
Could Be Wise

In another case, involving my wind-powered generator, I made such progress with improvements and inventive steps that I again had to withdraw my application to keep my options open. If I hadn't done so, it would have been published as an abandoned patent application in Australia this time and could have been cited against any later, related patent, including one of mine—with my improvements! So a published patent, even an abandoned one, can affect a later application you might make by making parts of your later claims invalid. In other words, if your abandoned prior application can be viewed by anyone, you could be in trouble if you tried to file another similar patent.

I learned the value of withdrawal prior to publication of my patent application the hard way, early in my inventing life. At that time I was so convinced that my new invention was a revolutionary breakthrough in the mushroom industry that I rushed into immediate, premature filing before I had fully tested the machine and worked out the bugs.

That early filing caused me extreme financial problems. The problem was with worldwide patenting due one year from my filing date. I was left with having to make the prototype, test it, eliminate bugs, get new parts tested, build a new machine based on my findings, promote it (write my letters), ship it halfway around the world to a mushroom conference, and find a licensee, all in 11 months—a virtually impossible task.

I did it, but I was in a very poor negotiating stance with my licensee, as I explained in Chapter 6, and was left with only two weeks in which to patent worldwide. I did not at the time realize that I could have withdrawn my patent application and refiled at a later date in order to have an extended time to refine my machine, and my then–patent attorney was not about to volunteer such information to me! These decisions have to be made by the inventor; you alone must know all the facts.

Had I waited six months (until after I had refined my machine and overcome some of the major problems) or had I withdrawn it after six months, I would have found life considerably less stressful and my costs greatly reduced (besides getting a greatly extended royalty income span). I was so intent on getting protection for my revolutionary invention that I lost sight of the necessary steps I needed to take to ensure its eventual success.

I thought someone might hear about my ideas and beat me to the patent office, which I now see was an unrealistic possibility. Was I doing all this inventive work in the middle of a mushroom-growing area where there was risk of others seeing and stealing my invention? No, I was on the remote island of Tasmania, the island state of Australia, where I was effectually the only grower of mushrooms. That was some 25 years ago, and I know better now. I'm poorer but wiser.

Another example of my premature filing was with my Relax-a-Flex Comfort System. I came up with a new type of mattress that had no springs, no water, but yet was not an air mattress. The system was lightweight and infinitely adjustable as to comfort, even for two people who wanted different settings. It was quite a major breakthrough, so I thought, "This will revolutionize the whole bedding industry."

And it might, eventually, after I'm dead and gone. But I was so sure it would be an instant success and be sought after by the bedding industry that I immediately went ahead and filed a patent; then I started making models and finding suppliers that could make the specialized parts, only to find that the technology for making the parts did not exist but had to be developed from the ground up.

About 18 months later, thinking to quickly get it off the ground, I took a small working model to a large bedding manufacturing show. Everyone I demonstrated it to was highly impressed with the obvious comfort level it could achieve. Then two executives took me aside (I thought they were going to make me an offer) and said, "Gordon, your new bed has many advantages. It's such a radical change from the present industry. It does not need anywhere near the amount of machinery as do the present spring mattresses. Also, we have no doubt that it is the ultimate in sleeping comfort.

"But Gordon, you don't understand the industry. The bedding industry is locked into making mostly spring mattresses and foundations. It is not interested in making the best mattress; it is interested only in selling mattresses at a profit. And your idea of a nondeteriorating mattress is not acceptable to the industry. The bedding industry relies for its survival on a constant periodic change of mattresses by the consumer."

That day I learned a great lesson as to how the business mind works. It's very self-protective and will not make any changes unless forced to do so, by either competition or financial necessity. Individuals love my mattress and never want any other. But the bedding industry, as a whole, is a hard nut to crack and is unlikely to go for any radical change that is not of its own making, or forced upon it. As an example, waterbeds have had a very rocky time over the past 20 years.

To Patent Or Not To Patent; It's A Real Question!

In more recent times, I have tended to try a different approach to filing, an approach that seems to work better and is considerably less costly. I wait as long as possible, then I file, but if I encounter any problems I had previously been unaware of, I withdraw within the first 10 or 11 months, either to refile immediately if I am continuing to work on the invention, or to shelve it if there seems to be a lack of interest or I have encountered too many technical problems that need further work later on when I have the time.

There is a financial advantage to waiting. The inventor's aim is to put his or her invention on the market with a minimum of delay in order to maximize the protective period—usually 20 years from filing. An inventor who prematurely files and wastes this protective period is at risk of losing a considerable amount of money that he or she would have received toward the end of the patent cover.

For example, suppose you file too early and it takes you five additional years to refine and bring your invention to commercial acceptability. Once you start selling, it takes another six years to get market acceptability for your invention and for sales to begin to take off. You are left with the possibility of only five years of good royalty returns on your invention.

Inventors
Always Seem
To Be
Defending
Themselves

But if you could get rid of that first "wasted" period (or get a good new patent later) prior to marketing—by waiting four years before filing—then you would gain perhaps five years at the other end. That would extend your five years of good royalty return by another four years of potentially even far greater returns, giving you about nine years of good end-of-patent cover!

It seems a truism that sales figures for a good exclusive item increase dramatically each succeeding year. By filing later, you might actually receive five to ten times more return! I am, of course, assuming that you can file later safely and that you have not exposed yourself to premature public disclosure. You and you alone must weigh the relative risks with the potential financial gain and the prevailing circumstances.

Withdrawal and refiling allows you to have your cake and eat it too. A patent attorney will rarely recommend withdrawal or delay because of the chance mentioned earlier of an identical (or similar) invention slipping in before your possible publication, or general public exposure through third parties. Your attorney would not want to take the blame for any possible miscalculation on your part! You will have to make that decision.

But I say withdrawal can be an avenue to allow you to delay while you still have possibilities for substantial coverage for the future. Filing and withdrawing gives you time for improvement and time to find a licensee. The law may allow you too little time otherwise, especially for filing in other countries. If you have no intention of foreign filing, the general 18-month or greater period before publication by the patent office may be more workable. At least you have a longer time before you decide whether or not to withdraw.

Somewhere in my mind, I usually have three or four inventions I am ruminating on. I now know from past experience that I can do real justice to only one at a time, so I just "sit" on those that I feel can wait, because they have lesser potential or are harder to get off the ground, and concentrate on that special one. The ones I do not proceed with I tell very few people about (and not in detail). I just put them on the back burner. From time to time, I just think about them and make written notes or make a homemade model.

On the one I decide to proceed with, I first refine it, making a plan or prototype, after which I file a preliminary local patent (through my patent attorney) with the broadest possible description. (I do this as insurance.) If I have not already done so, I then proceed to canvass potential interested people, hinting only of the broad possibilities of my invention and giving no specifics as to how I will achieve the end result. If I get any inquiries, I am prepared to give specific details *only* if the inquirer signs a nondisclosure statement. If the inquirer is willing to sign a minimum royalty licensing agreement, I am willing to file internationally as necessary. But this is a rarity.

Generally I have no firm commitment within the first 12 months, so if my prototype development has proceeded well and I am confident of eventual success, I advise my patent attorney to withdraw my patent application from the patent office and simultaneously refile with any added claims or advantages I have found since my first filing. I would withdraw and refile a second time—and have done so—if I still had confidence in the invention.

But if I decide to abandon the project for the time being, for any reason, I would still withdraw, so that at a later date, if I again wanted to proceed with the invention, I would not find that my previous filing could be used against me. This procedure can be used, however, only if the invention has been kept confidential and has not been published or exposed to general public knowledge.

A Change In Direction Always Takes Much Energy

These suggestions are designed to help you use the patenting system to your long-term advantage. There are many computations to any invention, not the least of which is your ability to afford your potentially rewarding hobby.

Disadvantages of Patent Application

Patents are not always good for the original inventor. This could be the case with a complex chemical formula that would be hard, if not impossible, to duplicate without the published details, but that could be easily read in any granted patent. Delayed approval by government authorities might delay marketing so much that protective time could run out.

You may have an invention that can be duplicated only through a published patent specification. In these circumstances, a closely held knowledge of the invention or formula might prove wise if the invention cannot be duplicated without specific information. We have all heard the story of how the Coca-Cola key formula has never been registered and is a closely held secret shared, reputedly, by only three people at any one time.

Invalidation of Patents

Industrial
Secrets Are
Never
Published

Once granted, patents can be invalidated at any time for a number of reasons, the most common being prior disclosure by use or publication by yourself or others; that is, the patent subject matter became public knowledge prior to the patent's original filing date.

Usually, it is sufficient for anyone to prove that your invention was published in such a manner as to advise the public of its essential details. As I have said, you need to be careful about talking to reporters. Everyone likes to have their invention recognized, but to indulge your local newspaper reporter before filing could be costly later, just as would be testing your invention at a show with dated brochures.

Then there could be that very rare occurrence when someone else has made a prior allied invention but neglected to file a patent. If that person (or anyone) is able to show and prove that theirs is identical to yet occurred before yours, then that would be sufficient evidence but such a rarity that I myself have never heard of it happening! I believe, as a general rule, that an individual's prior verbal knowledge of your invention, without specific details, is not sufficient to invalidate your patent. If otherwise, anyone could invalidate any issued patent just by claiming they had thought it up or had prior knowledge—clearly a totally unreasonable claim. However, circumstances will alter cases like noses alter faces!

Invalidating An Existing Granted Patent

Ironically, action to invalidate a granted patent almost always occurs only after the patent has been found to be successful! Invalidating patents costs money—so the invention would normally have had to be successful! Others then want to jump on the bandwagon of success and will often go to great lengths and expense to invalidate a patent. A case in point was the success of the "WorkMate," a handy work bench sometimes called a work horse, invented by Ronald P. Hinkman and now marketed by Black & Decker for the home workshop market worldwide.

The inventor originally canvassed the major home-tool companies with a view to licensing his product. All, including Black & Decker, turned him down, so he started making and marketing it himself with such great success that he was later approached by Black & Decker for an exclusive license, which he concluded under reasonably favorable terms.

Black & Decker were themselves so successful in promoting and selling the multiuse home workbench that some large companies wanted to have a piece of the pie and started to make their version of the Black & Decker unit themselves, which resulted in several costly defense actions. The most serious challenge was from a Japanese corporation that thought they could break the patent by showing a key feature near-exact general copy of the Work Mate that had been produced several hundred years earlier! They really thought they had a watertight case, as there was great visual similarity between an old bookbinding press and the new Work Mate!

The case went to the British high court for the final decision, and the fate of the patent hinged essentially on one word in the patent. It was determined that the application was invented and designed specifically for the home workshop and not as a bookbinding press. The validity of the patent was therefore upheld. This example demonstrates the value of having a patent that is correctly worded by someone whose job it is to ensure that it is: a qualified patent attorney or agent.

Good Inventions Do Not Guarantee Financial Success For Their Inventors

Unfortunately (as with Thomas Davenport, the inventor of the electric motor and Nicola Tesla, the inventor of the AC 60 cycle and so many of the electrical benefits we have today—wireless, strip lighting, and remote-controlled motors), such great original conceptual thinkers did not reap financial benefits or full recognition during their lifetimes. But today their contributions to human progress are more recognized—they will, I believe, go down in history long after left brain–dominant financial geniuses such as J. P. Morgan and John D. Rockefeller are forgotten.

Two Major Breakthrough Inventions

The Electric Motor

In the 1830s a man by the name of Thomas Davenport was trained as a "smithy"— that is, he was adept at making and fitting horseshoes and repairing farm equipment such as iron plows and farm implements. He must have been somewhat restless,

The More You
Succeed, The
More You
Have To
Defend Your
Patent

not content to make a steady living in his vocation. One can imagine him as a trusting sort of person, dealing with the local people in his rural area of New England.

As was normal at that time, at local fairs the latest technical innovations would be shown and demonstrated. It was here that he saw the marvel of a 30-pound magnet picking up a 300-pound piece of iron. Few people even today could associate a large magnet with an electric motor, but at that time no such electric motor existed, not even the thought of one. But Thomas Davenport suddenly visualized converting the linear power of magnetism to rotary-power magnetism. The ramifications for the potential uses of this process must have been almost overwhelming to him, even in those days.

From that first concept, Davenport worked feverishly to make his idea for a rotary shaft driven by magnetism (today known as an electric motor) work. Imagine the immense problems he must have encountered in making every part individually by hand. By trial and error he had to work out coil sizes and lengths, and how to insulate under hot working conditions. Then there were the lubricated bearings and the contact for supplying the constant power to the motor while it rotated. You may think you could have done it, but remember that Thomas Davenport, the genius, was breaking new ground at almost every turn, forcing with his mind thought patterns that really were new and revolutionary. He solved all the major difficulties virtually singlehanded.

Too bad that his brilliance extended only to that one area of inventing. I wish I could report that he reaped his just rewards financially. Unfortunately, his trust

in others in the business community was misplaced. He did not know how to exploit his invention to his own financial gain. He was too right-brained.

After much difficulty and personal hardship and with the help of some friends, he finally obtained a U.S. patent in 1834, yet within ten years he was dead, a poor, destitute man who will still go down in history as one of the world's greatest inventors. He never lived to receive his just financial rewards or the general approbation of society. His contemporaries just did not understand or realize the enormity of his breakthrough technology and its importance to the future progress of mankind. Surely modern society could not be so advanced without the electric motor and its multitude of uses.

The Wave Of Success Is As Fickle As The Wind

The Hydrofoil

To illustrate the time frame for the development work necessary to refine a new conceptual breakthrough to the point of financial viability, here is the chronology of significant events in the development of the hydrofoil, which is only now being commercially accepted worldwide.

1907 Wilbur and Orville Wright conduct experiments with a hydrofoil catamaran on the Ohio River.
1911 Alexander Graham Bell witnesses tests of a 1.6-ton hydrofoil conducted by Enrico Forlanini on Lake Maggiori, Italy.
1919 Bell's hydrofoil HD-4 sets a world speed record of 70.85 miles per hour at Baddeck, Nova Scotia.

1927 Baron Hanns von Schertel begins experiments with hydrofoil craft in Germany.

1935 Baron von Schertel abandons the full-submerged foil configuration and adopts the surface-piercing configuration with a hoop foil.

1937 The Cologne-Dusseldorf Steamship Co. places with the Sachsenberg Shipyard the world's first order for a commercial passenger hydrofoil.

1941 von Schertel and Sachsenberg launch the 17-ton German minelaying hydrofoil V-6.

1947 The U.S. Office of Naval Research, Bureau of Ships and Bureau of Aeronautics initiates a research program to develop the hydrofoil craft concept.

1951 The Canadian Navy begins to explore the military potential of hydrofoil craft and contracts with Phillip Rhodes to build the five-ton hydrofoil *Massawippi* (R-100).

1952 von Schertel founds SUPRAMAR A. G. in Lucerne, Switzerland, and completes the hydrofoil PT-10. It begins the first commercial hydrofoil passenger service on Lake Maggiori.

1952 The U.S. Navy sponsors the construction of a number of hydrofoil test craft. The *Lantern* (HC-4) experimental hydrofoil is constructed by the Hydrofoil Corporation of America; the experimental *Carl* hydrofoil (XCH-4) is completed by John H. Carl and Sons, and the hydrofoil test craft *High Pockets* is built by Baker Manufacturing Co.

1953 The U.S. Navy focuses on hydrofoil landing craft. *High Pockets* conducts demonstration of hydrofoil capability for Chief Naval Officer Admiral Carney.

1954 Gibbs and Cox, a New York naval architecture firm, begins modification of a Chris-Craft hull that becomes the first fully submerged hydrofoil craft with an electronic autopilot control system. The craft is named *Sea Legs*.

1954 The Rodriguez Shipyard in Messina, Sicily, is licensed to build hydrofoils of SUPRAMAR design.

1957 *Sea Legs* makes its first flight.

1957 The hydrofoil test craft *Halobates* is completed by Miami Shipbuilding Co. The U.S. Army contracts with Miami Ship to build the Flying *Dukw* amphibian hydrofoil.

The preceding was gleaned from the book *Twenty Foilborne Years*, prepared by William M. Ellsworth; the information was released by the David Taylor Naval Ship Research and Development Center. This chronology is fairly typical of the progressive (and sometimes nonprogressive) development of a breakthrough technology.

You will need to be careful that your new invention does not threaten any particular portion or segment of society. There are numerous examples of a new invention being so advanced for the society it's invented in that it is perceived as a threat to that society. The reaction can be severe for the inventor—even life-threatening.

In a story from ancient Roman times, an angry mob of weavers who perceived a threat to their livelihood looted and destroyed the premises of a superior, quicker weaver. They could not accept progress that threatened them, so they killed the weaver who was better than they were!

We hope that today's society is more receptive to new ideas. Nevertheless, do not expect to make a fortune with your new technological breakthrough. But with proper development of your left-brain skills, you may be lucky. It increases the chances that your name will go down in history, which would ultimately be longer lasting than monetary gain and better for your eternal ego.

What Is Obvious To You, Is Not To Another

The Importance of Action Against Infringers

When you believe that your patent is being infringed, you will need to get evidence of it. Such evidence must be in a form that enables you to convince a judge that there is indeed an infringement.

It is obvious that such evidence might be a sworn affidavit by an expert stating what he or she has seen the infringing article, or brochures, or descriptive information are available. But by far the best evidence is provided by photographs of the infringing article showing clearly the infringing part or parts. Sometimes it might be difficult to find these. If you took a photo of a machine from a distance, such a photo might not be acceptable in a court of law, because it would not show how it works. Close-up photos from many angles are best.

I knew that an owner-operated small manufacturing business was infringing one of my new composting machines, and I thought that I could go to see the infringed machine in the manufacturer's workshop. I took my patent attorney with

Infringers Only
Infringe If It Is
Profitable To
Do So

me, hoping that we could work out a deal. Imagine my disappointment when I arrived at the infringer's premises and was refused admission, and moreover the owner gave a blank refusal to discuss anything whatsoever. The owner's accountant and legal adviser met us outside the work premises and were rude and abusive to us while neither admitting nor confirming our suspicions. Such actions by infringers can be very frustrating and expensive to the inventor, which any future legal settlement may not adequately address. That is why I will make every effort and reasonable sacrifice in order to work out some mutually acceptable business and royalty arrangement.

Where multicountry patents are involved, be careful where you commence infringement action. You may think that if you find an infringer in a country where you have patent cover, then you should take legal action in that country. This may not be your best action for a number of reasons: (1) The infringers may export all or most of their production to various countries and destinations. (2) The country may have an expensive or cumbersome legal system that does not give the aggrieved party (which is you) a reasonably quick settlement. (3) You may find that (especially if you have no established licensee in that country) the government bureaucracy does not lend you the extent and type of assistance you will need in order to win and stop further infringements.

License the Infringer

Often, the first you hear about an infringement is the communication of one or more or your licensees that they have located an infringing article. They'll insist that you do something about it right away. They say it is affecting their business

and sales. You are put on the spot. If you refuse and do nothing, your present licensees will, and quite rightly, most probably refuse to pay you any more royalties until you take appropriate action. So you are forced to take action of some kind.

Your best, least painful action is to get your infringer to accept a license that is somewhat equitable to those of your other licensees in other countries. This might not always be possible, especially where you may have already given such rights to another licensee that may not have a presence in that country. If your controlling licensee will not or cannot grant a license to the infringer, then you'll begin to have more difficulties. You have to make it less or not profitable for the infringer to infringe. How do you do this? There are several approaches, all costly to you, though some more than others.

> Some Countries Prevent You From Taking Out Your Fair Share

Foreign Legal Systems

Do you view the infringer's country as having a cumbersome, outdated, or expensive legal system? If the answer is no, then action in that country could prove beneficial. You will first need to find a qualified legal firm to represent you. Only in a very straightforward case (and where you have lots of general income) should you get your own local legal counsel to work through a represenative in a foreign country, you would tell your attorney to tell the other attorney (doubling up costs).

You would most likely find it best to approach your favorite patent attorney, explain your dilemma, and ask him or her to locate a good patent attorney who can represent you in an action in that country. In the United States only one patent attorney is required. In England, France, and many other countries, you need two representatives. One should be the patent agent adviser, and the other the actual advocate who pleads your case in front of the judge or judges. The two work hand-in-hand and will (normally) need to be paid separately.

In this case it is the patent agent (the person or company who normally processes patent applications for clients) whom you need to approach and convince that there is an actual infringement taking (or that has already taken) place. Initially, the agent normally writes preliminary letters to the infringer, pointing out the errors of their ways and suggesting they cease and desist from further infringement. A personal visit to the agent, even in a foreign country, would be most helpful to you in establishing a good rapport and working relationship.

I have found patent attorneys, patent agents, and advocates worldwide to be most sympathetic and helpful to the individual inventor. Work done is excellent, and the charges for such excellent work are often not as high as for large corporations doing similar work. It seems to me that many patent attorneys have an inordinate protective feeling for "underdog" private individual inventors, especially those of limited means who are up against unscrupulous infringers (of which there are many, I have found).

If you find that the projected costs are simply beyond you, then your other available approach is to take action against the *receivers* of the infringed products as opposed to the sellers or manufacturers. This will cause the receivers to incur considerable defensive or other costs that will rebound on the original manufacturer, giving them a bad name and possibly making their continued infringement unprofitable or emotionally too stressful—to the extent that they may come to you to seek terms for settlement.

Patenting
In Some
Countries Have
Hidden Costs

Foreign Bureaucracies

One problem with an infringement action in a foreign country is the level of bureaucratic assistance or nonassistance you may get there. There is no point in initiating action where your problems are multiplied through a biased bureaucratic system that favors the established infringer and any political clout they may have. You are then regarded as the foreign interloper trying to stop a "legitimate" business and cause hardship to the country's citizens. You become the bad guy.

How can you tell whether the country you are dealing with may be antagonistic to your efforts at stopping an infringer? There are clues, fortunately. Ask your patent attorney's opinion about the country in question, especially the type and degree of his or her success in prosecuting the granting of patents in that country. If your own experience has been poor in a given country, and it has been expensive getting your own sometimes rather inadequate patent there, then this would be an indication. Your patent attorney can help you a great deal in this regard.

I, for example, have always had extreme problems in prosecuting patents in Taiwan and Eastern European countries. What is obvious in Western countries seems not obvious to examiners in non-Western countries. The process of obtaining patents (or even lesser valued, utility patents) in these countries becomes quite costly and time consuming. Licensing deals may be forthcoming in such countries, but I've gotten the feeling that they can never be fully satisfying or enforceable by the inventor, even with high legal cost.

Some countries put limits on the amount of royalty that can be charged and the amount that can be taken out of the country. And, to add insult to injury, some countries tax any royalty at the highest rate possible before the inventor gets a penny—overall, a no-win situation. Know the country's laws before you patent in them.

Fortunately, you have several options open to you that will depend on the extent and scope of the infringement. Your patent attorney can advise you on the specifics. But in general, I have found that going for the importers and/or end users is best, with also a possibility of getting shipments turned back or put into bond by the customs authorities upon proof that there is an unauthorized shipment of patent-protected product coming into the country. Have Chapters 1 to 9 confused you? If not, go on to "catch-all" Chapter 10. If yes, start at Chapter 1 again!

Inventors Should Be Aware, There Are Wolves In Sheep's Clothing

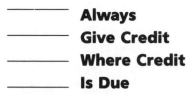

10 The Catch-All Chapter

Prior to this chapter, everything, unless noted, was written by me without substantial reference to other works. I hadn't read many! However, after I completed the main part of my manuscript I gleaned other more technical information from all sorts of different places, much of which may be of great help to inventors, entrepreneurs, and technically minded people. I have written more information to clarify its value. I certainly do wish that I had access to something like the following when I first started inventing to help me find those specialized sources of help. I thank author Gary S. Lynn for some of the general headings and public knowledge resource material used in this chapter, which came from the book *From Concept to Market* (published by John Wiley & Sons). Although a lot of this resource material is directed to the United States, you will find it interesting wherever you live. The appendix is a separate gold mine of information for those seeking inventor organizations. Appreciation must also be given here to the Minnesota Resource Center for much of the assembled information in the appendix. They have even more available, so write to them for additional specific help. Their address is Minnesota Resource Center, 231 East Second Street, P.O. Box 71, Redwood Falls, MN 56283.

Protection for Your Efforts: Sorting It All Out

What have you created? Can you patent it? Can you copyright it? Can you register it as a trademark, or perhaps is it a trade secret you wish to safeguard? There are great differences between all these.

Patents

To get a patent you need to convince the patent examiner that you have a new, useful, and not obvious process or product. It cannot be copyrighted, registered as a trademark, or kept as a trade secret.

Patents,
Copyright,
Trademark
And Trade
Secrets Are All
Different

The patent office does not guarantee the validity of the patents it issues, nor will it have anything to do with initiating any action on a patent after it's granted. The holder of the patent has to defend it at his or her expense. The patent entitles the owner to prevent others from making, using, or selling the patented product in the country of issuance—that is, if someone does make, use, or sell in the patented country, it is up to the patent holder to initiate appropriate action.

Copyright

A copyright protects a person's "expression"; books, musical works, plays, paintings, sculptures, computer programs, and movies would be covered by copyright. The copyright should be registered through your legal representative, but is often not until it becomes necessary for a legal action; then delays occur. A © symbol, in any case, should be placed on all copyrighted material. Essentially a copyright cannot be patented, kept as a trade secret, or normally registered as a trademark, though if you prepared a work of art that also included a trade name, you might attach both a copyright symbol and registration mark (®). Doing so would tend to warn off would-be copiers.

Trademark

A trademark or trade name is used to identify the goods and services of the trademark owner. Trademarks can and should be registered in each country you wish to be covered in at the appropriate government office. Initial filing fees vary from country to country, and there are generally renewal fees. However, there is no time limit on how long one can hold a trademark; it can theoretically last indefinitely and also be sold or transferred to others at any time. Some countries require separate registration of a single trademark to be carried out where it is used in separate classes of goods.

Generally, unlike with a granted patent, the owner of a registered trademark may, with suitable back-up information, request a country's customs service to disallow importation of an unauthorized shipment bearing the owner's trademark. Essentially a trademark cannot be patented, registered, or copyrighted or kept (by definition) as a trade secret. A registration mark (®) should be placed close to one side of the trademark to denote it as a registered trademark. You may put a trademark for a common law trademark that is not registered, which is more difficult to defend in case of violation.

Trade Secrets

A formula, pattern, device, tool, mechanism, or a compound of any of the preceding that is of particular value to the owner can and is protected providing that no one can deduce the secret independently; that is, that no one has had unlawful access to the secret. Not many trade secrets can stand the test of time. Secrets are often found out by analysis or reverse engineering. Coca-Cola is perhaps a notable exception, though today there are many colas on the market that probably come very close to the original Coca-Cola formula (or present-day formulas). By definition, though, a trade secret is generally protected by law from unlawful possession. A trade secret cannot be patented, copyrighted, or registered as a trademark.

If you are interested in a more detailed overview of these topics, write for a *Guide to Intellectual Property Protection*, available free of charge from the Minnesota Small Business Assistance office at 900 American Centre, 150 East Kellogg Boulevard, St. Paul, MN 55101.

Those wanting more specific current information on United States copyright should write to the Copyright Office, Library of Congress, Room 40, 101 Independence Avenue, Washington, DC 20559 (phone (202) 479-0700).

For more on patents and trademarks, contact the U.S. Patent and Trademark Office, Washington, DC 20231 (phone (703) 557-3158).

This can all be very confusing for the lone individual inventor to begin with, but on the positive side, all this detailed reading will strengthen your left-brain attributes!

Third Worlds
Are Known
But Not
Second And
Fourth

Third-World Technology

If you feel that your new invention has benefits for the so-called Third World, you will need to assess the benefits to yourself as well. Generally, marketing in the poorer countries of the world is difficult for the supplier, not because the product is not wanted or needed, but because the price the people there can afford is often lower than what the product can be manufactured for. In addition, there is very often the problem of getting money out of the country, so that even if the product is manufactured in the country, getting basic profits or royalties becomes difficult,

if not impossible, except using a barter system. Some countries levy heavy taxes on profits (royalties) too.

All of this means you have to be careful—after going to considerable expense to obtain patent cover in such countries, you may find yourself with a negative cash flow! Make inquiries about the country or countries you plan to market in.

If you know that your invention will benefit people in those countries but that you are not in a position to be a philanthropist, a good idea would be to contact the consulate or embassy of the proposed country and inquire if their country has a ministry that covers what you have to offer. Then contact it directly. If your offer is accepted, you never know, you may be invited to visit the country as a guest of the ministry, with all expenses paid, and offered a special deal!

From a practical standpoint, probably your best approach to selling to the less-advantaged people of this world is to license a company that already has access to the markets. Such a company is established and knows the ropes of how to penetrate the government bureaucracy and get payment, so that you can in turn get your royalty without risk.

What type of technology does your invention cover? Would you like to know more about what is out there already for the poorer nations of the world? I have found a wealth of such information available from Intermediate Technology Publications Ltd., 9 King Street, London WC 2E 8HW, England. They can send you a concise booklet listing their whole range of publications. Their books, available by mail, are directed at those who need simplified, less costly products or machinery, such as might help financially disadvantaged societies. If your invention is in this category, I recommend that you look through the list of books offered by this charity-supported publishing house.

Do Not Be Greedy

The hotter your invention, the less greedy you should be, though being greedy normally comes naturally to those who think they are sitting in the driver's seat. However, people and corporations usually enjoy more long-term success when they share their own success with others. I knew a person who made several million dollars by being greedy. He had no real lasting friends—many whom he had cheated hated him fiercely. No one would help him when he needed help. By way of illustration, consider the invention of the sailboard, which spurred the windsurfing craze worldwide. The inventor patented the sailboard principle with a very strong main claim and many subsidiary claims. When he saw the almost instant popularity of the product, the inventor, patent in hand, refused to license anyone unless they put up a lot of cash, even before discussion. This prevented much growth and further expansion of the market while keeping the sales price higher than it might otherwise have been. Naturally, the product was infringed by an increasing number of manufacturers—reaching over 100 worldwide. When the inventor (who would not allow general licensees) took legal action, all the infringers joined together to fight him. They initially succeeded in stripping all ancillary claims from his patent, except the key one for the toggle sail connector. Next, the interested parties pooled their money to finance searching every possible publication and prior art, from no matter what source. The search continued for month after month at a

cost of huge sums of money. Finally, they hit the jackpot! In an obscure 1930s
publication there appeared a photo of a toy ironing board with a sail and mast
connections. The inventor's last remaining claim was forfeited! Greed had led to
total failure, which would not—could not—have occurred had the patent holder been
satisfied with allowing his eventual infringers to have acceptable licenses. The
infringers would not have ganged up on him to bring about his downfall. You may
think this story is just an exception or an unlucky experience, but as I have
previously indicated, the better and more acceptable an invention, the more likely
it is to be infringed. If an infringer wants a license, let them have it; somehow,
they then become your friend instead of your enemy. An infringer who does not
want a license will become an enemy to you and all your other licensees as well.

When I give an exclusive license, I now have a clause stating that if the
exclusive licensee does not satisfy the demand, then they have to either satisfy
that demand within three months or sublicense; otherwise I, the licensor, have
the right to sublicense others to meet the demand. This has the effect of making
my exclusive licensees nonexclusive licensees if they don't satisfy the legitimate
demand.

Good Advice Is Best Sought From Those Qualified To Give It

You and Your Patent Attorney

As an inventor, you have to educate your patent attorney. Give him or her complete, thorough details regarding your invention.

A patent agent does not normally voice any concern that your invention is not going to sell or make you any money, nor should you expect him or her to, because it is neither the function nor within the normal expertise of a patent agent.

You should expect your agent to give you an honest opinion as to the likelihood that you will be issued a good and valid patent.

Your attorney's goal is to get you the broadest possible claims bearing in mind the prior art.

In the event that you decide to license your invention, your agent should be prepared and competent to advise you whether your proposed license is a good one, and if not, what is needed to make it good.

He or she should tell you what future maintenance fees might be due, and when, as well as the minimum fees and costs of trying to get a patent.

Adding new claims and/or material will probably be possible later, but it will cost you more.

For overseas parallel applications, you will have to be very careful in your timing. Your patent attorney is the one to advise you in this area.

Patent applications are generally rejected the first time. This is to be expected. Your best approach is to seek good advice from the person who can best give it—your patent agent.

Game and Toy Inventions

If you are trying to interest a game or toy manufacturer in your idea, you may have less than a 1 in 100 chance of success. Most toy and game manufacturers have their own energetic in-house development departments. If you go through a game broker or agency, your chances of success are improved by a factor of five. The reason is that game and toy manufacturers prefer potential new products to be evaluated or screened by a broker in accordance with their particular lines of interest. Bear in mind that demand in this area is divided unequally: 80 percent for toys and 20 percent for games. Therefore, your chances for success are less with a game by a factor of five!

For the preceding reasons I recommend that you approach a specialized broker for all toy and game ideas. You can contact any appropriate toy or game manufacturer and ask them for a list of brokers they deal with.

One such reputable broker in the United States is Excel Development, Inc., whose address is 7007 Dakota Avenue, Chanhassen, MN 55317; Fax (612) 934-1118 or phone (612) 934-1200; contact Andrew Berton or Michael Marra. If they like what you have, they will consider making a prototype at no cost to you—a very valuable offer if all you have is an idea with drawings (naturally their service costs or recoverable by them.) One nice thing about them is that they tend to explain in detail at the beginning your chances of success or failure, and decline to waste your money or their time on products that for the time being are nonviable. Remember: Games and toys tend to be hot items one day, cold the next. After the first hot item hits the scene, all related copies tend to be failures, so you need to be original for the greatest chance of success.

Help for Prototypes

If you feel you need professional help for your models, try to get local help—the nearer the better—so that you can be in constant personal contact to give day-to-day help as necessary. Your local university may want to participate; however, I have found that the best choice is a company I would like to license. The company gains confidence in your product. If all else fails, a visit to your local public library will most likely enable you to find that specialized prototype manufacturer you are looking for.

Independent Verification of Tests

Having verification that your product has been tested by an independent laboratory and proven to be a certain percent longer-lasting than the competition, or a certain percent safer, stronger, or more durable adds credibility to your product. This authentication can be very useful when you market your product and also enables you to work out any bugs that may develop during testing.

Locating a testing laboratory is not difficult. The telephone book's Yellow Pages are one source, and the following two directories can provide you with a

list of testing facilities that should be able to conduct your performance tests. You might also call the American Council of Independent Laboratories in Washington, DC, to get the names of laboratories near you; their phone number is (202) 877-5872.

- Directory of Testing Laboratories, American Society for Testing and Materials, 1916 Race Street, Philadelphia, PA 19103
- Directory of the American Council of Independent Laboratories, 1725 K Street, NW, Washington, DC 20006

Non-Disclosure Agreements

The type of nondisclosure agreement you use is a personal preference. If you make it too simple, you may not be covered. If you make it too tough or complex, your prospective licensee or helper will refuse to sign it on the grounds that they could be too exposed to future legal action through circumstances beyond their control. Here are several such possible forms to use as a guide. Make any adjustments you feel your particular situation warrants, then run the agreement by your patent attorney before you submit it to your potential licensee or helper.

Sample of Nondisclosure Agreement (On your letterhead)

Our company agrees that, in consideration for access to information submitted to me or our employees by (your name or company), our company will:

1. Keep all information relating to models, drawings, discussions, and printed material in strict confidence within our company.
2. Disclose this information solely to individuals who have signed a Nondisclosure Agreement with (your name or company) or who have written approval from (your name or company) to receive or have access to the information.
3. Not make any contract or agreement of any kind with anyone outside our company on any idea submitted without prior written approval of (your name or company). Furthermore, we agree not to use, either directly or indirectly, any such information provided by (your name or company) for our own benefit or for the benefit of any person, firm, or corporation.

Understood and agreed this

_____ day of _____ 19 _____ .

_____
Signature (Manufacturer's authorized representative)

_____
(Print the signer's name)

_____
(Title)

_____
Company

_____
Signature (Your representative)   Date

_____
(Print your representative's name)

Sample of Confidential Disclosure Agreement

This Agreement between _____(your name or company)_____ , the Discloser, and the undersigned Disclosee sets forth the terms and conditions of the disclosure of certain confidential information relating to (your product) by the Discloser to the Disclosee:

Written
Confidential
Agreements
Are Fine,
Verbal Not So

    The Disclosee agrees to receive said confidential information in confidence and to hold the same in confidence for a period of five (5) years from the date of this disclosure:

    The Disclosee agrees not to disclose to any third parties, other than to the extent it is necessary to disclose to employees of the Disclosee, and agrees to inform said employees of the confidentiality of the information so disclosed as soon as it is done so:

    It is understood between the parties hereto that confidential information shall mean conceptual, technical, or operational information relating to the above-identified apparatus or process disclosed by the Discloser to the Disclosee either directly or indirectly in writing or by drawings or by inspection of experimental apparatus:

    This agreement shall not be construed to grant the Disclosee any license or other rights except as noted herein. But the Discloser is interested in licensing suitable interested parties, and would therefore be well disposed to negotiating a suitable license with the Disclosee.

Dated this _____ day of _____ , 19_____ .

DISCLOSER: DISCLOSEE:

Sample of Secrecy Agreement

This Agreement, made this _____ day of _____ ,
19_____ , by and between ____(you)____ , a corporation (hereinafter
referred to as _____); and ___(them)___ , a division of _____
(hereinafter referred to as _____):

    WITNESSETH:

    WHEREAS, ____(you)____ represents that it has designed a new and unique device to be used as a (your product) and desires to explore with ____(them)____ the potential for ____(them)____ to become a Licensee of ____(you)____ in distributing and manufacturing said device; and

    WHEREAS, ____(you)____ desires to explore with ____(them)____ such potentials;

    NOW, THEREFORE, the parties hereto agree as follows:

    1. ____(you)____ will make a disclosure of all of the information necessary to evaluate the device to ____(them)____ . This disclosure may include written information relating to the design, structure, and technical performance of the device, as well as oral presentation of the device's capabilities. ____(you)____ will be available to answer questions concerning the device's operation and will

answer all questions necessary for ___(them)___ to make a business decision regarding the device. All written data disclosed to ___(them)___ by ___(you)___ shall be marked by ___(you)___ as being confidential and proprietary.

2. All disclosures made by ___(you)___ concerning the device are made in strictest confidence. It is understood and agreed by ___(them)___ that it will not, without ___(your)___ written consent, reveal to any third party any confidential written data provided to it hereunder; will not duplicate (except one copy for archive purposes) any of such data; and shall keep all such data in a safe and secure place that is inaccessible to third parties. Notwithstanding paragraph 5 hereof, ___(they)___ may retain one copy of such data solely for its archives.

3. ___(their)___ obligations under the preceding paragraph shall not apply with respect to any information disclosed *to third parties* hereunder which

a. was in ___(other's)___ possession prior to disclosure hereunder; or

b. is or becomes generally available to the public; or

c. is made available to ___(them)___ by a third party who, as far as ___(they)___ can reasonably determine, did not acquire such information under an agreement of confidentiality with ___(you)___ ; or

d. is independently developed by ____(third parties)____ .

4. Obligations to maintain the secrecy of ____(the invention)____ information shall terminate three (3) years from the date of this Agreement.

5. All information furnished to ____(them)____ by ____(you)____ shall be returned within sixty (60) days from the date of this Agreement.

6. This Agreement shall be interpreted and construed in accordance with its English language meaning under the Laws of the State of ____(your state)____ , USA.

7. This Agreement represents the entire agreement between the parties hereto and supersedes any oral or written understandings, proposals, or communications heretofore entered into by, or on account of the parties and may not be changed, modified, or amended except in writing signed by the parties hereto.

IN WITNESS WHEREOF, the parties hereto have executed this Agreement as of the day and year first above written.

WITNESS: (to signature)　　　　　____(corporate entity)____

_____ By: ____(authorized signature)____

WITNESS: (to signature)　　　　　____(corporate entity)____

_____ By: ____(authorized signature)____

> Too Many Restrictions In Agreements Make Them Less Watertight!

Agreements for Helpers

Saying to an individual whose help you want, "When my invention is successful, I'll reward you," or some similar statement, means nothing and does not reflect what will actually happen if you are successful. I always spell out what I want from someone else and what I will give them; it motivates the other party to give their best. It usually needs to be a simple statement of intentions between you. The agreements can take many forms. Usually, the less complicated, the better. The following are two examples of such agreements I have given to others. If your needs are complex or need to be more formal, as with a business entity, I advise you to seek legal advice beforehand.

My Wind Power Generator Agreement #1

I, Gordon Douglas Griffin, agree to pay five percent to F.R. from all royalties received from New Zealand and Australia in consideration for copyright assignment on all present and future wind generation drawings done by him, work done and to be done in the future in connection with Gordon Griffin's wind power generation invention. This agreement shall carry forward for a period of not less than three years from the last time work is carried out by the above on behalf of Gordon Griffin's wind generator project.

Signed _____ Dated _____

Signed _____ Dated _____

My Wind Power Generator Agreement #2

I, Gordon Douglas Griffin, agree to pay ten percent to _____ from all royalties received by me from Tasmania and Australia in consideration for work done and to be done in the future in connection with my wind power generation invention. This agreement shall carry forward for a period of not less than three years from the last time work is carried out by the above on behalf of Gordon Griffin's wind generator project.

Functions to Be Performed

1. Coordinating the services and functions of Prof. M. D. of Hobart; F. R. of Devonport; B. E. of Devonport; B. T.; and any others that may be advised from time to time.
2. Refining mechanics of wind power generator and determining the best performance under differing criteria according to information received from those in point 1.
3. Carrying out necessary work and adjustments in order to achieve the practical application of point 2.
4. Supplying a brief and concise outline of work done and progress achieved each month together with any conclusions or recommendations for future refinements.
5. Though there is no specified activity to be carried out daily or weekly, it is expected that the initial trial of the wind generator at least for farm use would be completed and preparatory results obtained within the first three months of this agreement, whereas further work and refinement will be carried out according to the success or otherwise of this project according to the results already obtained.

It is agreed that 15¢ per kilometer will be paid for traveling, and all other direct expenses will be reimbursed promptly on the submittal of a statement outlining the reasons for the expenses.

Signed _____   Dated _____

Signed _____   Dated _____

Keeping a Diary or Log

Though keeping a daily log can be very helpful, this may be difficult for some people to do. Some just don't have the time to sit down and pursue a left-brain function!

It is, however, very important to keep all receipts for all expenses in connection with your invention in a separate file categorized by date—such things as the following:

1. Telephone accounts showing when you have called somewhere in connection with your invention
2. Receipts for work done by people
3. Purchases of parts and raw materials
4. Fees by professional people

5. Travel expenses by whatever mode of transport

6. Any other categories of incidental expenses

The file is a meaningful way to cover two main areas of later possible benefits.

A.   The sequential listing of all associated expenses ensures that you had the concept first; you have the accumulated receipts to prove it. Then, a potential infringer can never claim first concept and obtain a valid patent. You can always take action to invalidate their patent, though your need to do so would be most rare and unusual.

B.   The main benefit I have found in keeping your financial records scrupulously correct is that you can normally claim all such expenses as legitimate deductions on your income tax. You may be audited the first time you claim, but once you are accepted as an inventor, life with the tax collector is much less stressful. Some expenses may have to be capitalized for write-offs over several years; other out-of-pocket expenses are usually allowed for the year of expenditure. Your tax accountant will tell you what you can and cannot do regarding your expenditures. If you wish to know the latest rulings and information on owning your own business (inventing is a business) so far as taxes and write-offs are concerned, write to your local internal revenue office for the latest publications available.

One's Memory
Tends To
Adjust To
Wants Rather
Than To
History

Disclosure Document in the United States

As I have already said, from a practical standpoint your aim is to delay the time of actual, final filing on that mature, marketable invention so that you can maximize your eventual financial rewards. Trying to file early because you think someone is going to steal it is usually counterproductive. Your invention will most probably improve in some aspect; then you will have to refile (at additional expense). In any case, you will usually lose momentum with a product that might have been good had you waited to be sure that you did indeed have the "ultimate mousetrap."

Even in light of all this, your invention may be a special case.

The United States (like most countries) has its own special ways of dealing with patents, one of which is that the first person to file for a patent may not be the first person to get a patent. It will depend on who is the first person to have the concept and how diligently that person pursues the development of that concept—a complex arrangement not followed by any other country, to my knowledge. To facilitate the process, the United States patent office has instituted a document disclosure program that is designed to protect the person who has the original idea (though not the inevitable improvements to that idea, unless further disclosure documents are supplied). In my case, I would have to file new, improved disclosures each week, if I entered the program, but that is because my inventions can always stand constant improvements! Can yours? If in doubt, ask your patent attorney to explain the benefits, latest rules, and fees of the document disclosure program. You may not have to be a United States citizen to participate; you only need a United States address for correspondence.

To proceed, send the Patent Office a letter along with your invention record, explaining your desire to have this information kept under the document disclosure program.

You should be aware that you can be excluded from obtaining a patent if you have publicly disclosed your invention in a printed publication, or offered it for sale, more than one year prior to filing a patent application (only applicable in the United States—it is prior to filing in all other countries). Even if you were awarded a patent and you had publicly offered your invention for sale more than one year prior to applying for that patent, in the United States your patent would be found invalid if challenged. If you confidentially disclose your idea to others, the one-year clock does not start. Also, though it is true that you have a one-year grace period for a U.S. patent, a public disclosure any time before you file a foreign patent application can invalidate a foreign patent. If you think your product has international sales potential, and many do, talk to your patent attorney or agent to find out about various cost-effective ways to obtain patents in foreign countries, such as a European application with designated countries. Your attorney can also tell you more specifically about when your one-year clock starts to tick!

Warnings from the United States Patent Office

The two-year retention period should not be considered a grace period during which the inventor can wait to file his or her patent application without possible loss of benefits. In establishing priority of an invention, the inventor must also be diligent in developing the invention. He or she cannot just submit for the disclosure document and do nothing else.

Warnings To
Inventors
Always Ought
To Be Noted

Inventors are also reminded that any public use or sale in the United States or publication of the invention anywhere in the world more than one year prior to the filing of a patent application on that invention will prohibit the granting of a patent.

If the inventor is not familiar with what is considered to be "diligence in completing the invention" or "reduction to practice" under the patent law, or if the inventor has other questions about patent matters, the Patent and Trademark Office advises him or her to consult an attorney or agent registered to practice before the Patent and Trademark Office. *The Directory of Registered Patent Attorneys and Agents Arranged by States and Counties* is available from the Superintendent of Documents, U.S. Government Printing Office, Washington, DC 20402. Patent attorneys and agents may be found in the telephone directories of most major cities. Also, many large cities have associations of patent attorneys that may be helpful.

The preceding is official advice. But please note:

If all else fails and you have no option but to file personally, then make every effort to see your patent examiner on a one-to-one basis! He or she will most likely help you avoid the grossest mistakes. Examiners are human, too! But you would be in for a difficult left-brain experience if you processed your own patent entirely by yourself. And you would almost certainly obtain a patent of less commercial value than one obtained through an experienced patent attorney or agent—unless you just want a piece of paper!

Sources for Locating Trade Associations

See the appendices for a helpful listing of informational addresses. However, you may need help in finding trade association publications for additional background on your particular invention. The following may be of help, but remember that your local librarian is always most willing to aid you in your particular need. Your library has updated access to many sources that you could not normally locate by yourself.

Directory of European Associations
Gale Research Co.
2200 Book Tower
Detroit, MI 48226
(Over 7,000 entries on associations in every nation of Eastern and Western Europe)

Encyclopedia of Associations
Gale Research Co.
2200 Book Tower
Detroit, MI 48226
(Over 16,000 national and regional associations, their addresses, contact person, and number
    of members)

Encyclopedia of Associations, Vol. 1
National Organization of the United States, Biennial, 14th ed.
Gale Research Co.
2200 Book Tower
Detroit, MI 48226
(Trade, business, professional, labor, scientific, educational, fraternal, and social organizations
    of the United States)

**Help For The
Well-Minded Is
Always
Available**

National Trade and Professional Associations of the United States, 1984
Klein Publications, Inc.
Box 8503
Coral Springs, FL 33065
(4,500 national associations, executives, addresses, and number of members)

National Trade and Professional Associations of the United States
Columbia Books, Inc.
Suite 300
917 15th Street, NW
Washington, DC 20005
(Approximately 4,300 national associations, addresses, executives, and number of members)

Evaluation of Your Patent

If you are the type of person who enjoys making charts in order to get an overall picture, proceed to develop your prototype charts and criteria information so that you can present them to qualified persons for evaluation. If not, get someone to help you.

My experience is that outside evaluators do not have the vision of the inventor/ entrepreneur. They are usually hesitant to give a positive report on anything. This is quite understandable, as professional evaluators need to keep their jobs! They are reluctant to stick their necks out on anyone's behalf, especially with litigation being so prevalent in today's society. They are conservatively factual with their opinions, basing them as conditional on many unlikely occurrences. Quite a left-brain exercise!

Many worthwhile projects have been stifled by being subjected to critical evaluations. As in governments or a business run by committee, no one wants to go out on a limb and disrupt the status quo. If it wasn't for a persevering executive at Xerox, we would not have such efficient copying machines today. At a critical point in Xerox's development, successive teams of evaluators were contracted to evaluate potential sales of copying machines in the late 1950s.

Evaluations Are Often Clinical And Negative

They concluded that there were insufficient potential sales of copying machines to warrant such large corporations as IBM and Kodak getting into the market. Five thousand units sold annually was suggested as the high end of sales! In reality, however, world sales have broken each previous year's sales records continuously for over 30 years, and are likely to keep increasing with the opening up of Eastern Europe to capitalism.

So much for evaluations. However, they do serve their purpose, if only to give the final decision maker (you) something to disagree with, or to help you pinpoint previously unforeseen negative points. To lend substance to an evaluation the evaluator would have to be a professional in that field or be under the direct supervision of a university department—engineering, agronomy, marketing, and so on. The normal evaluations we come across are soil, quantity (material), structural, water quality, and so on. There are a great many of them doing essential work in government and industry. Being professional they are naturally protective of their individual line of expertise and may be hard pressed with things out of the normal, such as new processes and inventions in their field, many of which have historically not lived up to original expectations.

Librarians Are
One Of The
Western
Hemisphere's
Secret
Weapons!

The cost for an evaluation may be upwards of $150, depending on range, depth, and scope. It should conclude with a summary of findings and a section estimating the likelihood of success. Although the evaluation may seem to answer questions as to the commercial potential of your invention, you should remember that the people performing the evaluation often are not experts in your specific inventive application. They may not know, for instance, that using the competitor's product may result in user injury in a particular application and that yours would not. Do not expect a 99 or 100 percent rating. It was reported that only one percent of all the inventions submitted to a particular university for evaluation received a score of 50 to 100 out of a possible score of 100.

Patent Searching by Yourself

If you have the time but not much money, you may wish to make a patent search for your own invention for possible similarities to others. The best place in the United States to search is in the Public Search Room, U.S. Patent Office, 2221 Jefferson Davis Boulevard, Arlington, Virginia.

It is much easier to complete a search at the U.S. Patent Office, or at any central patent office, because the patents there are filed by subject. Also, there will generally be more knowledgeable people present to help when you get stuck. If you want to search Beds, for example, you could go to the file for beds/mattresses, and most of the relevant patents would be there. On the other hand, in the U.S. Patent Depository Libraries, the patents are filed according to patent number, not by subject, making your work more difficult and time-consuming. Many of the inventor organizations will help you with your inquiries if you contact them (see list in Appendix 1).

Patent Depository Libraries

In the United States, many Patent Depository Libraries now offer the classification and Search Support Information System (CASSIS). CASSIS is a computer data base that can reduce your searching time by listing for you all the relevant patent numbers you might need without your having to look them up. A search can be done in minutes and usually without charge, or for a minimal charge of normally less than $50.

CASSIS does not give a complete listing of all issued patents, only the more recent ones. CASSIS can search for key words in a patent as well as patents cited as references in other patents, such as beds, sleep, mattresses, couches, and so on, which will help you get started.

Patent Searching

The world is so rapidly changing that today's knowledge can be obsolete tomorrow. For reasons previously stated, I do not recommend you (the inventor) do a final search for novelty on your invention. It's not your skilled, full-time job, and to rely on it for a later challenge to your patent might be very unwise as well as financially disastrous. However, new library technology can often show you if there is an obviously similar product; such information could be highly beneficial to you, especially in keeping you from developing something that has already been patented. Your failure to find a similar invention does not guarantee that there will be nothing prior to your own invention. It will depend on whether your invention is really something different or if it's just a rehash of something your subconscious mind had registered during another time.

One Can Have Too Much Of A Good Thing. Enough Help Is Enough!

Of course, using a computer data base for finding the types of information you require is terrific—the list of services and information offered is updated and expanded monthly. In the United States you could start with Dialog Information Services, 3460 Hillview Avenue, Palo Alto, CA 94304; (800) 334-2464, (415) 858-2700.

Other Patent Search Help

Other companies offer computer searches somewhat similar to CASSIS. These include the following:

Mead Data Center
9443 Springboro Pike
P.O. Box 93
Dayton, OH 45401
(513) 865-6800; outside OH, (800) 227-4908 [Lexpat]

BRS Information Technologies
555 E. Lancaster Avenue
St. Davis, PA 19087
(215) 254-0233; outside PA, (800) 468-0908

Permagon InfoLine, Inc.
1340 Old Chain Bridge Road
McLean, VA 22101
(703) 442-0900; or outside VA and Washington, DC, (800) 336-7575

Typical fees for these patent services vary but are approximately $100 for a subject search, $40 for a list of up to 100 patent numbers in a given class, and $80 for searches listed by an inventor's or a company's name. (That's if you really want to know how many patents have been issued worldwide in the name of, say, Gordon D. Griffin!)

You can obtain most of the information you need by doing your own patent search, and you need not spend the extra money to use these services if you live close to a Depository Library, though you would need to be familiar with computers. Personally, I would rather pay—time and travel is money! Computer searches should be used only as a supplement to your own final search, because the computer data bases contain only the more recent patents, usually after 1960. Also, you can obtain copies of patents at the Patent Depository Libraries or request them directly from the central U.S. Patent and Trademark Office or its branches. I have found that my patent attorney's searchers have supplied me with enough relevant copies of interested prior art (patents) to satisfy both our needs. Searches can be a good tool, but you should not absolutely rely on them to obtain a valid patent!

Basics for Performing the Patent Search
Outline

First, have lots and lots of spare time.
The basic procedure for performing a patent search is as follows:
1. Identify into which classification your invention falls, such as beds, mattresses, couches, and so forth.
2. Get a listing of patents in that classification(s).
3. Check the patents cited to see which ones, if any, are relevant.
4. Review the patents that appear to be similar to your idea.
5. Make copies of the patents that appear similar to your invention (for your patent attorney to review).
6. Fill out a search report (obtainable from your Patent Office).

Available Publications

When you perform your search, the following U.S. government publications will be generally helpful in whatever country you happen to reside:
1. *Index to Classification*—to determine the class and subclass of your product.
2. *Manual of Classification*—to locate a more specific detailed subclass.
3. *Classification Definition*—to check whether your class/subclass is correct.
4. *U.S. Patent Classification-Subclass Listing*—to get a listing of patent numbers in each class and subclass.
5. *Official Gazette*—issuance of the similar patent so you can review its brief drawing and summary to see if it is relevant to your invention. This may help your patent agent in wording the application and claims on your application.

Looking for Class and Subclass

Searching Does Not Always Result In Finding

If you cannot determine the class and subclass you need, the U.S. Patent Office will do it for you if you send them your request (many other countries give similar assistance). Do not be specific—your request is not kept confidential. In other words, do not disclose any confidential information regarding your invention.

Patent Search Sequential Work

Sequential Steps to Take	What You Should Do
Define product	List features of product
Index to Classification	Record class and subclass
Manual of Classification	Locate detailed subclass
Classification Definition	Confirm class/subclass
Patent Classification–Subclass Listing	Record relevant patent numbers
Official Gazette	Review synopses of patents
Full patent copy	Determine if your invention infringes
Record findings	Document search results
Modify product	Redesign if infringement exists

You will find everyone very helpful; nevertheless, doing your own search is a rough assignment. There are no guarantees of success. You will, as I've said, have to have a professional search done at a later time if you want to have a tighter patent. It would be wrong for your patent attorney to rely on your search; it would be wrong for you to rely on it too. Two wrongs do not make a right. In addition, there is always a delay in getting correct information, due in part to the continuous processing of patents through to granting and publishing (or, in most foreign countries, first publishing, then granting—sometimes. There is usually a no-man's-land of 12 to 18 months at least where no search is possible, even by the patent attorney. That is the time between your search and patent applications that have been applied for but not issued or published.

You must be the judge as to your own best initial approach to the searching process. My personal feeling is that when I have my invention where I want it (and not before then), I would rather pay my $500 to $1,200 for a proper, professional search for novelty and be done with it! But then we are all different, and I have to say that this exercise of the left brain has some long-term benefits. Still, I would rather read a technical book to achieve the same thing—less painful!

Direct Government Help

Several U.S. governmental organizations that can help you, frequently at no or with only nominal charge. The following are worth contacting:

National Innovation Workshops (NIW)
Office of Energy Related Inventions
National Institute of Standards and Technology
Gaithersburg, MD 20899

**Asking
Questions
Does Not
Guarantee
Good Answers**

The NIW gives seminars six times a year in different cities. Subjects include patents, licensing, estimating the value of your invention, marketing, inventions documentation, raising money, starting your own business, and sources for assistance. Contact them to find out the time and place of the next NIW seminar nearest you. These workshops are an excellent and economical way to learn about commercializing your invention or at least to get some idea of what's out there! They are biased toward energy related fields but have a great deal of other good background information for inventors.

Service Corps of Retired Executives (SCORE)
U.S. Small Business Administration
1441 L Street, NW, Room 100
Washington, DC 20416
(400 chapters throughout the United States)

SCORE can help you almost anywhere. It operates worldwide, especially in Third World countries. This group can put you in touch with retired business executives who can counsel you on a variety of questions, from helping you identify the best channel of distribution to assisting you to raise money. There may be some charge for their active help, but it could be well worth it; someone else's experience can be a great teacher to you!

Center for Innovation
P.O. Box 3809
Butte, MT 59701
Emphasizing new products and inventions related to energy, agriculture, and mining.

Getting Help in Business

Getting Firm
Quotations
Saves
Palpitations
Later

Helping inventors is a business in itself—there is a lot of help out there if you know where to look. Of course, getting help does not guarantee success; it just betters your chances if you have a good, viable invention.

Going It Alone (Marketing)

If you have decided to go it alone and start a business with your own and perhaps others' capital, it's a tough, somewhat risky approach. If it's your only choice, there are ways to improve your chances—to gather information that will prevent you from starting a business that past history has proved cannot succeed. No one wants to fail in a business, especially when good information can prevent the trauma of failure. Most businesses fail due to a lack of good preplanning, and most fail during the first five years.

Why not contact your government to see what help they can offer? In the United States, the Small Business Administration (SBA) is a good place to start. Many other countries have set up government agencies to help people like you. They will at least steer you along paths that are safe.

The Small Business Development Center (SBDC), 1441 L Street, NW, Washington, DC 20410, (800) 368-5855, sponsors nationwide assistance programs for small businesses. Approximately 500 universities and colleges participate in this program. Usually a university graduate student or faculty adviser will provide on-

Going It Alone
And Getting
Help Can Pull
You In Two
Directions

site management counseling. Remember though that their technical management helps you in the theory; there is no substitute for actual experience.

Trade Shows

Another good way to get knowledgeable people to help evaluate your invention, especially if you have filed a patent, is to attend industry trade shows to show manufacturers and manufacturers' representatives your rough prototype or photos (preferably after they sign the appropriate nondisclosure agreement). Ask them what they think and whom they would recommend as the best company to approach for licensing your product. Sift through their advice for truthfulness. Others may not always give you their best advice for fear of competition, especially if they like what you have but cannot use it themselves.

Opportunities for U.S. Small Businesses

The Procurement Automated Source System (PASS) is a national computerized directory of over 160,000 small businesses that supply goods and services. This directory provides these firms with a valuable marketing avenue for entering the federal marketplace or expanding their existing federal contracts. U.S. government purchasing agents actively use PASS to find potential suppliers. You can benefit by listing your firm in the PASS directory to increase your marketing opportunities. The U.S. government is the nation's largest buyer of goods and services, having spent over $180 billion each of the last three years. Although no one can guarantee

a new business, listing your firm in PASS is an effective addition to your regular sales efforts.

Listing your company in PASS is free. The greater the number of companies in the directory, the more valuable PASS is to its users, and ultimately to you. You can obtain a PASS Company Profile form from your local SBA office or by writing to U.S. Small Business Administration, PASS Program-Mail Code: 6256, 1441 L Street, NW, Washington, DC 20416.

Marketing Is The Pillar Of World Economies

Finding Potential Sellers or Manufacturers

Some of you may already know who you want to approach and how to go about it. Chapter 4, "Marketing," covered this subject exhaustively based on my experience.

It is always possible that your idea or invention needs special treatment, and you need access to further information to locate the right company.

For my automatic self-cleaning pollution filter, I had to use specialized information to locate the actual manufacturers and installers of such equipment. A painstaking effort, I'm afraid.

Your local librarian should be able to locate those registers and publications you feel are appropriate. Here are some for the United States:

Thomas Register of American Manufacturers
Lists over 115,000 U.S. manufacturers with addresses and products.

Dun and Bradstreet—Million Dollar Directory
Companies worth over $500,000 are listed with summaries.

Standard Directory of Advertisers
Directory with products of 17,000 firms.

Always ask your reference librarian for the names of directories of specific industries you are interested in.

If you wish to check up on any company in more depth to find out its specifics, several sources are available that should assist you. Here are some of them:

Encyclopedia of Associations
Gale Research Company
2200 Book Tower
Detroit, MI 48226
Five volumes—a comprehensive list of national trade associations and organizations of the
    United States. Note: Gale Research also has a lot of international informational
    publications.

Trade shows can be excellent sources of information. To learn when the applicable trade shows are scheduled, refer to:

Trade Shows and Professional Exhibits Directory
Gale Research Company
2200 Book Tower
Detroit, MI 48226

Trade magazines can also provide a wealth of information on a particular industry. Ask the reference librarian to locate the names of periodicals published in your industry.

The computerized library searches that I mentioned earlier are also available at most major public and university libraries.

Proper Evaluation by Interested Corporations and Others

The smaller companies you deal with, and some of the not-so-small, will evaluate your invention on a one-to-one basis with you personally, once you have their signed nondisclosure agreement. This happens in the majority of cases. However, large corporations and foreign companies will often wish to evaluate your product through their own in-house staff. Your help in this regard could be impressive to them, especially in such countries as Germany and Japan where such matters are often treated more formally. Once matters move to an appropriate stage, supply them with as much background information and technical help as you can. Set it out in a sequential manner. If you are not used to the correct manner of submission to large (especially foreign) companies, approach the SBA or SCORE for the assistance you may need to pull all your material together into a proper approach. Also don't forget the confidential agreements should be returned to you, as appropriate, prior to full disclosure to large corporations.

Would-Be Help from Developers and Brokers

I have previously indicated my less than enthusiastic opinions on inventors paying brokers for outside help. The success rate for the inventor is not good. It's not so much what they tell you they will do for you as what they *don't* tell you they *will not* do! The problem exists worldwide.

The Minnesota Inventors Congress says that "rip-off" firms are now again increasing in number, as does England's Institute of Patentees and Inventors. A New York Special Committee on Consumer Affairs investigated invention brokers in 1978. The New York committee found that most brokers do not engage in outright fraud. They are meticulous in fulfilling the terms of their written agreements! However, the services they perform for the inventor are usually of poor quality and rarely benefit inventors. Just about the only people getting rich from the services of the invention developers are the developers themselves, who make their money not from selling inventions, but from their fees gained by selling somewhat worthless contracts to starry-eyed inventors.

The More You Are Impressed With Words, The More Problems You Face

Brokers spend large sums of money on advertising in do-it-youselfer magazines. They offer free information on how to make money from your invention. When an inventor responds, the broker sends a packet of materials, including a beautiful color brochure listing testimonials and endorsements by public officials. The inventor fills out their nondisclosure agreement and mails it to the broker (which means almost nothing and can later prove harmful to the inventor's rights). The broker promises to evaluate the invention for its commercial feasibility, which means only that they will have one of their salespeople contact the inventor.

After initial contact by the broker to the inventor and after the inventor expresses some interest, the broker will propose a preliminary agreement by which a market analysis and patent search will be performed. The cost to the client is often $500 (or more).

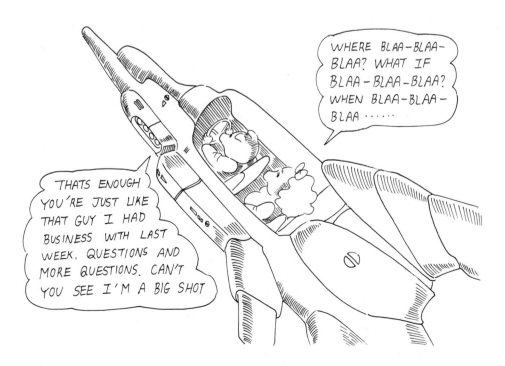

After about a month the inventor will receive a phone call suggesting he or she hurry to the broker's office. Over the phone, the broker may tell the inventor that the patent has great potential, or that the company has decided to take a chance on him or her.

The results are reviewed with the inventor in abstract, complex (left-brain) terms, ensuring that the inventor does not understand the actual results of the search. The inventor gets the impression that the broker would not proceed unless they had achieved promising results from their evaluation. However, in reality an evaluation was never fully completed. The broker may also allude to possible sales and royalties to pique the inventor's interest and anticipation. The broker may talk in terms of making millions selling to only 10 percent of the market.

The broker will explain their "deal" for the client. For $1,000 or more, and sometimes for a percent interest in the invention, the broker agrees to develop and promote the invention. This promotion usually consists of patent application preparation, often done in a shabby manner and charged to the inventor. Drawings cost approximately $100 (in 1978; now more) each for poor, often incorrect schematics. Also, the broker will "promote" the invention by preparing a one- or two-page black and white descriptive sheet on it. They will look up companies in *Thomas Register* to obtain names of manufacturers in the same field and send them cheap "Dear Sir" letters, enclosing a copy of the black-and-white sheet. Needless to say, the results from this shoddy approach rarely if ever produce any results.

You can do a far better job yourself, saving your money in the process. I have dealt with this matter earlier in this book, but I need to reemphasize it due to the seriousness of the matter and the pain and frustration it too often causes people who cannot afford the financial losses, let alone the heartache. The rip-offs continue worldwide!

However, I do know that there are some decent people and organizations out there genuinely willing and able to help you at reasonable remuneration—value for money, in other words. You may have to go out and find them—they won't come to you!

Treat a solicitation to help you from anyone seriously, and don't divulge anything without appropriate safeguards. If you are really impressed with the other party, they should not mind you asking them some basic questions, such as the following:

1. Do they have a particular industry or specialty?
2. How long have they been in business?
3. What are some projects they have worked on in the past?
4. How many full-time personnel work for their company?
5. How many inventions have they handled that proved to be commercially successful? (If it's one in ten or thereabouts, you should be encouraged.)
6. How many active clients do they currently have?
7. Ask for three or four names, addresses, and phone numbers of people whose inventions they have successfully marketed. Would they have any objection if you contacted them?
8. What are their fees?
9. Specifically, what services will they provide?

Finding Licensees

If your invention doesn't seem to fit into the normal range of products, getting help might seem difficult, especially if it's a breakthrough, new technology that society does not realize it needs.

There are numerous magazines available dealing with all types of subjects. You may be able to locate that special interested licensee by placing your own appropriate, nonspecific advertisement in one of them. Remember, always present responders with nondisclosure agreements to sign before you communicate any meaningful information to them. Watch carefully what you say during any phone inquiries. Here are some magazines that may fit the bill:

In Business
The JG Press
Box 323
18 South Seventh Street
Emmaus, PA 18049

Industrial Research and Development Magazine
Technical Publishing
1301 South Grove Street
Barrington, IL 60010

International Invention Register
Catalyst
P.O. Box 547
Fallbrook, CA 92028

Casing The
Opposition
Can Pay
Dividends

International New Products Newsletter
6 St. James Avenue
Boston, MA 02116

Invention Management
85 Irving Street
Arlington, MA 02174

Mindsight
P.O. Box 6664
Woodland Hills, CA 91356

Product Design and Development
Chilton Company
Chilton Way
Radnor, PA 19089

The Review of Scientific Instruments
American Institute of Physics
335 45th Street
New York, NY 10017

Evaluating the Competition

You may wish to see what's out there in the marketplace. Go to one or more appropriate exhibitions or conventions. Just walk around and observe, take notes, and talk to people. I have been to all types of these gatherings. The format is

generally the same worldwide, large and small, but what you see on the floor is significantly different. I have found the biggest to be the best, but also the most frustrating after days of walking interminable aisles (which seem like miles) day after day. Don't think you can adequately see any large exhibition in a day or two. For example, if you decide to go to the International Exposition of Inventions in Switzerland, plan to attend for at least one week. Take daily notes too; otherwise you will later forget important observations, people you met, and products you saw. This advice is very important no matter what conference or exhibition you attend. Here is a list of some of the larger, more important conventions you might like to attend in the U.S. and worldwide:

Attending Exhibitions Is Fun; Exhibiting More So

United States Invention Conventions

Invention Convention
International Convention Services
1645 N. Vine Street, Suite 611
Hollywood, CA 90028

INVENTECH Expo
Inventors Workshop
International Education Foundation
3537 Old Conejo Road, Suite 120
Newbury Park, CA 91320

National Inventors' Week Exposition
Patent and Trademark Office
Washington, DC 20231

California Inventors' Council
Box 2096
Sunnyvale, CA 94087

New Products Technology Development Conference
P.O. Box 12793
Research Triangle Park, NC 27709

International Conventions

International Exposition of Inventions
Messezentrum Nurenberg
D-8500 Nurenberg 50
West Germany

Business World Exhibition
1801 McGill College Avenue, Suite 970
Montreal, Quebec H3A 2N4

Hanover Fair
Deutsche Messe-und
Ausstellungs-AG
Messengelande
D-3000 Hanover
West Germany

Knowing
Where To
Start Is Better
Than Knowing
Where To
Finish!

Techno Tokyo
Promotion Division
Nihon Cogyo Jimbocho Chiyoda-ku
Tokyo, 101 Japan
Held in odd-numbered years only, usually in the spring.

INOVA
S.A. TECHNOEXPO
8 Rue de la Michodiere
75002, Paris, France
Odd-numbered years only.

International Exposition Inventions
Secretariat du Salon
8, Rue due 31 Decembre
Ch 1207 Geneve
Switzerland
Held in April.

Flanders Technology International
International Jaarbeurs
Van Vlaanderen VZW
ICC Floraliaplaeis, B-9000
Ghent, Belgium
Odd-numbered years only.

Predrafting Patent Applications

If you are interested in helping your patent attorney (and educating him or her about your invention), draft a good patent application. Draft out the best preliminary outline you can. This will also save you money and give your patent attorney more background information to strengthen the drafting on your behalf. I always supply the maximum background information I can.

Following this outline will help your patent attorney and keep you out of trouble if you have to prepare your initial patent application yourself, though I have already warned you of the many dangers you may face if you try to go all the way alone!

1. Title: A heading that describes your invention.
2. Background: Previous related patents that you have submitted.
3. Comparison to similar products (prior art): Discuss prior inventions, including a list of previous patent numbers and what the patents tried to accomplish.
4. Advantages and disadvantages: List the advantages of your invention and indicate why yours is specifically better than the prior art. Also, list any disadvantages you have not overcome. Your attorney may be able to suggest ways to help you overcome these failings.
5. Drawings: Include drawings of your invention along with sketches of other possible alternatives to your invention. Give detailed descriptions of each drawing.
6. Descriptions: Describe in detail how your invention works. Explain the drawings, components parts, and their functions. Describe as many alternatives as possible to accomplish the same function. If those rights are challenged in court, judges frequently review the description portion of the patent to determine the inventor's purposes.

Starting A Corporation

Your friends might tell you that to save the corporation costs involved, you should register a business name—something that I do not recommend, as most new businesses fail. The possible burden of you having to declare bankruptcy at a later date and losing all your (and your family's) assets is too much of a burden to carry. A corporation will let you sleep more peacefully at night! Ironically I have also found that tax authorities seem to look more kindly on company expenses than they do individuals'! So these are the steps you will need to take to start and run your own company, not necessarily in the following order.

1. Decide that you are going to start.
2. Incorporate.
3. Build a working model of your product.
4. Secure orders or letters of intent to purchase your product.
5. Prepare your business plan.
6. Obtain funding.
7. Develop sales channels.
8. Begin manufacturing the product.

In the United States, SCORE, Service Corps of Retired Executives, provides free business consulting to small companies. SCORE has over 10,000 retired and active executives available to assist you. They can help you with most of the steps from incorporating your business to selling and marketing your product—all at no

**The Less You
Give The Less
You Get**

or only nominal charge. But don't expect the impossible—they are not you! You
should be the leader!

Getting Outside Investment

To get financial help, you will need a business plan. Your potential investors will
look at your product, your plan of action, your presentation, your personal background of previous success (if any!), and the possibility of your paying them back
with interest and a possible additional share of the profits.

If outside capital is what you must have, then approach the whole matter
correctly and thoroughly. It cannot be done quickly. It will likely cost you, too!
Get some professional help. After you have roughed out all the main requirements,
do your very best, but be prepared for disappointments. Topics that should be
covered in the plan include the following:

- Management: The education and past experience of principals in your
  organization.
- Product: The features and benefits of your product and why it is better than
  the competition.
- Market environment: A general profile of your potential customers, the current
  status of your competition, and the impact of the competition on your business.
- Distribution: How your product gets from producer to consumer.
- Funding: Money needed and how it will be used.
- Status of the business: Background and history of the company.
- Future prospects: Likelihood of other or new products.
- Financial: What the pro forma balance sheet and income statements would in-
  dicate. Don't forget, SCORE and the SBA are set up specifically to help small
  start-up businesses.

Whole or Partial Manufacture of Your Invention by Others

There are distinct advantages to contracting the manufacture of your invention
to third parties. Choose one carefully. The advantages are as follows:
1. You need make no investment in plant and equipment.
2. You have fewer personnel needs.
3. You have reduced capital requirements.
4. You have reduced start-up time.
5. You avoid plant maintenance and equipment obsolescence.

The added advantage is that it is one less thing for you to worry about. You
will have enough work to do taking care of all the other areas that concern you.

One of the biggest advantages is that your controlling manufacturer, upon
your success, will almost certainly be interested in an expansion of your agreement,
even to the point of their later taking over the whole business at a substantial
profit to you, while you retain a continuing royalty from sales!

Of course, it is very important to have a full license agreement with them,
even if there are no royalties or other payments to you. A nonexclusive license

would stipulate that the product they produced could be sold only to you (your company) or someone else you specifically authorize in writing. Such a license agreement would be easier to enforce and could get upgraded as appropriate.

Mail Order Selling Can Be A Good Way To Test The Market

Mail Order Possibilities and Direct Marketing

I have known several inventors who were moderately successful at direct sales of their inventions.

Perhaps your invention lends itself to such marketing—you and you alone must be the final judge. It will be your money at risk. Don't let an advertising agency talk you into a big direct-advertising promotion. Go slow to begin with. Go carefully. Do not squander your precious resources in the first flush of anticipated success. If your invention is going to be successful, it will be, even if for safety's sake you proceed slowly and carefully. If it's not going to be a success, no amount of your money or anyone else's is going to change it!

There are lots of helpful books and directories you can get at your local library about direct mail order marketing.

The Sales Representative

If you decide that your invention is best suited to selling through representatives, then you will need some type of agreement setting out what you expect of them and conversely what they may expect of you. Such agreements need to be comprehensive with large numbers of sales representatives or fairly simple with only one or two. This is where SCORE can be of most help to you, wherever you live.

Not Sure What to Do?

If you are unsure of all the many left-brain technicalities contained in this chapter, I suggest that you start again to read chapters 1 through 9 to reinforce the basics for the inventor's life and often right-brained–dominant thinking. The information in the Appendix could be very, very helpful to you (whether you are right- or left-brain–dominant) by helping you get in touch with like-minded people through inventor organizations. At inventor's association meetings, inventors generally like to meet other inventors. I have found that the first time it's a unique, yet pleasant experience!

Bibliography

Baker, Kenneth G. "The Comparative Analysis of Models for Use in New Product Screening Decisions." Ph.D. diss., University of Oregon, 1980.

Betts, Jim. *The Million Dollar Idea.* Point Pleasant, NJ: Point Publishing Co., 1985.

Betts, Jim, and Noreen Heimbold. *New Products.* Point Pleasant, NJ: Point Publishing Co., 1984.

Blanchard, Kenneth, and Spencer Johnson. *The One-Minute Manager.* New York: Berkeley Books, 1982.

Buggie, Frederick D. *New Product Development Strategies.* New York: Amacom, 1981.

Business Publication Rates and Data. Wilmette, IL: Standard Rate and Data Service, 1987.

Business Services and Information: The Guide to the Federal Government. Philadelphia, PA: Management Information Exchange, 1978.

Carnegie, Dale. *How to Win Friends and Influence People.* New York: Simon and Schuster, 1948.

CASSIS User's Manual. Washington, DC: U.S. Government Printing Office, 1985.

Churchill, Gilbert, Jr. *Marketing Research,* 3d ed. New York: Dryden Press, 1983.

Colgate, Craig Jr. *National Trade and Professional Associations of the U.S. 1987.* Washington, DC: Columbia Books, Inc., 1987.

A. Coskun, ed. *Technology Transfer.* Westport, CT: Quorum Books, 1985.

Daniells, Lorna M. *Business Information Sources.* Berkeley, CA: University of California Press, 1985.

Direct Mail List: Rates and Data. Wilmette, IL: Standard Rate and Data Service, 1987.

Dougherty, David E. *From Technical Professional to Entrepreneur.* New York: John Wiley, 1986.

Dufour, Patrick, and Carol Niemir. "Idea Screening in the U.S." Ph.D. diss., Northwestern University, 1978.

Eisenberg, Richard. "Financing Your Venture." *Money,* December 1982, 73-94.

Ellsworth, William M. *Twenty Failborne Years.* U.S. Navy, 1986.

Elster, Robert. *Trade Shows and Professional Exhibits Directory.* Detroit, MI: Gale Research Company, 1985.

Famualao, Joseph. *Handbook of Personnel, Forms, Records, and Reports.* New York: McGraw-Hill, 1982.

Federal Government Directory of Information Resources in the U.S. Washington, DC: U.S. Government Printing Office, 1974.

Freimer, Marshall, and Leonard Simon. "The Evaluation of Potential New Product Alternative." *Management Science,* February 1967, 279-292.

Gendron, Mary. "Here are Ten Factors that Determine HBA Product Success." *Supermarket,* May 1977, 31.

Goldscheider, Robert. *Eckstrom's Licensing in Foreign and Domestic Operations.* New York: Clark Boardman, 1984.

Goldscheider, Robert, and Gregory Maier. *1986 Licensing Law Handbook.* New York: Clark Boardman, 1986.

Gregory, James, and Kevin Mulligan. *The Patent Book.* New York: A&W Publishers, 1979.

Grissom, Fred, and David Pressman. *The Inventors Notebook.* Berkley, CA, Nolo Press, 1987.

Groosswirth, Marvin. *The Mechanix Illustrated Guide to How to Patent and Market Your Invention.* New York: McKay, 1978.

Gruenwald, George. "Seven Steps Toward New Product Success." *Advertising Age,* April 27, 1981, 52.

Gruenwald, George. *New Product Development.* Lincolnwood, IL: NTC Business Books, 1985.

Hall, Chuck. *How to Make Money from Inventions.* Melbourne, Australia: Rala Publications, 1983.

Hamburg, Bruce. *1984-1985 Patent Law Handbook.* New York: Clark Boardman, 1984.

Hartman, Susan, and Norman Parrish. *Inventors' Source Book.* Berkeley, CA: Inventors Resource Center Publishers, 1978.

Hooper, Meredith. *Everyday Inventions.* Landen, UK: Spring Books, 1960.

Hopkins, Davis S. *New Product Winners and Losers.* New York: The Conference Board, 1980.

Kasunic, Vivian, and Anne Wallis. *Lawyer's Register by Specialties & Fields of Law,* 2d ed. Cleveland, OH: The Lawyer to Lawyer Consultation Panel, 1979.

Kenyon, Joan, ed. *The American Lawyer's Guide to Leading Law Firms.* New York: American Law Publishing, 1983.

Konold, William, Bruce G. Tittel, Donald F. Frei, and David S. Stallard. *What Every Engineer Should Know About Patents.* New York: Dekker, 1979.

Kotler, Philip. *Marketing Management: Analysis, Planning and Control,* 6th ed. Englewood Cliffs, NJ: Prentice-Hall, 1988.

Kuczmarski, Thomas D. *Managing New Products.* Englewood Cliffs, NJ: Prentice-Hall, 1988.

Larsen, Egon. *Ideas and Inventions.* Landen, UK: Spring Books, 1960.

LaSalle, Roger. *So You Want to Make Your Million by Inventing.* Melbourne, Australia: L. Eastlane, 1984.

Lent, Constantin. *How to Invent, What to Invent.* New York: Pen-Ink Publishing, 1966.

Leonard-Barton, D., and W.A. Kraus. "Implementing New Technology." *Harvard Business Review*, November–December 1985, 102–110.

MacCrachen, Calvin. *A Handbook for Inventors.* New York: Scribner's, 1983.

Manual of Patent Examining Procedure. rev. ed. Washington, DC: U.S. Department of Commerce, Patent & Trademark Office, 1986.

Martindale Hubbell Law Directory. Summit, NJ: Martindale-Hubbell, 1987.

McGuire, Patrick E. *Evaluating New Product Proposal.* New York: The Conference Board, 1973.

Melville, Leslie W. *Precedents on Industrial Property.* Landen, UK: Sweet Flexwell, 1965.

Midendorf, William. *What Every Engineer Should Know About Inventing.* New York: Dekker, 1981.

Midgley, David F. *Innovating and New Product Marketing.* New York: Halsted Press, 1977.

More, Roger A. "Risk Factors in Accepted and Rejected New Industrial Products." *Industrial Marketing Management*, February 1982, 9–15.

Paige, Richard E. *Complete Guide to Making Money with Your Ideas and Inventions.* New York: Barnes & Noble Books, 1973.

Park, Robert. *The Inventor's Handbook.* White Hall, VA: Betterway Publications, 1986.

Patents and Trademarks Style Manual. Washington, DC: U.S. Patent and Trademark Office, U.S. Government Printing Office, 1984.

Pessemier, Edgar A. *New Product Decisions.* New York: McGraw-Hill, 1966.

Pope, Jeffrey. *Practical Marketing Research.* New York: Amacom, 1981.

Pressman, David. *Patent It Yourself.* Berkeley, CA: Nolo Press, 1985.

Quelch, J. "How to Build a Product Licensing Program." *Harvard Business Review*, May-June 1985, 186–197.

Rivkin, Bernard. *Patenting and Marketing Your Invention.* New York: Van Nostrand Reinhold, 1986.

Rom, Walter O., and Frederick W. Winter. "New Product Evaluation Using a Bayesian Dynamic Program." *Journal of the Operational Research Society*, March 1981, 223–232.

Rosenbloom, Richard S., and Francis W. Wolek. *Technology and Information Transfer.* Boston, MA: Harvard University Press, 1970.

Sheth, Jagdish N., and S. Ram. *Bringing Innovation to Market.* New York: John Wiley, 1987.

Silver, David A. *Up Front Financing.* New York: John Wiley, 1982/1988.

Smith, Keith. *Energy Works. Home Energy Systems.* Melbourne, Australia: Nelson Publishers, 1985.

Statistical Abstract of the U.S.—1986, 106th ed. Washington, DC: U.S. Department of Commerce, U.S. Government Printing Office, 1986.

Stobaugh, Robert, and Louis Wells, Jr., eds. *Technology Crossing Borders.* Boston, MA: Harvard Business School Press, 1984.

Udell, Gerald G., and Kenneth G. Baker. *Pies II Manual for Innovation Evaluation.* Whitewater, WI: University of Wisconsin, 1980.

Urban, Glen, and John R. Hauser. *Design and Marketing of New Products.* Englewood Cliffs, NJ: Prentice-Hall, Inc., 1980.

1988 U.S. Industrial Outlook. Washington, DC: U.S. Department of Commerce, U.S. Government Printing Office, 1988.

Verified Directory of Manufacturers' Representatives. New York: Manufacturing Agreement Publishing Company, 1982.

Weller, Don. "Protecting Your Product." *International Trade Forum,* January 1982, 13–15.

Wonder, Jacquelyn, and Priscilla Donovan. *Whole Brain Thinking.* New York: Valentine, 1985.

Appendix
Acknowledgment

I must here give grateful recognition for certain resource information that I have included in the appendix, some of which was first gathered by the Inventors Resource Center.

Besides providing information on areas pertinent to the interests of inventors, developers, students of creativity, and problem solvers, and elementary and high school students, the Inventors Resource Center's publication *Inventors Resource Bibliography* has much additional information. Their information covers books and periodicals pertaining to creativity, problem solving, thinking and learning, business resources (including local SCORE chapters), regional educational cooperative service units, higher education programs and services, United States federal and state government agencies, school creativity programs, and audiovisual materials. They make information available on all areas, and it is constantly being updated. I highly recommend this publication.

The Inventors Resource Center has been expanding its services for over 30 years. They can put you in touch with inventor-oriented organizations. They can also give you information about exhibitions and educational programs where you can meet other inventors and experts and get referrals, literature, and so on. They also offer walk-in services.

You can reach them by phone at (800) INVENT-1 (Minnesota only) or (507) 637-2344, or you can write Inventors Resource Center, P.O. Box 71, Redwood Falls, MN 56283.

Appendix A

Inventor organizations set-up for helping individual inventors.
United States by State, also United Kingdom and Australia.

Alabama

Alabama High Technology Assistance
  Center
University of Alabama at Huntsville
336 Morton Hall
Huntsville, AL 35899
(205) 895-6409

Alabama Inventors Association
3409 Fountain Circle
Montgomery, AL 36116

Decatur Inventors Guild
1403 Office Park West, Suite J
Decatur, AL 35603

Economic and Industrial Development
1100 Fairhope Avenue
Fairhope, AL 36532
(205) 928-3002

Arkansas

Arkansas Inventors Congress, Inc.
AIDC/Energy Division
One State Capital Mall
Little Rock, AR 72201
(501) 371-1370

California

California Inventors Council
P.O. Box 2732
Castro Valley, CA 94546

California Inventors Council
P.O. Box 2096
Sunnyvale, CA 94087

Innovation Expo
City of Modesto
P.O. Box 642
Modesto, CA 95353
(209) 577-5473

International Trade Administration
USDOC-450 Golden Gate Avenue
Box 36013
San Francisco, CA 94102

Inventors Licensing and Marketing
  Agency
HQ/Inventor Center USA
3201 Corte Malpaso #304A
Camarillo, CA 93010
(818) 998-7404

Inventors of California
215 Rheem Boulevard
Moraga, CA 94556

Inventors of California
250 Vernon Street
Oakland, CA 94610

Inventors of California
P.O. Box 158
Rheem Valley, CA 94570

Inventors Workshop International
  Education Foundation
3201 Corte Malpaso #304A
Camarillo, CA 93010
(805) 484-9786

Robert Kuntz
1107 9th Street, Suite 301
Sacramento, CA 95814

National Congress of Inventor
  Organizations
P.O. Box 158
215 Rheem Boulevard
Moraga, CA 94556

National Inventors Foundation
345 West Cypress Street
Glendale, CA 91204

Patent Information Clearinghouse
1500 Partridge Avenue, Building 7
Sunnyvale, CA 94087

Silicon Valley Entrepreneurs Club I
Techmart Building, Suite 3241
5201 Great American Parkway
Santa Clara, CA 95054
(408) 562-6040

Inventor's Resource Center
P.O. Box 5105
Berkeley, CA 94705

Technology Transfer Society
11720 West Pico Boulevard
Los Angeles, CA 90064

Colorado

Affiliated Inventors F undation, Inc.
2132 East Bijou Street
Colorado Springs, CO 80909
(303) 635-1234

IBM—Department 985
P.O. Box 190
Building 001-3
Boulder, CO 80302

National Inventors Cooperative
   Association
P.O. Box 6585
Denver, CO 80206

Rocky Mountain Inventors Congress
P.O. Box 4365
Denver, CO 80204
(303) 443-3818

U.S. Department of Commerce
625 Broadway #680
Denver, CO 80202

Governor's High Tech Cabinet Council
3271 S. Clay
Englewood, CO 80110

Connecticut

Field Publication
The Children's Weekly Reader
245 Long Hill Road
Middletown, CT 06457
(203) 638-2752

Inventors Club of America
RD 87
Andover, CT 06232

Society for Advancement of Invention
   and Innovation
9 Sylvan Road South
Westport, CT 06880

Inventors Association of Connecticut
9 Sylvan Road South
Westport, CT 06880

District of Columbia

American Enterprise Institute for Public
   Policy
1150 17th Street, NW
Washington, DC 20036

Associate Advocate for Capital
   Formation and Venture Capital
SBA
1441 L Street NW—Room 101C
Washington, DC 20416

Documentation Administrator
U.S. Patent & Trademark Office
Washington, DC 20231

Energy Related Invention Program
CE-12
U.S. Department of Energy
Washington, DC 20585

NRCM Database
Resources Analysis Section
General Reading Rooms Division
Library of Congress
Washington, DC 20540

Office of Legislation and Internal Affairs
Patent & Trademark Office
Washington, DC 20231

Office of Program Coordination
Main Commerce—Room 5894
Washington, DC 20230

Small Business Administration
1441 L Street, NW
Washington, DC 20416

U.S. Department of Commerce
Office of Technical Commercialization
14th & E Street NE—Room 5712
Washington, DC 20230

Florida

Central Florida Inventors
The John Young Museum
Loch Haven Park
Orlando, FL 32802

Central Florida Inventors Council
4849 Victory Drive
Orlando, FL 32808

Central Florida Inventors Council
6402 Gamble Drive
Orlando, FL 32818

Central Florida Inventors Council
4855 Big Oaks Lane
Orlando, FL 32806

Daytona Beach Community College
P.O. Box 1111
Daytona Beach, FL 32015

Dr. Dvorkovitz & Associates
P.O. Box 1748
Ormond Beach, FL 32075
(904) 677-7033

Innovative Products Group Inc.
2325 Ulmerton Road
Clearwater, FL 34622

The Inventors Club
Route 11—Box 379
Pensacola, FL 32514
(904) 433-5619

NASA—Southern Technology
  Application Center (STAC)
University of South Florida
College of Engineering
Tampa, FL 33620
(813) 974-4222

Palm Beach Society of American
  Inventors
P.O. Box 766
Palm Beach, FL 33480

Florida Entrepreneurship Program
Bureau of Business Assistance
Division of Economic Development
Florida Department of Commerce
107 W. Gaines Street, Room G-26
Tallahassee, FL 32399-2000

Society for Inventors and Entrepreneurs
306 Georgetown Drive
Casselberry, FL 32707

Society of American Inventors
P.O. Box 21624
Tampa, FL 33622-1624
(813) 221-2343

Tampa Bay Inventors Council
P.O. Box 2254
Largo, FL 34649

Tampa Bay Inventor's Council
805 West 118th Avenue
Tampa, FL 33612
(813) 933-9124

Georgia

Economic Development Library
Engineering Experiment Station
Georgia Institute of Technology
Atlanta, GA 30332

Patent Assistance Program
Georgia Institute of Technology
Atlanta, GA 30332-0999

Inventor Associates of Georgia
637 Linwood Avenue, NE
Atlanta, GA 30306

Inventor Associates of Georgia, Inc.
P.O. Box 38229
Atlanta, GA 30334

Inventors Association of Georgia
241 Freyer Drive, NE
Marietta, GA 30060
(404) 427-8024

Inventors Club of America, Inc.
P.O. Box 450261
Atlanta, GA 30345
(404) 938-5089

Hawaii

Inventors Council of Hawaii
P.O. Box 27844
Honolulu, HI 96827

Statewide Strategy for High Technology
  Growth
High Technology Development Corp.
220 South King Street, Suite 840
Honolulu, HI 96813

Illinois

Argonne National Laboratory
Energy and Environmental Systems
  Division
Mail Stop 362-3A
Argonne, IL 60439

Chicago High Tech Association
53 West Jackson Boulevard #1634
Chicago, IL 60604-3704
(312) 641-0311

Inventors Council of Chicago
53 Jackson Boulevard, Suite 1041
Chicago, IL 60604
This is a very active club in Chicago
  with over 3500 members and provides
  invention evaluations free of charge.

Technology Commercialization Center
Northern Illinois University
DeKalb, IL 60115
(815) 753-1238

Indiana

ARAC
611 North Capitol
Indianapolis, IN 46204

Indiana Inventors Association Inc.
P.O. Box 2388
Indianapolis, IN 46206

Indiana Inventors Association Inc.
612 Ironwood Drive
Plainfield, IN 46168

International Association of Professional
  Inventors
Route 10—4412 Greenhill Way
Anderson, IN 46011
(317) 644-2104

International Association of Professional
  Inventors
818 Westminster
Kokomo, IN 46901

International Association of Professional
  Inventors
RR #1—Box 1074
Shirley, IN 47384

The Inventors and Entrepreneurs
  Society of Indiana, Inc.
P.O. Box 2224
Hammond, IN 46323
(219) 989-2354

Iowa

Inventure
Drake University
210 Aliber Hall
Des Moines, IA 50311

Kansas

Kansas Association of Inventors
Business Industry Institute
Barton Community College
2015 Lakin
Great Bend, KS 67530
(316) 792-1375

Kansas Technology Enterprise Corp.
112 SW 6th Street #400
Topeka, KS 66603
(913) 296-5272

Kentucky

Alternative Energy Development
  Program
Division of Alternative Energy
  Development
Kentucky Energy Cabinet
P.O. Box 11888
Lexington, KY 40578-1916

Center for Entrepreneurship
School of Business
University of Louisville
Louisville, KY 40292

Louisiana

Louisiana Innovation Program
Louisiana Department of Commerce
P.O. Box 94185
Baton Rouge, LA 70804

Maryland

KSI Technical Sales
10615 Keinlock Road
Silver Spring, MD 20903

Odetics, Inc.
557 Arundel Drive
Severna Park, MD 21146
(301) 261-1610

Office of Energy Related Inventions
National Institute of Standards &
  Technology
Gaithersburg, MD 20899

Massachusetts

Innovation Invention Network
132 Sterling Street
West Boylston, MA 01583

Innovation Invention Network
13 Benjamin Road
Worcester, MA 01601

Innovative Products Research and
  Service
P.O. Box 335
Lexington, MA 02173
(617) 862-5008

Institute for Invention & Innovation
85 Irving Street
Arlington, MA 02174

Inventors Association of New England
4 Baron Park Lane, Suite 1
Burlington, MA 01803

MIT Innovation Center
School of Engineering
Cambridge, MA 02139

Michigan

American Association of Inventors
Business Office
5038 Kasemeyer
Bay City, MI 48706

Inventors Center of Michigan
Ferris State University/MRPC
1020 East Maple Street
Big Rapids, MI 49307
(616) 796-3100

Inventors Council of Michigan
6175 Jackson Road
Ann Arbor, MI 48103
(313) 663-8000

Michigan Tech Small Business Center
Michigan Technological University
1700 College Avenue
Houghton, MI 49931
(906) 487-2470

Minnesota

Austin Public Library
201 2nd Avenue, NW
Austin, MN 55912

Countryside Council
P.O. Box 78
Marshall, MN 56258
(507) 532-9641

Midwest Inventor's Society
P.O. Box 335
St. Cloud, MN 56301

Inventors Education Network
P.O. Box 14775
Minneapolis, MN

Faribault County Development Agency
City Hall—Room 100
Wells, MN 56097

Greco Inc.
P.O. Box 1441
60 Eleventh Avenue, NE
Minneapolis, MN 55413

Inventors & Designers Network of
Minnesota
P.O. Box 268
Stillwater, MN 55082
(800) 247-2574, ext. 380

Inventors and Technology Transfer
Society
Inventors Club of Minnesota
P.O. Box 14775
Minneapolis, MN 55414

Inventors Resource Center
129 Bedford, SE
Minneapolis, MN 55414
(612) 379-7387

Midwest Inventors and Innovation Work
P.O. Box 14235
St. Paul, MN 55114

Minnesota Entrepreneur's Club
Business and Technology Center
511 11th Avenue South
Minneapolis, MN 55415
(612) 375-8103

Minnesota Inventors Congress/Inventors
Resource Center
P.O. Box 71
Redwood Falls, MN 56283
(507) 637-2344 or (800) 468-3681 (MN
only)

Minnesota Inventors Hall of Fame
P.O. Box 2045
Minneapolis, MN 55402

Minnesota Project Innovation Center
Supercomputer Center
1200 Washington Avenue South, Suite
M100
Minneapolis, MN 55415
(612) 338-3280

Research and Development/3M
2235S02 3M Center
St. Paul, MN 55144

Society of Minnesota Inventors
20231 Basalt Street
Anoka, MN 55303

South Central Educational Cooperative
Service Unit
1610 Commerce Drive
North Mankato, MN 56001
(507) 389-5101 or (507) 389-1425

Southwest Regional Development
Commission
Economic Development Planner
2524 Broadway Avenue—Box 265
Slayton, MN 56172
(507) 836-8549

State Documents
Legislative Reference Library
645 State Office Building
St. Paul, MN 55155

West Central Minnesota Initiative Fund
Norwest Bank Building—221 West
Washington
P.O. Box 641
Fergus Falls, MN 56537

Young Inventors Fair
Metro ECSU
3499 Lexington Avenue North
Arden Hills, MN 55126

Mississippi

Confederacy of Mississippi Inventors
4759 Nailor Road
Vicksburg, MS 39180

Mississippi Society of Scientists and
  Inventors
P.O. Box 2244
Clinton, MS 39056

Gulf Coast Breeder
109 East Scenic Drive
Pass Christian, MS 39571
(601) 452-2007

Confederacy of Mississippi Inventors
1415 Post Road
Clinton, MS 39056

Mississippi Research and Development
  Center
3825 Ridgewood Road
Jackson, MS 39211
(601) 982-6425

Mississippi Inventors Workshop
4729 Kings Highway
Jackson, MS 39206

Society of Mississippi Inventors
P.O. Box 5111
Jackson, MS 39296-5111
(601) 984-6047

Missouri

Center for Business Research and
  Development
Southwest Missouri State University
Springfield, MO 65804

Inventors Association of St. Louis
P.O. Box 16544
St. Louis, MO 63105

Columbia Venture Club
Missouri Ingenuity, Inc.
T-16 Research Park
Columbia, MO 65211

Missouri Energy League Company
826 Crestmere Court
Jefferson City, MO 65101

Montana

CFI Inc.
Division Montana Energy Research &
  Development Institute
P.O. Box 3809
Butte, MT 59702

Nebraska

Kearney Innovation Network
Chamber of Commerce
P.O. Box 607
Kearney, NE 68848
(308) 237-3101

Lincoln Inventors Association
P.O. Box 94666
Lincoln, NE 68509
(402) 471-3782

Omaha Inventors Club
c/o U.S. Small Business Administration
11145 Mill Valley Road
Omaha, NE 68145
(402) 221-3604

Sarpy County Economic Development
  Department
Regional Inventors Fair
1210 Golden Gate Drive
Papillion, NE 68046
(402) 593-2331

Nevada

Mike Planin and Herbert C. Schulze
P.O. Box 6070
Incline Village, NV 89450

Technology Council
1755 East Plumb Lane #152
Reno, NV 89502

New Hampshire

Franklin Pierce Law Center
2 White Street
Concord, NH 03301

New Jersey

National Society of Inventors
141 Ridge Dale Avenue
Madison, NJ 07940

American Society of Inventors
402 Cynwyd Drive
Abesecon, NJ 08201

National Society of Inventors
539 Laurel Place
South Orange, NJ 07079
(201) 596-3322

National Society of Inventors, Inc.
P.O. Box 434
Cranford, NJ 07016

Office for Promoting Technical
   Innovation
Department of Labor and Industry
Trenton, NJ 08625

Princeton University
Woodrow Wilson School
Princeton, NJ 08544

Technology 4 Children (MIIT)
New Jersey Department of Education
225 West State Street, CN 500
Trenton, NJ 08625
(609) 292-5720

New Mexico

Organization of NM Innovators
P.O. Box 30062
Albuquerque, NM 87190

New York

Buffalo Public Schools
453 Leroy Avenue
Buffalo, NY 14214

Center for Technology Transfer
SUNY—College at Oswego
209 Park Hall
Oswego, NY 13126

Innovative Design Fund, Inc.
866 United Nations Plaza
New York, NY 10017

Pan Hellenic Society Inventors of
   Greece in USA
2053 Narwood Avenue
South Merrick, NY 11566
(516) 223-5958

SUNY Farmingdale
Lupton Hall—Route 110
Farmingdale, NY 11735

Syracuse University
204 Maxwell Hall
Syracuse, NY 13210

Syracuse University
Merril Lane
Syracuse, NY 13210

North Carolina

Society of American Inventors
P.O. Box 7284
Charlotte, NC 28217

North Carolina Technology Development
   Authority
4216 Dobbs Building
430 North Salisbury Street
Raleigh, NC 27611

North Dakota

Center for Innovation and Business
   Development
Box 8103—University Station
University of North Dakota
Grand Forks, ND 58202

Innovation Institute
Box 429
Larimore, ND 58215

North Dakota Inventors Congress
Jamestown Chamber of Commerce
Box 1530
Jamestown, ND 58402
(701) 252-4830

Ohio

Columbus Inventors Association
2480 East Avenue
Columbus, OH 43202
(614) 267-9033

Inventors Club of Cincinnati
18 Gambler Circle
Cincinnati, OH 45218
(513) 825-1222 or (513) 922-9462

Inventors Council of Dayton
140 East Monument Avenue
Dayton, OH 45402
(513) 439-4497

Ohio's Thomas Edison Programs Seed
   Development Fund
Ohio Department of Development
65 East State Street, Suite 200
Columbus, OH 43266-0330

Ohio Department of Development
Division of Technological Development
30 East Broad Street
P.O. Box 1001
Columbus, OH 43266-0101

Inventors Council of Ohio
191 Illinois Avenue
Westerville, OH 43081

Inventors Council of Ohio
Dayton Chapter
P.O. Box 77—800 Livermore Street
Yellow Springs, OH 45387

Ohio State University
302 D Hagerty Hall
1775 College Road
Columbus, OH 43210

TechEx
Suite 1000—65 East State Street
Columbus, OH 43215
(614) 460-3543

Oklahoma

Invention Development Society
8502A SW Eighth Street
Oklahoma City, OK 73128

Inventors Assistance Program
Oklahoma Department of Commerce
6601 Broadway Extension
Oklahoma City, OK 73116
(800) 443-6552 or (800) 522-6552

Oklahoma Inventors Congress
P.O. Box 75635
Oklahoma City, OK 73147

Rural Enterprises, Inc.
Wes Watkins New Product & Process
   Fair
P.O. Box 1335
Durant, OK 74702

Oregon

College of Business Administration
University of Oregon
Eugene, OR 97403

Western Inventors Council
P.O. Box 3288
Eugene, OR 97403

Western Inventors Council
School of Business
Oregon State University
Corvallis, OR 97331

Pennsylvania

The Invention Convention
The Franklin Institute
20th & the Parkway
Philadelphia, PA 19103
(215) 448-1174

Pennsylvania Technical Assistance
   Program (PENNTAP)
501 Keller Building
University Park, PA 16802

University of Pittsburgh
Forbes Quadrangle
Pittsburgh, PA 15260

University of Pittsburgh
College of Business Administration
Pittsburgh, PA 15260

American Society of Inventors
P.O. Box 58426
Philadelphia, PA 19102-8426

American Society of Inventors
545 Hughes Road
King of Prussia, PA 19406

American Society of Inventors
1710 Fidelity Building
123 South Broad Street
Philadelphia, PA 19109

South Carolina

Inventors Association of South Carolina
2222 Terrace Way
Columbia, SC 29205

National Institute for Inventors
A Division of P. D. Distributors, Inc.
P.O. Box 1465
Seneca, SC 29679

South Dakota

College of Engineering SDSU
Engineering Extension
Brookings, SD 57006

SD School of Mines and Technology
Physics—Room 220
Rapid City, SD 57701

South Dakota Inventors Congress
P.O. Box 1113—26 South Broadway
Watertown, SD 57201
605-886-5814

Tennessee

Martin J. Skinner
856 Nelson Drive
Kingston, TN 37763

Appalachian Inventors Group
P.O. Box 388
Oak Ridge, TN 37830

Tennessee Inventors Association
P.O. Box 11225
Knoxville, TN 37939

Texas

Baker, Kirk & Bissex P.C.
3555 Timmons #700
Houston, TX 77027
(713) 790-9316

Technology Business Development
Texas Engineering Experiment Station
Texas A&M University
310 Wisenbaker Engineering Research
  Center
College Station, TX 77843-3369

Dallas–Forth Worth Patent Association
500 Baker Building
Fort Worth, TX 76102

Bill Fly
Box 30400
Amarillo, TX 79120

Houston Inventors Association
600 West Gray Street
Houston, TX 77019

Innovex, Inc.
Suite 1125–LB37
4144 North Central Expressway
Dallas, TX 75204
(214)265-1540

Inventor's Expo 88
P.O. Box 927
Abilene, TX 79604

E. A. Kisseling
15402 Wandering Trail
Friendswood, TX 77546

Richardson Independent School District
Richardson, TX 75081
(214) 470-5202

Texas Innovation Information Network
  System (TIINS)
Infomart, P.O. Box 471
1950 Stemmons Freeway
Dallas, TX 75207
(214) 746-5140

Texas Inventors Association
4000 Rock Creek Drive #100
Dallas, TX 75204

University of Texas–Arlington
Continuing Education Program
528 Campus Center
Arlington, TX 76019

Utah

Intermountain Society of Inventors and
  Designers
P.O. Box 1514
Salt Lake City, UT 84110

Utah Technology Finance Corp.
419 Wakara Way, Suite 215
Salt Lake City, UT 84108

Virginia

Ralph Dorr
316 Southland Drive
Danville, VA 24541

Invent America
U.S. Patent Model Foundation
510 King Street, Suite 420
Alexandria, VA 22314

National Patent Council Inc.
Suite 301, Crystal Plaza #1
2001 Jefferson Davis Highway
Arlington, VA 22202

National Society of Professional
  Engineers
1420 King Street
Alexandria, VA 22314
(703) 684-2842

National Technology Information
  Service
U.S. Department of Commerce
5285 Port Royal Road
Springfield, VA 22161

Washington

Batelle
Pacific Northwest Labs
P.O. Box 999
Richland, WA 99352

Inventor's Association of
  Washington, Inc.
P.O. Box 1725
Bellevue, WA 98009

Innovators International Project
P.O. Box 4636
Rolling Bay, WA 98061

Inventors Association of
  Washington, Inc.
P.O. Box 2684
Seattle, WA 98125-2684

Northwest Inventors Association
723 East Highland Drive
Arlington, WA 98223

Reynolds Engineering Company
3060 West Lake Sammamish Parkway
Redmond, WA 98052

Wisconsin

Center for Innovation and Development
206 Fryklund Hall
University of Wisconsin–Stout
Menomonie, WI 54751
(715) 232-1252

Midwest Inventors Group
P.O. Box 1
Chippewa Falls, WI 54729

Wisconsin Innovation Service Center
402 McCutchan Hall
University of Wisconsin–Whitewater
Whitewater, WI 53190

Australia

Victorian Innovation Center
First Floor—Building C-2
Hawthorne Technology Center
192 Burwood Road
Hawthorne, Victoria 3122, Australia

Inventors Association of Australia

The Boot Factory
27–33 Spring Street
Bondi Junction
Sydney NSW 2022

Malaysia

Invention and Design Association of
  Sarawak
93764 Kuching
P.O. Box 3292
Sarawak, Malaysia
082-412604

United Kingdom

Institute of Patentees and Inventors
Suite 505A
Triumph House
189 Regent Street
London W1R 7WF

Institute of Inventors
19 Fosse Way
Ealing, London W13 0BZ
ENGLAND

Profile

Gordon D. Griffin was born in London, England in 1930 and currently resides in the United States. He has had varied commercial experience, both running his own businesses (in mushrooms and lava rock) and promoting his own inventions. His experience as a young boy just after the Depression and in war-torn London during the Second World War prepared him well for the deep, practical thoughts he has put toward this book and his many and varied inventions. He knows that an open, fertile mind does not guarantee instant success; on the contrary, he has observed firsthand how inventions can fail financially. His inventions include the following:

- Seat belt safety device that prevents a motor vehicle from starting if the seat belt is not fastened
- Antitheft device for motor vehicles
- Motor transmission mechanism (to replace tracks on heavy equipment)
- An improved mushroom-composting machine
- Cross-mix composting machine. Automatically picks up, aerates, waters and restacks organic materials.
- Automatic mechanical watering device for gardens and agriculture (works based on soil moisture needs)
- Solid-state solar-powered collector (retro fit for heating buildings and water)
- Solar-powered portable pool heater
- Relax-a-flex Comfort System (a new type of infinitely adjustable, long-lasting mattress)
- Wind-powered generator (for agricultural use)
- Automatic pollution-control filter system (to remove precipitates from heavy industry)
- "Biography" (a board game played by up to six people who create their idea of the perfect life)
- Apparatus for control of virus (controls body temperature in humans for a time sufficient to kill virus particles)
- Hand-tite pipe fitting (for plastic pipe)
- Six universal pipe fittings for plumbers (to effect 6,480 different plumbing combinations)
- Control valve for flood irrigation (agricultural)
- Storm damage–proof qualities for wind power–gathering device.

This book is aimed primarily at helping the individual inventor in all of us who needs encouragement and financial rewards to succeed and to continue inventing. Mr. Griffin's more than 35 years of expertise in the inventing field has enabled him to develop several formulas that will help give inventors and would-be inventors the ability to assess properly what they have invented; to take sequential steps to maximize financial returns on "good inventions"; and, conversely, to be able to recognize early an invention that may be financially nonviable before it cripples the inventor.